985
Von
c.1

Von Hagen, Victor Wolfgang
    Highway of the sun.   Duel; Little,
1955.
     320 p.   illus., maps, 32 photos.

1. Inca Highway expedition, 1952-1954
2. Incas I. Title

6.00

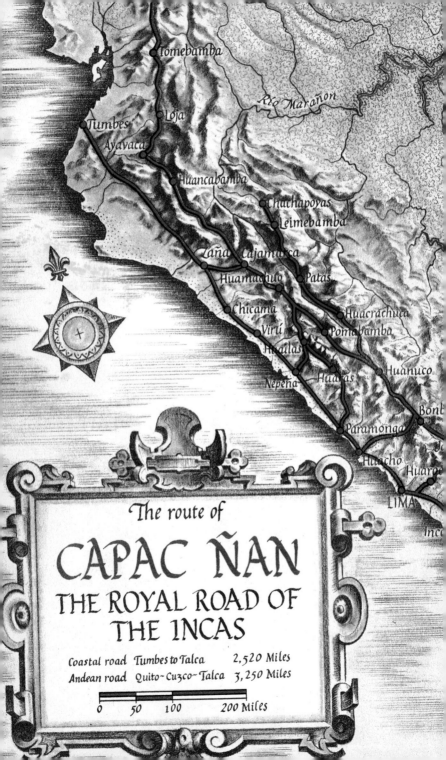

The route of

CAPAC ÑAN
THE ROYAL ROAD OF THE INCAS

Coastal road Tumbes to Talca   2,520 Miles
Andean road   Quito~Cuzco~Talca   3,250 Miles

0   50   100   200 Miles

QUITO
Tumbes
Chachapoyas
LIMA
CUZCO
SANTIAGO
Talca

13
6r

Machu Picchu
Apurimac Bridge
-huaman
Colorado
Nazca
Acari
Chala
Andahuailas
CUZCO
Cailloma
Macusani
Sicuani
Ayaviri
Juliaca
Puno
Moquegua
Sandia
Huancane
L. Titicaca
Guaqui
Tacna
Hurina

PACIFIC OCEAN

Lee Hu

Books by Victor Wolfgang von Hagen

Exploration

OFF WITH THEIR HEADS (1937)

ECUADOR THE UNKNOWN (1938)

JUNGLE IN THE CLOUDS (1940)

ECUADOR AND THE GALAPAGOS ISLANDS: A HISTORY (1949)

HIGHWAY OF THE SUN (1955)

Biography

SOUTH AMERICA CALLED THEM (1945)

MAYA EXPLORER, THE LIFE OF JOHN LLOYD STEPHENS (1947)

FREDERIC CATHERWOOD, ARCHITECT (1950)

THE FOUR SEASONS OF MANUELA (1952)

Ethnology

THE TSATCHELA INDIANS OF WESTERN ECUADOR (1939)

THE JICAQUE INDIANS OF HONDURAS (1940)

THE MAYA AND AZTEC PAPERMAKERS (1943)

For Younger Adults

RICHES OF SOUTH AMERICA (1938)

QUETZAL QUEST (1939)

TREASURE OF TORTOISE ISLANDS (1941)

MOSQUITO BOY (1943)

SOUTH AMERICA ZOO (1948)

HIGHWAY OF THE SUN

HIGHWAY
of the Sun

by *gang*

VICTOR W. VON HAGEN

With 4 Maps
and 32 Pages of Photographs

Duell, Sloan and Pearce · *New York*
Little, Brown and Company · *Boston* · *Toronto*

DUELL, SLOAN AND PEARCE—LITTLE, BROWN
BOOKS ARE PUBLISHED BY
LITTLE, BROWN AND COMPANY
IN ASSOCIATION WITH
DUELL, SLOAN & PEARCE, INC.

Published simultaneously in Canada
by Little, Brown & Company (Canada) Limited

PRINTED IN THE UNITED STATES OF AMERICA

To the memory of
Sigmund Gildemeister

. . . The roads of the Incas were the most useful and stupendous works ever executed by man.

— ALEXANDER VON HUMBOLDT

Contents

I	The Grandest Road in the World	3
II	In the Beginning . . .	8
III	The Floating Road	24
IV	Towers of the Dead	45
V	Into the Carabaya Country	56
VI	Cuzco — the Four Quarters of the World	81
VII	Somewhere, Lost Vilcabamba	98
VIII	Apurimac: the Bridge of the Great Speaker	121
IX	The Sanctuary of the Hawk	136
X	The Highway of the Sun	161
XI	The Road to Chachapoyas	186
XII	The Unliving Desert	204
XIII	The Marked Desert	217
XIV	Chala: the Fourth Quarter	234
XV	The Kingdom of the Moon	253
XVI	A Great City Called Tumpiz	276
XVII	The End of the Road	293
	Acknowledgments	307
	Bibliography	309
	Index	315

Illustrations

Maps   9, 85, 255, 277

Photographs   306–307

HIGHWAY OF THE SUN

I

The Grandest Road in the World

It was 1548. At the side of a road which went on out across the bare Andes, a young soldier was keeping his vow to write down the "wonderful things of these Indies." Pedro Cieza de León looked again at the stone-paved highway he had followed for so many leagues and then he slowly wrote:

> Accordingly the Inca constructed the grandest road that there is in the world as well as the longest, for it extends from Cuzco to Quito and was connected from Cuzco to Chile — a distance of 800 leagues. I believe since the history of man, there has been no other account of such grandeur as is to be seen on this road which passes over deep valleys and lofty mountains, by snowy heights, over falls of water, through the living rock and along the edges of tortuous torrents. In all these places, the road is well constructed, on the inclining mountains well terraced, through the living rock cut along the riverbanks supported by retaining walls, in the snowy heights built with steps and resting places, and along its entire length swept cleanly and cleared of debris — with post stations and storehouses and Temples of the Sun at appointed intervals along its length.

In the four hundred years since the young traveler wrote this, much of this grandeur has been laid waste by the insults of time; much is in ruins, many of the superbly made halting-places of the road reduced to formless mounds. Here and there, during the inter-

3

vening centuries, explorer-archaeologists have wandered over the empty spaces of Peru and have painstakingly pushed away the debris of time to ferret out some of the clues with which to reconstruct an empire. But between what is known and what is not known lies an immense hiatus, and between what we know of the ancient cities along the road and what we do not know is a great gap. We know only that the thread which bound the widely separated communities was the Road — that ubiquitous overwhelming Road — which Cieza de León described as the "grandest and longest in the world."

What then if this fabulous road were to be found and followed from end to end? What if one were to employ the techniques now available in the scientific fields of archaeology and geography, and were to make use of advanced methods of travel such as the double-transmissioned truck and the airplane? Would it not then be possible to discover the route taken by its various roads, and so make their heights and lowlands accessible to those who would search for the many forgotten cities? And if these were found might they not reveal the secret of how the Incas lived, how by building their amazing roads they were able to communicate with almost telegraphic speed with the most remote sections of their empire?

To travel this ancient route, seeking to find some light on the enigma of the history of Man in the Americas, was my dream. Until now much of this history had been a mystery — one with scale, plot and drive. There were clues to be found from which deductions were to be made — there was the drama of suspense and continued novelty. Where did the ancient roads lead and what would one meet on the way if they were followed?

Movement is as old as the earth. And Man is of the earth. Since earliest times he has been a great roamer. As early as 10,000 B.C., Man the Traveler opened a route to the Baltic to obtain amber,

4

"that special act of God." The earliest man-made roads were built to obtain salt; the oldest Roman road was the *Via Salaria,* the "salt road" to Ostia.

Persia excelled in good roads "crowded with men on the King's business." The caravan trade, extending its way into India, found roads already built; for, ever since man invented the vehicular wheel in 3000 B.C., traffic had rolled out of the larger Indian villages. Alexander the Great said of these same roads, built of clay-made brick with stairways of broad steps and low treads easily climbed by laden camels and lined "with all manner of trees bearing fruits," that they were the best he had ever seen.

Egypt too had its roads. As early as 3000 B.C., a ten-fathom-wide road had been built by King Cheops for the purpose of transporting the huge limestone blocks destined for the Great Pyramid. "The road," said a certain Greek geographer, "was not much inferior, in my judgment, to the pyramid itself." There were ancient many-gated roads in Africa over which one moved across the desert. Sennacherib the Assyrian built his royal road and made "it shine like the light of day." Darius the Persian constructed another from Susa to Babylonia, spacing it with stone markers and posthouses. In Crete there were wagon roads which led to the palace of Knossus. The Greeks became systematic road builders, extending their roads into Sparta; and, even at this early date, they prepared a manual on road repairs. Most of these early routes were luxury highways and over them moved obsidian, amber, gold, jade, silver, emeralds; and for delicacies, Greek fruits such as olives, figs, lemons, almonds. Spices were carried to every destination; silks came over the caravan routes, frankincense and perfumes from Arabia.

The Romans constructed the first road system. Now for the first time the "road" was open to all, without tolls or prerogatives. It was no longer exclusively one road only for the luxury trade, or reserved for royal travel. Pompey built his roads over the Alps;

Africa was traversed by a Roman road network from Gabes to Tebessa; Emperor Claudius built roads in Britain. On all of these, milestones were commonplace while posthouses mushroomed all along a Roman way. At the height of the Empire, the longest continuous road ran from Antonine's Wall in Scotland to Jerusalem, a distance of three thousand miles. Even during the declension of Rome the building of roads went on in Spain, in France and in Africa.

After the seventh century the upkeep of roads throughout Europe and along the Mediterranean rim was neglected, and by the sixteenth century for a traveler to arrive in Madrid he needed "a falcon's eye, an ass's ear, a monkey's face, a merchant's word, a camel's back, a hog's mouth, a deer's foot." For a thousand years Europe's roads remained quagmires. It was Napoleon who rebuilt the Roman Road in the nineteenth century.

Yet during these same centuries, far across the world a people called the Incas built a road system which bound together all the discordant elements of their land — the desert, the mountains, the jungles — and was in many respects superior to any European road network. "Nothing in Christendom equals these wonderful roads in Peru," said a literate conquistador. "The great Inca road from Quito to Cuzco is as much used as the road from Seville to Triana and I cannot say more . . ."

During my many years of exploration through South America I had heard much about and had seen fragments of these fabulous royal roads of the Incas. Now at long last I was determined to seek the reality of these ancient stone arteries and, wherever they might lead — through jungles, across deserts, over towering mountains — to follow from the starting point to the end this great Inca highway system — these roads which for centuries bound the Inca empire together and which, like the Persian highways, caused the downfall of a great and ancient civilization.

The Grandest Road in the World

This, then, is the story of the six people — two women and four men — who formed our Expedition and who began, in the winter of 1952, to seek out the remains of the "most useful and stupendous works ever executed by man."

As the fog begins to rise from the Andes like a theatrical drop curtain, the Expedition's caravan slowly makes its way across the bare roof of Peru. Not a tree, nor plant, nor bird voice animates this void; the only moving thing is our caravan of two cars, rolling out over the *puna* toward Lake Titicaca.

I I

In the Beginning . . .

W E CAME upon the lake at the end of the day. It was, we later remembered, the same hour of the same day of the same month that the first white man chanced upon it in the year 1553. At 12,500 feet above the surface of the sea, Titicaca lay immense and shimmering and as blue as the heavens — almost on a level, it seemed, with the sky.

Over the lake a fleet of grass balsa boats, hurrying before a following wind, was sailing toward Puno, gliding over the glass surface without disturbing its polished water-skin. Far in the background like a painted backdrop were the snow-draped peaks of the Bolivian Andes, biting into the sky with their glistening white glacier-teeth and so sharply outlined that we could not believe they lay forty miles distant.

The truck caravan came to a halt, and for a brief moment we sat there spellbound by the magnificent sight. Then Silvia von Hagen, my wife, bundled heavily against the almost arctic bite of the cold, stepped from the truck and scrambled up to the top of a rock.

"I never dreamed it would be so beautiful," she said as she pointed to a small distant figure. "Look, you can see the bright color of the Indian's skirt, and see how the golden color of the grass is reflected in the lake."

After the upward climb from Arequipa and the drive across the

8

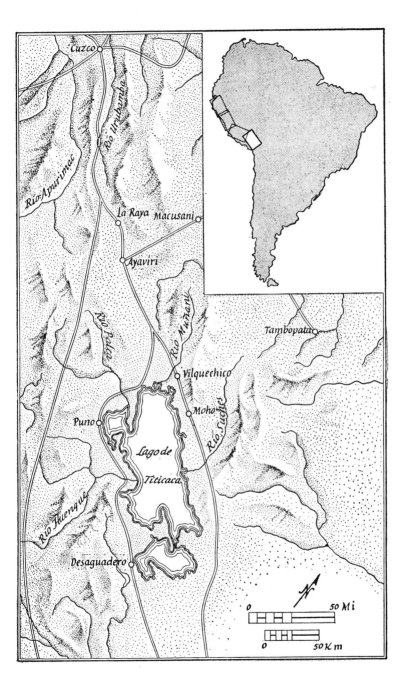

cold, treeless and sombre *puna*, it was a stirring experience to come in this twilight hour upon Titicaca. For five thousand years, people have lived and died about the shores of this great lake. Amoeba-shaped, it is over one hundred and thirty miles in length and forty miles, more or less, at its greatest width, and as deep as the Atlantic Ocean off the coast of Massachusetts.

One river flows out of this Gargantuan lake to curve about the grass-bound *puna* and empty many hundreds of miles southward into a lesser lake in Bolivia, from whence the brackish waters filter down to form salt-swamps at Argentina's borderlands. This lake and its fringes of good soil had for centuries supplied the "all" for ancient peoples who lived along its shores — fish in abundance, water for crops, fertile earth, a plenteous supply of the reeds which took the place of wood for building material for houses and for balsa boats. Around its shores lived large bird-colonies of gray-suited ibis, ducks and black-winged flamingos. From one of the lake's islands, it is legended, came the first Inca King. The environs of the lake still remain the most thickly populated section of the Andes. Indian in custom and language, these people live much as their ancestors lived centuries before.

Across the *puna* we could see the path of the Inca road, a fragment of that fabulous highway which had not been annealed by time, moving up from the lake to where we stood on the bare land. Together Silvia and I drank in the scene. Lake Titicaca in the foreground, and the ancient road marching across what seemingly was the top of the world . . .

I had traveled a long road since that day in 1934 in the Ecuadorian Andes when I saw for the first time a fragment of the Inca road. It was at the ruins of Ingapirca and I was on my first expedition to South America, and very young. From the summit of what had been an Inca fortress I had seen a clearly defined road, several yards wide and bordered by a stone wall undulating over the treeless land.

"That, Your Grace," my Indian guide had said then, touching the brim of his felt hat, "is the Inca road." I had followed it for some miles until, at the edge of a canyon, it disappeared in a tangle of masonry. Was this a part of that great Royal Road system I had heard about? Did this road really lead to Cuzco, fifteen hundred miles to the south, and to Tucumán in Argentina, three thousand miles away? In time the Royal Road became a sort of obsession; it was always in my thoughts. Later, when I was exploring the Maya ruins in Yucatán, I walked a stone causeway that connected the sea with the Maya capital and I thought again of the Incas and wondered about their road: "Some day I must . . ." I promised myself.

Throughout all the intervening years, I was haunted with the idea of rediscovering that road. Now I realized that all my other expeditions to South America were merely a preparation for the exploration of these ancient highways of a great and dead civilization. After all these years of hoping that someday such a thing could be done, it seemed at the moment scarcely credible that we were now on the heights of Titicaca, about to begin the exploration.

The flags of our caravan beat time with the wind. From the smaller truck, the red and white banner of Peru flew above the American flag. On the larger, a fiery red Power Wagon, the blue ensign of the American Geographical Society — its device, U B I Q U E, encircling a design of the world — beat violently at its jackstaff.

I had felt from the beginning that our Expedition was to be basically engaged in geographical research. Where the ancient road ran, why one route and not another had been selected by the Inca's engineers, was, in this "doubled-up world" of Peru as the Spaniard called it, primarily a geographical study. Therefore, in the early stages of planning for this expedition I had sought out the American Geographical Society.

For a century this Society has sent expeditions to the far reaches of the globe and their blue ensign has floated over many an isolated region. Latin America had, for many years, been a focus of their interest and their famous long-term project of an accurate mapping of all the Americas from pole to pole has kept the Society very close to developments in Hispanic America. The Director of the Society agreed to our association with the Society, allowed us to make use of the prestige of its name, and in the months that followed, assisted us in preparing our field maps.

On October 12, 1952, the American Geographical Society made the first formal announcement of the Expedition:

> The most novel and one of the most ambitious archaeological and geographical expeditions of modern times will begin when Mr. Victor von Hagen leaves for Peru. In cooperation with the Society, Mr. von Hagen will direct an intensive two-year study of a forgotten and almost incredible world, the thirteenth-century highway of the ancient Incas whose remains still stretch for ten thousand miles along the west coast of South America. The Inca Highway began . . .

The geographical rediscovery of the Inca Royal Road, of course, had to be closely related to archaeological research, for the ruins of the way stations (*tampus*) that once lined the highways throughout the entire length, when found, would have to be mapped, and such artifacts as came to light studied for the characteristic detail that would "date" the ruins and the road.

Although knowledge derived from archaeological research is more reliable than such information as might be found in writings about the road, we still had to begin with the early writings for basic information. I contacted Dr. John Rowe of the University of California, an authority on Peru and an old friend. We decided that everything ever written about the roads would have to be sought out and catalogued under regional headings, a task over which one of his young graduate students labored for more than a year.

The nature of such a geographico-archaeological expedition suggested a group of five or at most six members. I, as the leader, proposed to do the ethnographic work and concern myself principally with the actual discovery of the Royal Road and the co-ordination of the things we found with the evidence supplied to us from the literature; in addition I would make ethnological studies of the natives in the regions through which the road passed. Silvia, who is a textile designer, would be the staff artist and study the weaving techniques used in the ancient textiles found in the graves and would assemble our collections.

Silvia, who looks like an American, is in fact Brazilian. Born in Berlin, educated in the United States, tall and long-limbed, with dark hair matching her dark eyes, she has a fearful and passionate curiosity about life and, to balance it, a wonderful gaiety and sense of humor with a way of puncturing sophisms with thrusts of disarming frankness, and in addition she has a poet's feeling for nature, for the color of an autumnal tree, a bird in flight, a flower or a design in nature.

In 1952 I was lecturing at her college; later when we met, I found that she was from Brazil and that she was connected with a family long established in Peru. Being still in that period of "wanting" to organize this Expedition, I told her about the Inca roads — drawing, I suppose, as one will under these circumstances, the whole business in dramatic overtones. So, seduced by my own enthusiasm, our plan to seek out the Incas' roads developed in the counterpoint of her interest, and the Expedition suddenly left the dream stage and metamorphosed into being.

But coming into being was not just a matter of saying, "Let it be done." Our project called for travel within the three Perus: desert, jungle and mountain. Each region demanded a different type of equipment. For the heights we would have to be prepared to face an arctic cold; on the desert, a heat which during the day was as torrid as the Sahara's; while the jungle, insect-filled and dank, demanded yet another type of equipment. All this was expensive; there was the matter of raising money. Where were we to get enough to maintain five or six people in the field for two years and to purchase all we would need? I sought out foundations, institutions, museums — and there was nothing or next to nothing to be had from these sources. We next tried industry, and here we found there was interest; eventually, we had a promise for all the gasoline, cameras, medicines, batteries, tires, power generators, film, dehydrated foodstuffs and coffee, and transportation, that would be needed for the Expedition.

Thus it went on until, in June 1952 — the halfway mark set by ourselves — we had in services and materials more than half of the fifty thousand dollars needed to undertake the Expedition. With the feeling that we had passed the initial critical stage, I negotiated for the literary rights of the Expedition. The *New York Times* and its affiliate, the North American Newspaper Alliance, gave us a contract for a monthly article; *Life Magazine* wanted certain picture rights, and my publishers felt enough confidence in the project to make a substantial advance on contract. With this accomplished we had reached the mark set by Sigmund Gildemeister, Silvia's grandfather.

"If you can assure me," he had written, "that you can yourself raise more than half of what you feel you need, then I will match that half with dollars which you need for carrying out the Expedition."

Herr Gildemeister could have stepped out of Thomas Mann's *Buddenbrooks*. He had a gentle but worldly look, the inherent probity of a man who has come from a long line of Gildemeisters who played their role in the development of the free cities of the Hansa.

His parents had been married in Peru in 1853 and as a young man he had gone from Peru to Chile to look out for some nitrate interests. Eight years later he entered the family corporation. After the last war which he spent in the suburbs of Hamburg, the most bombed area of all Germany, he went to Brazil where he formerly had had business interests, there to re-establish himself. In a sense Sigmund Gildemeister had returned to the land which had launched him on what was to be a successful career. In him we, as the Spaniard has it, had found our *patrón*.

Now to the others who would form the Expedition. To carry out this program we needed one or two archaeologists, a topographer-draughtsman and a cinematographer. To take a larger group of people into this barren earth — where food, or its lack, is a very real and gnawing problem — would complicate matters. There were other considerations. For two years we would have to live on quite intimate terms with each other. Members of the Expedition would not only have to be expert at their particular tasks but they should have other talents and interests as well, for they would undoubtedly have to lend a hand in many ways. Then too there would be many physically trying aspects to our journey through low-lying arid desert, high altitudes and humid jungles. There would be many difficult hours and no matter how well organized the Expedition, there would be constant irritations.

So for our topographer, one who also happened to be an expert cameraman, we picked a New Yorker. In his late thirties Charles

Daugherty, the son of a well-known illustrator, had studied at Yale, worked under John Steuart Curry and learned about mapping during his five years in the Pacific as a Captain of the Engineers attached to Admiral Nimitz's staff. I had known him personally for years; quiet and effective, he was an able skier, inured to the cold and the heights. In the first weeks of our trek he grew a beard which gave him the look of one of El Greco's hollow-eyed saints.

It had not been easy to find a cinematographer, a specialist in the documentary film, one with the tough endurance needed to carry cameras over these high altitudes. In addition he would have to be a man of stability and patience, a quality he would have much need of in photographing the natives and ourselves, his principal actors. Had there been money involved perhaps it would have been easier to find such a one, but those who could afford to risk life for two years in perilous journeying for the sheer joy of adding a bit more to our knowledge of ancient man were not easy to come by. Such a one was Richmond Lawrence. He came all the way from a midwest university to announce himself ready to undergo any hardship or privation in order to film the phantom roads of the Incas. Born in Upper New York State, Lawrence had first been employed with one of the major film producers and so had a thorough knowledge of the fundamentals. After several years in the Army, he had traveled all over Mexico and Central America photographing the cultural life of the Indians. A small man, Lawrence we soon discovered, daily consumed an extraordinary number of cups of coffee — whether this gave him his endurance we were never to learn.

It was Silvia who suggested Dorothy Menzel as the Expedition's archaeologist. She was the young graduate student who had done such a remarkable job for me at the University of California on the research on the Inca roads. Who, asked Silvia, was better qualified? She had gone through four hundred years of literature written in several languages, selecting those passages which mentioned the roads; and at the end of a year, her research notes filled three huge notebooks. She had often said rather wistfully that she would like to come along as the Expedition's archaeologist.

It was an idea that presented certain problems. Dorothy had yet to finish her doctorate thesis and I was concerned about her ability to stand the strain. Her own field work had not, as she herself admitted, been too extensive. Moreover she was both unmarried and attractive; and for two years . . .

"I know, I know," Silvia had said with emphasis, for she heard this objection often: "*Never more than one woman on an expedition. . . .*"

I was still undecided. I talked the matter of an archaeologist over many times with the late Dr. Wendell Bennett of Yale University, who helped us formulate the archaeological approach. Even though he himself could not accompany us, he gave us without stint all of his available time. "He must be the right man, he has to be. And he must have considerable field experience. We have no such person now at Yale and, too, even two years will not permit extensive archaeological investigation at any given site. Your expedition from an archaeological standpoint is to be mainly reconnaissance and your man will have to go through Peru with blinders on his eyes so as not to run after every ruin. This will take a special type of man. I'll see what I can do . . ."

It was most important that the geographical rediscovery of the Royal Road be combined with archaeology. After finding the *tampus*, which appeared on the Highway every twelve to sixteen miles, experimental pits would have to be sunk and the potsherds studied for stylistic sequence. We would have to know if a particular section of the road was Inca or pre-Inca. While the pottery would give some evidence, the architectural styles of the buildings would also have to be studied so as to assign a definite period to each road station.

Highway of the Sun

It was now the fall of 1952. Ever since our marriage Silvia and I had lived Expedition, breathed Expedition. With six other expeditions in the craw of my experience, I had tried at the beginning to tell Silvia just what we were in for — yet in my most pessimistic moments I never thought the planning would be so involved. But we were now committed, and far enough along even to set a sailing date.

The matter of an archaeologist was still unsettled when we prepared to sail that December day in 1952. It was a day of calamitous rain when noon was but a thin solution of night. As the vessel was about to leave, the purser brought us a telegram from California:

HAVE MARRIED FRANCIS RIDDELL ARCHAEOLOGIST WILL TRY
TO DIVERT HIM FROM AMERICAN NORTHWEST ARCHAEOLOGY
TO PERUVIAN AREA. DOROTHY MENZEL RIDDELL.

The retiring sun was lighting up all the glacier-topped mountains on the far edge of Titicaca. The snow took on a variety of glowing pastel colors, shades beloved by the impressionists; streamers of mist floated by, glowing first red, then crimson, like the crests of a *dent du midi*. We took a last look at the thin ribbon of the Inca road, now blue-shadowed, entered our cars and started down to Puno, the major city on the lake.

At the gateway to San Carlos de Puno we were stopped by a red-and-white ridgepole that barred our entrance, and when we were approached by a guard, neat in powder-blue uniform and peaked visored cap, I saluted, pointed to the door of the car with its insignia of the running *chasqui* figure and the legend, INCA HIGHWAY EXPEDITION, and said, "Official car."

Carefully he examined our license plates. Then, as I handed him our much valued document — the decree granted us by President Odria of Peru which in broad and generous terms granted us "all aid and facilities" — he read it through after first summoning the Corporal of the Guard who in turn called the Sergeant. They all saluted; the ridgepole was raised and we drove on into Puno.

The cobblestoned street was filled with Indians moving at a half walk, half run, a mountain stride which they use untiringly for hours. It gave a lively cadence as if the whole town were hurrying toward something. The dun-colored houses which fronted the street were uniformly flat, forming as it were a continuous mono-lith, while the brilliantly colored ponchos of the Indians and the gaudy skirts of the *cholas*, openly and proudly half-caste, gave a joyous note. The *chola* women were particularly colorful as they trotted by with their high-crowned derbys set at a rakish angle, their numerous crinoline skirts, wrapped tightly around the waist, swelling out so that the wearers looked like animated tea cozies, their skin tints varying from bronze to yellow-red, their round full faces with dark almond eyes shaped like those of well-fed Buddhas. The males by comparison were dull birds of passage with the plum-age of black carrion crows and their ill-fitting black suits inevitably topped by large-brimmed black fedoras.

That night we stopped near Puno and put up in a rustic chalet at Haqui, a mile outside of the city. This was fortunate, for there was not another place in all Puno for passers-through like ourselves. A gracious lady who had read of our Expedition kindly made us the loan of her house for as long as we stayed in the region of the lake. The house, surrounded by high moldering adobe walls, had rooms made entirely of sun-baked brick. The largest of these Silvia marked for the kitchen study while the other three served for our bedrooms. Between the house and the shore were walls of high-growing *totora* reed, where unseen ducks cackled and frogs kept up a throbbing ululation throughout the long frigid nights. In a day's time we had put the place in working order. Our electric generator gave us our light; we had our own portable sanitation; and stoves, camp furniture and two gasoline heaters were installed. As for the water, which was always of questionable purity, we put up a large Lister bag in the patio and kept our Indian helpers traveling back and forth like processionary caterpillars, carrying water to fill it.

Puno has the "air-temper" of Burgos in Spain, noted for its ten months of winter and two months of hell or, to retain the Spanish pun, *Diez meses de invierno y dos de infierno.* The days are warm and sun-filled, although the shadows are always cellar-cool; but once the sun disappears it becomes bitterly cold. Actually Puno has two seasons, wet and dry: the dry or "winter" because it is cold; the wet or "summer" because it rains and is warmer. Although it was May, the edges of the lake and the pools on the road as well as the water in our Lister bag were frozen every morning. Yet no matter what the day or the food or the freezing night, our arctic sleeping bags of feather down provided the comfort that was denied us by the climate.

We acquired Francisco along with our chalet. His face like beaten bronze had a Mongolian cast of eye, Hyperborean cheekbones, and was fretted with an astonishing arabesque of wrinkles. Francisco was pleasant, ineffectual and affirmative. He answered "Arí" to everything, so we called him Arí.

We would have been lost, however, without his twelve-year-old son. He was already a miniature man and as astute as an Indian of thirty, yet at thirty he would know no more than at twelve. The original shape and form of what he wore when we first met, we were never to discover, since his clothes were so rainbow-patched. Where he needed his pants most he had nothing at all and at any moment we believed he would expose that which society insists be hidden. And so we decided to dress him befitting his new station as a personal servant to the Expedition. With his new clothes — tight-fitting, gray, coarse homespuns, a form-fitting jacket and a brightly colored *chumpi*-belt, sandals, a stocking cap with ear flaps to keep out the night cold, and a gaudy-colored poncho — Silverio was ready to attend us.

Since an Expedition, like an army, travels on its belly, organization of house and food had to take precedence over program and so, won to the logic of food, presently we went into Puno to augment our supplies. Puno is not, as Andean cities go, very old. It was nothing in ancient times and did not even appear as a formal city until 1668 when the Viceroy of Peru, by grace of a newly discovered silver mine, named it the Villa of San Carlos de Puno. Its streets are cobblestoned and progress on them is a little like bouncing on a pogo stick. The houses that face the streets are of uniform height and are uniformly painted. In Puno's center near the large square is its cathedral. A coldly austere edifice which bears in the midst of its intricate decorations the date AÑO DE 1754, the church is decorated in the mestizo style. Over the doorway an Indian-inspired St. Michael wearing a feather headdress and flounced skirt kills a dragon, while nearby mermaids, curiously popular with Indian sculptors, play their ukulele-like *charangos* as they float over the niches containing austere-faced saints.

From one cold shadowed street to another, Puno is a long market place with the main one in front of the railway depot providing the drama of the day. There shopping is not much different from being in an evening subway rush hour, except that here one is endangered by the loaded workers carrying out-sized baskets, or he may be spattered with gore from a cart in which a drayer is transporting the viscera of a flayed ox. Here too jousting is part of buying. Food is abundant. Vegetables range from purple potatoes the size of prunes to artichokes. There are bananas and avocados from the *yungas* hot-lands and enormous salmon trout from the rivers, shrimp from the coast and seaweed from the ocean. The butchers are women, shrouded in white wraparounds and wearing the brown, high-crowned trilibies. They wield an instrument shaped like a be-heading ax, and no sooner is the amount of meat gauged than the ax crashes down. You are then handed an undistinguishable mass of meat, bone and viscera. Apparently, from the toughness of the meat, the seventeenth-century Italian law of Lex Foscarini is strictly adhered to — oxen are not slaughtered until unfit to work in the fields.

In the open market, outside of the concrete walls, lies the traditional market. Here Indian women sit with much dignity before their offerings, which are placed atop woven mats laid over the cobblestones and heaped up with their specialties — earthen cooking pots, painted clay bowls, glazed clay figures, fish, seaweed, talismans, fetishes, potatoes, oca, frozen *chuno* potatoes and corn. There are no hucksters — the women merely wait. Man first knew peace from commerce and the market is as old as man in the Andes.

All manner of things are for sale here, including such standard simples as condor fat for rheumatism, starfish for headaches, aborted llama foetus for good luck and other equally unpalatable recipes for fertility and aphrodisia. Since the Incas did not have the money, trade was by barter, and so, even though the Indian has now had coins for five centuries, barter remains the trade technique. We watched an Indian woman who sat beside her offering of potatoes. They were stacked neatly on her woolen poncho, arranged like a diagram of chemical molecules. A buyer with her baby strapped to her back sat down, pulled a handful of beans from her blouse and offered to exchange them for an amount of potatoes. The vendor gave a disdainful glance at the offering and simply ignored her. The woman reached inside her blouse and pulled out another handful of beans and placed these on the pile. The vendor, now satisfied with the exchange, swept the beans into the fold of her skirt like a croupier pulling in lost chips while the buyer picked up her potatoes, stuffed them into her blouse, then pulled out a few more beans which she tossed down as a token of good feeling.

It took us only a short while to purchase the supplies which would complement our own dehydrated food store. That done we returned to Haqui, there to make ready for our reconquest of what Pedro Cieza de León called "the grandest road in the world."

III

The Floating Road

W E WERE now well on our journey into the past. The moment we left Puno to follow southward, first, the traces of the Inca road, we left the present and vaulted back four hundred years. And almost at once we were aware that we had undertaken a gigantic task. The Royal Road was here somewhere, buried under five centuries of earth-drift, but to find its course we would have had to track it much as one does the spoor of some gigantic prehistoric beast who had left its footprints in the sands of time. It was going to be, I was convinced, an engrossing sort of puzzle played on the blackboard of time. We had the literary research, the maps and borrowed aerial photographs, and these had dovetailed to form the picture. Our antagonists were time and geography. Yet, if in the first days we did not always find what we had hoped immediately to find — the broad expanse of the Royal Road running like a modern turnpike across the level land — we still had the land and the people of the land who filled in the vacuum.

Now our elaborate literary research was having its first full test. There was scarcely an hour of the day that I was not using our notebooks filled with information about the direction the Inca road had taken around the edge of the lake. For although the little villages mentioned in the research notes still retained their names, many of them had been moved from their original sites. That made for much geographical confusion and could — and often did — throw our survey of the road off for many miles.

No one helped us more than our "Cieza." We never thought of those who had centuries ago preceded us along these roads as mere "chroniclers" or disembodied authorities. Through the text of their books it was as if they were actually talking to us and, themselves, living.

Who for example was this Pedro Cieza de León who since 1553 has conducted his readers along the Royal Road? We knew no more of him than he chose to tell of himself, which was precious little. Anonymity was not uncommon in that robust century, for unless a man were well born and had his official scribes to record his deeds, little attention was paid to him, and few were bold enough to speak of themselves. So it was with Cieza. He was, in his society, nothing or less than nothing — an undernourished boy from the hovels of Seville who in 1532, at the age of fourteen, had signed on as a lolly-boy to a knight bound for the New World.

Don Pedro mentions nothing of his first years in the Americas. Yet when boys normally would be studying the arts of civilization, he was learning his in the savage school of experience. At twenty-two he began his journal. What inspired him, of all the conquistadores, to set down the events that took place before his eyes? What moved him to write? He was not, like many of the knuckleheads that surrounded him, an illiterate. That he could write was an achievement sufficiently startling in itself for those times, but he also wrote well — which is even more surprising; ". . . there came upon me a strong desire to write an account of some of the great and strange things that are to be seen in this new world; those which can be seen with my own eyes. . . ."

If a talent could be said to justify itself not by its originality but by its intensity and vitality, Cieza may be placed beside William

Dampier, the pirate, who while sailing the Spanish Main wrote his "Discourse on Winds" which he kept in the hollow of a bamboo tube. Despite long days in the saddle, living off the meager fare of the country, attacked by Indians, disturbed at night by the roll of dice and the coarse humor of soldiers frolicking with Indian wenches, Cieza wrote: "Ofttimes when the other soldiers were sleeping, I was tiring myself by writing. Neither fatigue nor the ruggedness of the country nor the mountains and rivers nor raging hunger and suffering has ever been sufficient to obstruct my two duties: writing my chronicle and following without fault my flag and my Captain."

Don Pedro, then, was our constant companion, and through his eyes, four hundred years to the day and year that he published his chronicle,[1] we saw the roads, the bridges, and better still the people who had wrought the road. "Of the lake of Bonbón and how it is supposed to be the source of the great river of La Plata. . . . Of the manner in which the city of Cuzco is built of the four Royal Roads which lead from it . . ." One places trust in such a man. Like those of his time, he paid his obeisance to God and his King. Beyond that, Cieza was exact and critical. What he himself did not see, what did not actually "transpire before his eyes," he sought out from others, weighed what he found, balanced it in the scale of his own experience, and then used it.

Long in the "Indies," Cieza returned to Spain in 1550 without any fortune, and in a sordid garret in Seville he composed his chronicles. Physically worn by years of hardship, living off poor wine, eating bread, garlic and olives, finding it difficult even to buy new pen quills and writing amidst all the squalor and filth of the Seville slums, he was, after thirty years in the New World,

---

[1] *The First Part of the Chronicle of Peru, which Treats of the Demarcation of Its Provinces and the Description Thereof, of the Foundations of New Cities, of the Rites and Customs of the Incas and Other Strange Things Delightful to Know,* by Pedro Cieza de León. (Seville, 1553).

old before his years and broken. "The hardships that had to be endured in those countries were so terrible. . . . Oh! to have gone there, damaged my conscience, wasted my time, and lost my teeth!"

Three years later some printer-publisher with a nose for a good thing published the first of the *Chronicles* and within a year they were translated into several languages. Unfortunately by that time Cieza was dead.

In this bare land, where we slowly followed the spoor of the Inca road, houses and people seemed part of the landscape. This region was the most densely populated in Peru. It was May and the time for planting. Everyone was in the fields, the very young and the very old. Women were predominant, as if to underscore the belief that agriculture was a female discovery and under the aegis of the earth-mother. Little girls, counterparts of their mothers, were setting down the patterns of existence which, with only slight variation, was to be theirs the rest of their earth-days. The windowless houses, made of adobe and thatched with grass, were clustered near sheltering rocks away from the fields. The winter wheat had not yet been harvested and the golden sheaths with the blue sky and the blue lake as backdrop was a picturesque setting for the lives of these Indians. In this, his own environment, the Indian is as one with his tradition-filled life. Love for the land, a yearning for land, a desire to have his own piece of land, is the dream of every Indian; he will starve for it, even kill himself working to get money to buy his own land.

The people of the lake, however, are quite unique in that here the old Inca system of the *ayllu,* or communally held land, is still in effect. The community is the "earth-cell." The land cannot be sold. It can only be worked, and as a member of the clan you are born into this earth-cell. Still the Indian does not seek the comforts of our civilization; he resists symbiosis with the white man.

The lake was always with us. It reflected like a mirror all the moods of the sky. At times it seemed more like the sea with the constant wind raising high waves and the opposite shore lost to view. Much of the shore was fringed with the tall reeds called *totora* which the Indian uses for his balsa boats, and from the shore the land retreated upward until it swept up to heights a thousand feet above the lake surface. It was in such places that the road ran, for its builders had always tried to avoid running their road through fertile land.

At first we were lost in a confusion of maps and overwhelming geographical detail. The Inca road, as traced in our research, went on both sides of the lake, separating into two parts the town of Ayaviri which lay above the northern end of Titicaca. The road which ran on the west side, where we were now camped, was named the Oma-suyu, while that which ran along the east side was called the Urco-suyu. At the southern end of the one-hundred-and-thirty-mile-long lake, the branches came together; southward the Royal Road continued into Bolivia and thence down to Chile and Argentina.

We had decided to follow the route on the west side by truck caravan when we could, by horse when vehicles failed us, and if needed, by foot. It was an enormous first project, for it took in the entire province which the Incas called the Koya. Charles Daugherty, who had a penchant for giving a code name for everything we did, called it "Operation Koya."

Aside from the trouble of trying to find the remains of any Inca road, we now began to have mechanical difficulties. This, of course, was to be expected at these high altitudes where the rarity of the atmosphere greatly affects the functions of any mechanism. First, our jeep had developed a death rattle and then the long fifteen-hundred-foot climb up the side of the Andes to Puno had done the jeep in. Stalled in the streets of the town, with the temperature at freezing, I sought out a mechanic called "the Master." He promptly diagnosed the problem as a "little nothing" and promised that before the sun came up over the roofs on the morrow it would be repaired and ready for the road.

However, when I called the next morning I found he had gone far beyond the call of duty. Jeep parts were strewn all over the dust-filled garage. The garage was a madhouse swarming with no less than a dozen Indian boys who acted as his assistants. The whole business reminded me of the theme of the "Sorcerer's Apprentice."

When I inveighed against this delay, he meekly replied, "Your Grace, tomorrow — tomorrow, Your Grace, it shall be ready."

There were many "tomorrows" and when at last we set off many days behind schedule, I noticed at once that the jeep was without sustained power and that the oil pressure seemed erratic. In that high whine and rasp of sound was the leitmotif of an Andean comedy of errors. At best we could move but slowly.

Within a fortnight, however, we had fallen into a rhythm. At the first real bite of the night we stopped, searched out a campsite, pulled the caravan around so that the cold winds would be broken and set to work. One of the trucks of our caravan, the Dodge Power Wagon, had been designed for the Expedition. It had a four-wheel drive and was capable of climbing in low gear up a sixty-degree angle. On the front there was a geared winch of tremendous power. We had built a special body for it with steel cabinets along the side with matching steel doors. In these, as Silvia planned, the food was so arranged that at any given time we could lower the door which then became table or cutting board, and so prepare our meals. Unless one has lived in lands where once out of the larger villages there is nothing to be had, one cannot fully appreciate what this rolling commissary meant. It had taken much precious time to think out the way to carry our food but we knew that all this careful planning would now be worth the time and expense given to it. We had worked out every detail carefully. We had our own electric power; we could sustain ourselves without contact for months if need be; with supplies and with our sleeping bags, tents and other related equipment we moved in our own self-contained world. Lawrence would set up the generator and within a few minutes we had electric light. Meantime, while Charles had set up the "facilities," Silvia and I would start work on the preparation of food. The sides of the Power Wagon were let down. At one end was the gasoline stove; in the center our plastic dishes and the spices; in the third cabinet was the food, mostly of the dehydrated variety. In time we would augment it when possible with fresh food, but the *puna* offered little variety and when you travel across it, you must be independent of all other sources or else most of the time will be spent in futile search for food. Canned goods were not for us. They were expensive, space-filling and wasteful.

On our first night out our menu consisted of duck *à la puna* with dry mushrooms and dehydrated carrots and onions. To this was added a handful of dehydrated spinach cooked in water with a soupçon of garlic powder and salt. From a moisture-proof envelope Silvia poured out a quantity of dried fruits which she made into the filling for a pie. The duck and the pie were baked in a flat oven on the third burner of the stove. Our coffee was Nescafé. By the time the beds were up, the double arctic sleeping bags unrolled and the stars had made their heralded appearance, dinner on the top of the world was ready. Then on this first night on the road as we lay back to allow our whole beings to enjoy what in this clime had been an arduous day's work, I thought back to our arrival in Peru.

*　　*　　*

The Floating Road

Silvia and I had arrived in Lima two months before the main part of the Expedition, so that we might make, as we thought, all the arrangements with the officials for the clearance of the vast impedimenta of the Expedition. Then came the day when Silvia and I had risen betimes and had gone down to the port of Lima to see the S.S. *Lena-Dan* come in with the other members of the Expedition and our vehicles and supplies for two years of exploration and study. The sea journey had filled our friends with a sense of expectancy; they were anxious to get cleared of Customs and into the field. I had played a fantastic game with the Customs. Possessed of an executive decree, which in general terms promised "everything," I had to give actuality to that "everything." Since in the lower echelons of the bureaucracy of Peru there is no executive power, decisions cannot be made at this level. Yet it was on this level that I had to work in order to get Customs clearance for the Expedition. The list headed by the two vehicles, a Dodge Power Wagon and a jeep, was a long one; cameras, film, surveying instruments, camping equipment, saddles, personal effects — all of these could be admitted on a temporary basis since these tangibles could be checked out of the country at the terminus of the Expedition.

"And what about these items?" said one official. Using his small finger as we use the index finger, he went down the list.

"There is here your first item — two cases of Daiquiris — those are mixed cocktails, I take it — and Martinis." He was correct. Our shipping agent had put these by mistake at the top of the list of a thousand different items.

"Now these cannot be admitted temporarily, since you shall not take them out again, I take it."

"Of course not, but you see . . ." And I explained how an enthusiastic sales promoter thought it might be nice to donate some mixed drinks to inspire us on some of the cold Andean nights.

"You shall need a permit . . ."

"But we really are not interested in the cocktails."

Now somewhat suspicious of all we carried, he went over the list item by item and there were thousands: thermometers, copying devices, cutlery, books, film splicers, machine tools, axes, machetes, gasoline stoves, altitude masks, oxygen-breathing devices for high altitudes. Day after day I would turn up at Customs in a freshly pressed suit; each afternoon I would leave, my temper frayed to ribbons. At last I called on the Finance Minister, an old friend. There were telephone calls and orders, more paper, more delay. At last it came to an end. A compromise was effected. A bond was offered for the Expedition's impedimenta in transit for a period of two years, the cocktails excepted, and after two weeks of effort, we were more or less ready.

Then gasoline had to be cached along the way — we could only transport a small amount. This we had to arrange with the International Petroleum Company. The foodstuffs destined for two years of travel had to be separated into stores for coast, jungle and Andes and a selection of the things we would take along for the first phase of the Expedition had to be made.

While all this went on, Silvia and I selected the maps offered us by the *Instituto Geográfico Militar* — those marked "Secret" had to be released to us. Some of these, based on aerial surveys, were wonderfully detailed. Later we went out to the Peruvian Air Ministry to select aerial photographs.

Ever since the Shippee-Johnson Expedition of the American Geographical Society in 1931 had photographed Peru from the air, the Government had worked steadily on a complete aerial mosaic of Peru. This project was of great value to us, for we could now select aerial photographs in the areas of our interests and obtain the copies at a small cost. These proved to be invaluable in our road search.

On the eve of our take-off, we summed up all we had — the research from the literature of chroniclers, knights, conquistadores, picaros, Incas, padres, travelers and archaeologists, correlated in three large black notebooks. Our specially prepared Inca Highway maps showing the road directions as deduced from that literature were supplemented by detailed Peruvian military maps and by the aerial surveys we had made in various air flights. These, with aerial photographs from the archives, completed our list of necessities — or so we thought. We believed, then, that with these assists we had lessened our research problem considerably and that we should the more easily find the roads.

This was oversimplification.

Even on the last day before we moved out, we were still frantically enmeshed in things undone and wanting. Then on the sixth of March, 1953, we went through a small official ceremony in Lima. We were interviewed, embraced, photographed. Then we set off and within an hour we had put Lima behind us, and were in the desert. That noon I sent off my first dispatch to the *New York Times:*

AFTER FIFTEEN YEARS OF DREAMING IT AND TWO YEARS PLANNING IT, THE INCA HIGHWAY EXPEDITION LEFT LIMA TODAY TO BEGIN ITS DISCOVERY OF THE FAMOUS INCA HIGHWAY SYSTEM . . .

After all these irritating complications the hardships of the Expedition now seemed as nothing. The most difficult part for us all was the adjustment to each other. Our first weeks of traveling over the *puna* in search of the roads were not always in wilderness that was "happiness enow." There were the natural irritations of propinquity. Then, too, we all suffered from the first onrush of *soroche*, altitude sickness, when our food never seemed to digest, headaches were frequent and tempers short. Self-control here was as necessary as breathing if our individual discomfort was not to take the form of anger toward one another. This is always a danger when persons unused to each other are thrown together on a continually intimate basis. Silvia held up well, although I could see that the enforced intimacy was galling; few women could have endured it day after day, night after night. Charles, under the pressure of altitude, withdrew into himself and was inclined at times to be uncommunicative. Lawrence, like most who live alone, became hyperefficient; a martinet over details, he grew short-tempered and explosive. I was equally irritating, for the altitude seemed to give me more energy — I have more than my share under normal conditions — and my pushing of the program certainly strained nerves that were already taut. And yet despite all this, animated by the tremendous challenge that our exploration offered, we were making good progress in searching out the Inca road.

By June we had followed the road down from the *puna* and arrived in the "Kingdom of God," the halfway mark between our starting point and the border of Bolivia, whither we were bound. At Juli, in the center of this "Kingdom," we drove into its small square dominated by a baroque cherub holding a fish which spewed water into a crisply carved fountain. Here the buildings about the plaza dated back to the sixteenth century. One with an ornamental doorway was now the jail; another had housed a printing press which issued early books — one of these, dated 1595, is a bibliographical rarity. A vast area about these shores of Lake Titicaca had been given by the Viceroy in 1576 to a militant order of God and at that time the Jesuits, gathering the Indians into villages, had imposed a veneer of Christianity over their paganism and had taught them to carve and decorate in the Spanish style. As a result in Juli today there are churches as astonishing as they are original. All through the Titicaca region we were to find such churches bordering the Royal Road of the Incas.

The Floating Road

By the time we arrived at Pomata, the next village on the road, we found that time had almost obliterated its traces. The low stone walls that had bordered it had been removed and used for the making of houses. In many places fields occupied the place where the highway had been. Only on the bare *puna* or on the high grass veldts which did not lend themselves to cultivation was the road to be clearly seen.

We had now to depend on other chroniclers for aid in locating the exact location of the phantom road. Our friend Cieza's scant and tantalizingly brief descriptions were not now enough to aid us.

It was here, at the little village of Pomata, that we began to consult the writings of another New World chronicler, one Poma de Ayála. He had also written a valuable documentation to the early history of the Inca. Compiled during the years 1567–1615, this contains in its thousand pages, hundreds of pen drawings at once lively and naïve. This strange old history — one could almost call it a comic book history of the Inca empire — came to light in 1908, oddly enough, in the Royal Danish Library at Copenhagen. Written partly in Quechua, partly in archaic Spanish, it reflected the author's origin, an Indian mother and a father who was one of the Spanish conquistadores. Poma de Ayála was apparently educated at the school for Indian nobles at Cuzco. As a young man he traveled about his estates, witnessed the degradation of the Indians, and took their sides in disputes with their Spanish overlords; and in time he began to work on his book.

The result was a profusely illustrated volume, difficult to read but invaluable as a sourcebook on the religious customs, dress, daily life of the Incas. It was of tremendous interest to us, especially so since under a chapter headed "TAMBOS" (*tampus*), Poma de Ayála had a complete listing of these wayside stations along the highway from Colombia to Chile. At this point at Pomata we came upon a succinct entry in his book: *Pomata pueblo tanbo rreal.*

From this we knew that Pomata, city of the royal *tambo,* had once been an official stop on the Inca highway, and that even though the road we sought had long since disappeared it had in fact passed this way. And so Pomata became one more historic link on the Royal Road of the Incas.

As the land became less fertile and less peopled, we were able to pick up longer stretches of the ancient Inca road. On the *puna* it ran unobstructed as straight as line and eye could make it, its width the standard measure of fifteen feet. Apparently it had been paved except where marsh lands had converted the land into a quagmire. Otherwise across the *puna,* as firm and hard as a macadamized road, the Inca road was laid down in a direct line, marked with a low wall usually made of stone mixed with a mud adhesive. The Andean earth here was subject to severe erosion due to the alternate assaults of sun and rain, those "insults of time" as the French have it, so that much of the original course of the road had been worn away. Occasionally, however, we could see enough of the old roadbed to mark it, measure it, and even travel this path of an empire. For many miles we followed the Royal Road over a land as vacant as the moon for while the Incas had made a practice of using the shortest route to get to their destination, their engineers had avoided any land that could be cultivated, so the road traveled through barren regions.

In this way we came to Zepita. Our research said very clearly: "*Cipita* (Zepita) *Village:* Royal Road near to the river bridge."

All day we searched for ruins of old Zepita and its Inca *tampu,* yet we found no indication of its remains. I questioned the old and the young, even sought out the padre, guardian of the church and the special amenities. He could tell me nothing. He was a singularly obtuse man who insisted that the road of the Incas here ran underground. Why, he could not say, except it was what was said in

36

these parts. Exasperated, I finally led him out back of his church and pointed out the plainly visible Inca road, but he still held to his original argument.

Beyond this little village, the littoral of Lake Titicaca is transformed into a grotesque tableau of sandstone and limestone sculptured by the winds. It had taken fantastic shapes and would have seemed uninhabitable except that wherever there was a purchase in the cliffs there was an Indian's house.

For three weeks now we had been skirting the lake. We were now at the border town of Desaguadero, the coldest spot on Titicaca. The cool shadows of night had fallen and the winds whipping across the lake carried a penetrating cold. We were dressed as we would be for the Arctic — sheepskin-lined jackets, fur gloves, stocking caps over ears.

I had expected to find a large river here, since the Desaguadero is the only river to drain the huge lake. But not until we drove along a reed-choked estuary did we see it. A hundred feet wide, marshbound on both sides, this river which marks the border between Peru and Bolivia was spanned by a battered wooden bridge with iron gates on either side strung with barbed wire and patrolled by guards. In Spanish times there were no such boundaries. The Inca road threaded its way through the fantastic cliffs of sandstone, crossed the river by means of a balsa pontoon bridge and went on to the next *tampu* station.

Here the *tampu* known as Cacha-marca was famous for its bridge. "In the days of the Inca," wrote Cieza, "there used to be a toll-taker who received tribute from those who passed over the bridge which is made of bundles of stalks in such a way that it is strong enough to allow men and horses to cross over it. . . ." Renewed every year this famous floating pontoon bridge was to endure for over eight hundred years and was still in place in 1864 when the American explorer-diplomat, E. George Squier, came upon it. Fortunately for us, he sketched it.

He came into the village of Desaguadero much as we did — tired, hungry, seeking a place to sleep. He arrived during a fiesta. Across the entrance to the little plaza were two crooked poles and stretched between them on ropes by way of decoration dangled silver spoons, silver goblets, silver soup tureens and night pots, cups, plates and strings of Spanish dollars, gathered from all the people of the village. Indians, drunk as Dionysus and barbarically costumed in ostrich plumes, beating drums and blowing at pan pipes, were dancing around the plaza. The elite of the town sat on mats drinking.

"The scene was droll and barbaric," Squier wrote later, "and we involuntarily checked our horses as we passed beneath the extraordinary string of treasures which garnished the entrance to the plaza."

The resident priest of the village "red of face, his glistening eyes watery and blinking," staggered forward, bottle in hand, gave them a drink and offered them the village. They took only a part of it, a small hovel on the floor of which Squier spread his bed, while his companion, Harvey the daguerreotypist, who carried an enormous primitive photographic apparatus with him, "contrived to dispose himself on some bags of barley in the corner."

When Squier died in the Great Blizzard in 1888, he was remembered chiefly as one of the five husbands of the formidable Mrs. Frank Leslie. Yet he had been *the* first important American archaeologist. Born in Upper New York in 1821 and with little formal schooling, Squier became a self-taught civil engineer and journalist. At twenty-seven he wrote his book on "Indian Mounds," the first book published by the Smithsonian Institution. At twenty-nine he was the American Minister to Central America and in 1863 he was named Lincoln's Commissioner to Peru. On the termination of his official duties, he traveled throughout Peru and eventually wrote a book on the archaeology of Peru.

The Floating Road

And now here at Desaguadero, with Squier's *Peru* as our guide, we were to try to relocate the site of this once famous balsa pontoon bridge, on the Royal Road of the Incas.

The village was empty and cold, but overlooking the river there was a hotel of sorts; and while there was no priest to welcome us with generous bottle, there was the official of the place who, having been advised of our probable arrival by the Prefect of Puno, gave us welcome.

It was freezing. We had already put on our arctic clothes. After a supper which seemed to congeal on our plates, Silvia gave up and took to the shelter of her sleeping bag. We stayed below, and in the light of a single gasoline lamp we talked over the details of to-morrow's building of the balsa bridge. The official, a youngish man in a black suit with matching black fedora who seemed warm enough although his hands were as red as parboiled lobsters, informed us that, on receipt of the telegram from our friend in Puno, he had set about to gather up the needed Indians.

"I work, you must understand, through my Indian officials, who are called gobernadores. They are usually elders of the villages, the best informed and respected. I have asked them to come here to-night to talk to you."

I indicated that this was very good and thanked him for what I considered to be a miracle of organization.

"But of course," he went on, "you must do the rest . . ." By that he meant the supplying of the common incentive — alcohol and coca leaves. "Unfortunately," he went on, "our Indians will not work properly without coca, and then if you give them in addition some alcohol, matters proceed faster."

I felt that I should go out at once and see, even at this cold hour, about these indispensable items but the official stayed me with one of his lobster-red hands.

39

"There is no need, Señor, of your going; I just happen to have here . . ." And he produced four large bags of coca leaves and several bottles of pure alcohol. By this time the Indian elders had arrived.

Each gave me a flaccid handshake, the white man's greeting which they perform limply. Each murmured a few words in sibilant Aymara, showing their stained teeth in a vacant smile of salutation. Their dress was a common one — pants, jacket and high woolen poncho. All wore the *chullo,* a crocheted stocking cap with earflaps, and all carried silver-headed sticks which are the wands of authority. I passed around generous glasses of "incentive," and after a while the chill of the atmosphere was noticeably warmed. The official spoke. "These scientists," he said solemnly, "have come here to Desaguadero to study the place where once the balsa bridge crossed the river. They want to assemble all the Indians, have them bring in their balsa, and before their eyes and their cameras they want to see how this ancient balsa bridge was made."

He went on to ask if they remembered how it was made. At this they fell into excited talk among themselves, although no one seemed to be listening to anyone else. The oldest of them all — said to be a century old — at first sat quietly munching coca leaves, deaf to the talk-talk, but when it had gone on for a few minutes, he raised his wrinkled hand. In the silence that followed he spoke.

It seems (so it was translated to me) that as a boy he had seen the bridge built; it had been the last of its kind. (If the old fellow really was a hundred that would have placed the erection of his bridge somewhat before the arrival of Squier in 1863.) The pontoon had to be renewed every year, the old man went on; and every year each Indian had to make and deliver a thirty-five-foot balsa. One bridge was built here at Desaguadero and another at Nasacara farther down the river.

I took Squier's book printed in 1870 and laid it in front of them.

The Floating Road

There on page 265 was a wood engraving of the balsa bridge at Nasacara, some fifty miles down the river to the southwest. It showed forty or more large balsas fastened together with ropes over which a reed road was laid. Two mules were crossing the bridge while women in native dress stood before stone towers to which the cables of the bridge were attached. Excitedly the Indian elders peered at the sketch, pointing to details of the bridge. Once again the old man held up his hand and, nodding as one who knows, said, "This is how the bridge was built."

Through our interpreter I spoke: "Well, this is how we want the bridge built. Follow it as the ancient ones did it. Don't change anything. Come in the morning with your balsas; come with ropes, matting and *totora* grass; come in native dress; come on time. I will pay all who work, I will give all who come coca. I will give all alcohol."

And as an earnest I passed another round of coca leaves.

The day for the bridge-building was clear, beautiful and cold. I never felt a New England winter-cold as intense as that in this village, which was on a direct line with the snow-topped mountains of Bolivia. From these the ice-laden winds raced across the lake, leaving a perpetual trail of what an eighteenth-century traveler called "frigorific particles." Charles, who had taken an early walk, had come back with his body ice-stiff from the cold, and with icicles in his beard. We prepared oatmeal on our paratrooper stove and drank multiple cups of coffee. It gave us courage to brave the winds.

There was no one in the streets at this hour. Our rendezvous was a spot where the rock from the eroded hills approached close to the lake. The lake itself was as rigid and as mirrorlike as glass. Around its shores ice clung to the reeds and fringed the moored balsa boats.

A bird walked across it to stand and peer uncertainly in the stygian water. The snow-topped mountains in the distance were deep blue at first, shadowed and shimmering; then glowing, first green, then red, and, as the sun mounted, gold. It was breath-taking. Now Indians began to arrive paced by the gobernadores carrying their silver-headed sticks. Since they spoke little Spanish and we no Aymara speech, I broke the cold of our relationship by ordering our carriers to pass out hatfuls of coca leaves.

At the signal, our Indians picked up their poles and made their way across the ice to their boats. Then the entire fleet of little boats, their *totora*-reed sails operating like Venetian blinds, sailed up the river toward the village.

Lawrence waited on the small wooden bridge that today connects Peru with Bolivia to photograph the balsas sailing in single file under the bridge; at a predetermined spot below the modern bridge, the first balsas came to anchor and the others began to pile up, each holding to the sides of the other for anchor. A Bolivian soldier, muffled up with only his nose visible, leaned on his rifle staring at us with unseeing eyes; a few dogs barked; and an old woman, come to gather water in an earthen-red pot, watched us curiously. That was all. The place was as empty as the sky. So we set about our business.

The reed boat is one of man's more fascinating inventions. It was perfected in those parts of Peru where there was no wood for boat-building. Around the littoral of Lake Titicaca, there is a profusion of *totora,* and it is this tubular reed, half an inch in diameter and eight feet in length, which furnishes the material for the boats. The making of reed boats is so ancient a craft that it is pictured on Peruvian pottery dating back to the first century B.C.

The reed is dried, made into four cigar-shaped bundles, the length of the bundle determining the size of the projected reed boat. (Although the Indians can and do construct boats forty feet long, capable of carrying sixty people, these are a rarity.) First, two of these bundles are tied with rope made from the twisted fibers of *ichu* grass to form the prow of the balsa boat. The other two, laid on top and off center, form the sides and the cabin of the boat. Using only such material as the lake offers, the balsa boat is completed within two days. Sails also are made from the *totora* reed. Since the balsa has no keel, it cannot tack and can only sail in a following wind, so propulsion is mostly by punting and, when the water is deep, by paddle.

The buoyancy of the reed boat is amazing. The Egyptians used a similar type of craft made from the papyrus, and the White Nile is still navigated by the Kinka tribesmen in boats made of a batch-reed, so similar to the reed boats of Lake Titicaca that the parallelism in human invention is startling.

Since man is a practical animal, he has made use of the floating bridge in many parts of the world, and here at Titicaca he made use of the reed boats as pontoons or foundations for the floating section of the Royal Road.

The centenarian who had remembered the original directed the building of our bridge, so we had only to record and to watch. The main anchor was two poles stuck into the low bank of the river. To this a grass rope was attached; and this, in turn, passed along to all of the forty balsas, was seized by the occupants and fastened to the wooden pegs that had been driven into the boats' sides. Within a short time all of the balsas were fastened together in a pontoon and anchored to poles driven in on the Bolivian side of the river. They were now stuffed with *totora* reed, forming a solid flooring. Then woven reed mats were laid on top and fastened to the sides. Although this was not as firm a bridge as that built by the Incas, it was a good facsimile. For that moment at least we had rolled back the flight of time, for there again a balsa pontoon bridge stood as it had centuries before.

The moment had arrived for the dedication of our balsa bridge. We had so concentrated on watching the building of the balsa that we were unaware that we were being watched. But when we attempted to photograph a line of llamas being urged across the bridge, the press of people was so formidable that Lawrence could not even see the bridge. We would have preferred complete indifference. Instead there was utter chaos. The onlookers helped themselves to the Indians' coca leaves. Bottles of alcohol disappeared; the llamas, stampeded by the mob, ran rather than ambled in their usual stately walk across the balsa bridge. And above the din of voices, the town savant — as drunk as the morning allowed — was attempting a speech, something about the greatness of the Incas.

All the carefully laid plans of balsas and men dissolved in this confusion. We had hoped to cross the bridge, and go on to Huaqui in Bolivia — where, according to Cieza, there were "buildings of the Incas," there to begin the survey of that section of the Inca road that ran through Bolivia and down into Argentina. But Bolivia was at the moment going through one of its periodic upsets, and our experience with the balsa pontoon project was so frustrating that we ended, for the moment, this phase of our search for the southern Royal Road — at Desaguadero.

However, the local savant, who was still trying in vain to make his speech, provided a measure of comic relief. For, angered at the lack of attention, he strode off across our balsa pontoon bridge. He had gone only a few yards when he stepped into a vacant pocket of *totora* reed and, like Mephistopheles, disappeared as if swallowed up by a trap door. The last we saw of him was his head, bobbing up and down in the river, with the natives who had been clustered around the balsa bridge running down the bank in pursuit of him.

I V

Towers of the Dead

W E WERE lost in a veritable forest of *chullpas*, the stone Towers of the Dead. There were so many of them that they took in effect the place of trees. It was an eerie feeling as we rode north to come across these extraordinary tombs on a barren plain. "I was truly astonished," wrote Cieza, who in his travels had wandered among these same towers of the dead, "to see how little these people cared for the living while they bestow so much care on the tombs . . . as if happiness did not consist in something else. On the plains . . . the tombs were built in the form of small towers . . . according to the rank and wealth of those who built them. They carry the corpse to the place where the tomb is prepared . . . there they burn ten or more llamas . . . kill the women, boys and servants who are to accompany him on his last voyage. All these are buried in the same tomb with the body. The mourners then walk along uttering sad and mournful songs . . . while an Indian goes before them beating a drum. The great tombs are so numerous that they occupy more space than is given to the living."

On our way back to Puno, Silvia and I had decided to have a look at the high plateau that overlooked the lake, hoping to discover that section of the Inca road we had missed on our southward survey. As the land was too precipitous for the Power Wagon to negotiate, Silvia and I, equipped with food and rifles, set off alone in the jeep. On our second day out we picked up the Inca road, lost it again, and then at Qutimbo we came to the forest of *chullpas*. As far as we could see there was nothing to relieve the eye except these stone burial towers. Fourteen feet high, some circular, others square, the Towers of the Dead were wonderfully fashioned of stone in the megalithic style, with huge polygonal rocks fitted together so exactly that even moss could not find lodgement. The corbeled vaults inside, almost as high as the towers, were of meticulous stonework. There were a few bone fragments lying about, and some bits of pottery — not much more, for these tombs had been sacked first by the Incas and later by the Spaniards, and so thoroughly that just who built the Houses of the Dead has never been discovered.

We wandered about the tombs for the rest of the morning, then in the afternoon set our course east, to search again for an elusive stretch of the Inca road.

We drove endlessly, the sky above us angry and overcast, gray and somber. The land was as vacant as the open sea — the undulating *puna* might have been its waves — and the lonely piercing cry of the gull, that of the seabird following the wake of a ship. Occasionally an Indian hovel would appear made of crumbling adobe and propped up against a lava boulder. Thatched with the same *ichu* grass which covered the plain, they were so well camouflaged that only on close inspection were we aware that these were houses.

We were up 14,000 feet. I had not at first paid any attention to the jeep, although I should have remembered that lack of oxygen would reduce its efficiency. Now it began to sputter and, like ourselves, seemed to be gasping for air. The oil gauge took to oscillating madly and I realized that something was terribly wrong. Although we were only seventy miles as the condor flies from Puno, we were in effect hundreds of miles from effective aid.

I tried to get to the top of the hill so that we could make a rundown in case we stalled, but we never got that far. Suddenly the jeep stopped dead as if it had struck a concrete wall. I looked at the motor — a rather useless procedure, for my knowledge of such things is small — and then unpredictably I was overcome by an immense weariness. I staggered back to get the tools and was so overcome with giddiness that I had to clutch the sides to keep from falling backward. Silvia climbed out to help me extract the tools and that was enough. She too turned a pale-green color and cupped her hands over her eyes.

As I clung to the car I knew that I had to force myself to do something about our problem, so I managed to propel myself forward and began to work on the engine. I released the brake and, on the assumption that a push might start the engine, went around back. One push and I slipped to the ground panting for breath. Silvia came back to find out what was happening and, seeing me down, her strength too took flight. We found ourselves lying there, both as completely done in as if we had just run ten thousand meters.

As we lay there, I could hear my heart pounding, fighting against the decrease of oxygen. Yet in a few minutes I felt completely recovered. I looked at Silvia. She was pale, her lips colorless; her pulse fluttered and her breathing was short and hardly audible. I stood up to get the medical box, and again the feeling of dizziness came over me. But this time I managed to stay on my feet long enough to boil a hypodermic needle, select an ampoule of caffeine sodium and inject it in her right arm. I followed this with an injection of adrenalin. Presently she fell into an exhausted sleep and I, wearied by this simple effort, lay down beside her.

There was a condor far up in the sky and I watched it gliding about effortlessly and wondered if it had any trouble with *soroche*. Then I recalled that physiologically a 12,000-foot elevation in the Andes was equivalent to 5000 in the Alps. At 0 feet of altitude, there is 760 mm. of atmospheric pressure. Here we were at 14,000 feet where we had only 430 mm. of atmospheric pressure, allowing us a mere 86 mm. of oxygen tension. At this elevation anoxemia or shortness of breath is a permanent condition, and *soroche* or acute mountain sickness is, for those not used to it, a little like experiencing death. I thought of Father José Acosta, a sixteenth-century traveler who was making his first trip across the Andes when it "came on him."

> Now some [said he] hold it to be a fable, and others say 'tis an exaggeration, but I will tell you what happened to me. There is in Peru a very high mountain range which they call Pariacaca; I went "upstairs" as they call it when you go up the highest part of the mountain range. There I was suddenly seized with such mortal anguish that I was of a mind to throw myself off the horse; I was seized with such retchings and vomitings that I thought that I should give up my soul, for after the food came up and the phlegm, then came bile and more bile, this one yellow and the other green until next I spit up blood . . . finally I declare that if it had gone on, I believe I would most assuredly have died. This *soroche* happened because the air is so thin and penetrating that it goes through one's bowels. . . .

I did far better than the good Father. Within an hour I was attempting to work on the jeep, inveighing the while against that stupid "master" mechanic at Puno, for in taking out the vitals of the car he had apparently pinched the oil line with the result that the motor was frozen and the bearings burned out. The car would have to be towed. Although a mere fifty miles from Puno, we might as well have been on the moon! We could not both walk it — that would be too much for Silvia, and I could not go alone and leave her. The cold was intense. Perhaps I could get some Indian at that last hut . . . I wakened Silvia and told her of my plans, then I was off, following the spoor of our tires, and in less than an hour — happily I was walking slightly downhill — I came across an Indian

48

house. The pale blue smoke mushroomed out from grass thatch, and after calling in vain for a few minutes I pushed against a door that hung so perilously on broken thongs that it almost fell at my touch. A small light from a cooking fire burned pallidly in the corner of a room as small and as bare as a prison cell. I could just see the people in one corner. I spoke in halting Aymara.

I explained; I imitated an automobile; I made noises of its dying; I tried as in a game of charades to explain my plight. I grant it was a poor performance but certainly, it seemed to me, they should understand *something*.

The group was seated around a large cooking pot. The men were dirty, the women disheveled. No one laughed, no one spoke. They swallowed and gulped in a kind of gloomy haste. A rather young woman, kneeling over the cooking pot extracting something with her fingers, had one enormous well-shaped breast exposed. To this a little boy clad only in a jacket, who had also been picking scraps, turned to suckle noisily.

Our only chance of getting out of our difficulty was to make these people understand, to buy their aid, and, if that failed, somehow to compel them to aid me. Forcing myself to be patient, I began again; they were unheeding — all but a young boy who detached himself from the huddling group.

"I understand Spanish."

Did he know Puno? He did. Could he possibly know the Mission of the Maryknoll Fathers?

"Oh, yes, I was taught to speak there."

Would he be willing for this amount of money — I held up a sizable amount — to take a message to Puno? For this too? In my right hand I held a mouth organ. . . . He was *most* willing. . . . I gave him the note asking for aid, the money, the mouth organ and a handful of coca leaves, and off he sped in the direction of Puno.

I returned to the stranded jeep where Silvia, now somewhat recovered, had the sleeping bag unrolled. We got out the paratrooper
stove, took out the dehydrated soups and other emergency rations,
gave ourselves a hot supper and spliced the main brace. Then, as
night fell, we crawled into our sleeping bags.

We were alone with the night. The wind howled across the *puna*
bringing with it wisps of snow. Crawling deeper into our sleeping
bags, we were dwarfed by the magnitude of the darkness.

Three days later we came back to the Expedition house at Haqui,
frozen and hungry and angry over the mishap that had used precious time, unnecessarily exposed us to danger, and lost us our jeep.
Shortly after our arrival I met the "master" mechanic. He now
chose the wrong moment to ask for more money — and to his surprise I showered him with a colorful array of curses. He grew truc-
ulent. He forgot his earlier obsequiousness and, as he came too close
for my physical comfort, I pushed him. That set him off like a
maniac. He came at me in the Puno free-style, legs and arms swinging. Whatever the gods that succored him, Master Pilón was in
their good graces that day. He offered so many opportunities for
me to break his head that I have often wondered how I managed to
withhold myself. As it was, I easily warded him off and no blows
were struck.

Two hours later I was drafting my cable dispatch to the *New
York Times*:

PUNO, JUNE 15: INCA ROUTE TRACED OFF LAKE TITICACA.
THE EXPEDITION IN SEARCH OF THE LOST AND FORGOTTEN
GREAT STONE HIGHWAYS OF THE INCAS HAS FINISHED ITS
FIRST SURVEY OF THE TOWERING LAKE TITICACA BASIN. THE
EXPEDITION WILL NOW SHAPE ITS WAY TOWARD CUZCO THE

Towers of the Dead

ANCIENT CAPITAL OF THE INCA EMPIRE. LIVING THROUGH THE FREEZING NIGHTS AND SEARING DAYS AROUND THE RIM OF THE HIGHEST NAVIGABLE LAKE IN THE WORLD HAS TAKEN ITS EFFECT ON BOTH THE MEMBERS OF THE EXPEDITION AND MACHINES. THE . . .

I was aware that the iron gate of the villa was being shaken vigorously.

"Francisco," I called. He appeared, his face an arabesque of wrinkles set in a smile.

"Arí," he answered.

"Whoever is rattling that gate, tell them to go away. I am busy working, writing."

"Arí."

The rattling went on.

Francisco was back again. "It is, your Grace, the mechanic Pilón . . ."

"Tell him to go to the devil."

"Arí. I have told him that, but he is there with the police, and they are armed with big rifles."

"Well . . ."

"It is as I say," insisted a blue clad officer of the National Police, "you must come with us. This man," and he indicated Pilón, who stood there in cat-swallowed-the-canary triumph, "accuses you of assaulting him. You must come within the hour and bring, if you have them, your witnesses."

My witnesses, such as they were, were scattered, so I was later than the set hour when I arrived at the Police Station. I found the Chief of Police in a paroxysm of rage. I had shown him grave disrespect by arriving late. I began to speak. I was silenced.

"Twenty-four hours in jail and then pay this man whatever sum he asks," he stormed.

One's private affairs in these Andean villages know no escape from prying ears. All is known to all, and every private act becomes at once part of the social fabric. Since nothing is private and everything is public, sides are taken at once and a whole village can be involved in an affair which is itself of little importance.

So this incident which anywhere else would have been a small dispute between mechanic and client had now mushroomed up to dangerous proportions. I was now about to be marched off for a tenure in jail. I was understandably in a thoroughly defiant mood since the Expedition was under the protection of the Government. Then as if someone had suddenly turned on the light of reason, the police captain came back, his face wreathed in friendliness. He understood our actions, the strain we had been under, the loss of time and equipment to the Expedition, and he apologized for the to-do. The mechanic, who had been sitting basking in his triumphs, was in utter bewilderment when he was actually shoved out the door.

What in the world had happened to change the picture? Silvia and I were still puzzling over this when we emerged from the Police Station to see Francisco Deza standing waiting for us with his quizzical smile reflected in his fine serious eyes.

"At your service," he said, lifting his hat.

"You did it?" asked Silvia.

"Well . . ."

Francisco Deza was the type of man that the early Spaniards had hoped would evolve out of the merging of the two bloods, native and Spanish. In him were blended the best elements of the two races. He spoke both languages with equal enthusiasm and, as Director of Rural Schooling, he had given his entire life to aiding the Indian within the framework of his own society. An avowed enemy of all Spanish rodomontade, he had wit, enthusiasm and direction. His house was book-filled. His wife, a charming woman who shared his interests, taught in an Indian school. Few aided our Expedition more than he. Once indeed he had saved Charles from imprisonment.

"I was backing up the Power Wagon," so Charles had reported the incident, "and I backed into a power line; I never knew it until the whole business began to fall down on me. In no time a policeman was at the window and before I could even say who I was — which would have been difficult as I don't speak Spanish — and that the damage would be taken care of, I was hustled off to jail."

But the affair of the "master" mechanic was far from ended. The matter continued to boil even as we carried on with our search around the lake. On a prolonged trip north, to the northern terminus of the lake, where the Rio Ramis enters Lake Titicaca, we traveled the path taken by the Inca road along the eastern side of Titicaca toward Bolivia.

On our return to Puno weeks later, I was asked to appear at the office of the Prefect where I was presented with an official document. This, he explained, was a charge to be laid before the Judge of the Criminal Section. In it, the mechanic accused me of assault and asked damages. . . . His claim? . . . That I had struck him with a heavy club breaking his arm, and that, therefore, he should be recompensed to the sum of five hundred soles for each day he had been incapacitated and, along with this, several thousand soles for punitive damages and . . . Medical affidavits? . . . Yes, there were several, attached to all these documents. . . .

Well, what did the Prefect wish us to do? . . . It seems that he wished to save us embarrassment, and so had held up the document and had not submitted it to the Criminal Section, intending to wait until he consulted with us. For once it was filed, it would set off a rain of events that he would find difficult to control. . . .

"But it is absurd, these charges and the amounts asked. We'll dispute it," I said.

"That, of course, is your privilege, Señor. It will take time, drag out for years; you have no idea of the vagaries of the laws of my country."

"Well, it can not matter much to us," said Silvia. "We shall be hundreds of miles from here."

"That is the point, Señora. You can be summoned back here at any time, which means your important work will be subject to constant harassment. Therefore, my advice would be . . ."

"To buy him off!"

He held out his hand in quizzical gesture. Who was it that said the human hand is about twenty thousand times more versatile than the mouth? That gesture conveyed everything.

Rising, I said: "We shall consider it."

All Puno, it seemed, was divided over the case. The episode was taking on a nasty turn. We were advised not to walk the streets after dark in Puno.

It was Francisco Deza who worked out the solution. One day he appeared at the door. "Come with me to the Public Notary; I have some papers for you to sign. I believe there is a way out."

In one of the cold little windowless niches that faced the main plaza, where the eighteenth-century Cathedral caught the first rays of a warming sun, we found the scrivener hunched over mounds of paper. Rising, he gave us a limp hand, asked us to be seated, and brought out a sheaf of papers.

"Our counterclaim," said Deza, who, fortunately for us had made our problem his problem, "accuses Pilón of criminal negligence, of sending you out in a car which was unserviceable. You will sign."

"Now," he said, pushing a second paper at me, "you sign this document. This will charge him for the loss of the jeep. That is

50,000 soles and for the purchase of your new pickup, another 90,000 soles. This, added to what you have lost each day through all this, makes our counterclaim 250,000 soles."

Some days later we met Francisco Deza at the Plaza. With an expressionless face he talked about everything except what we wanted most to hear. Then at last . . .

"Oh, about Pilón! You know he has dropped his suit? And, by the way, you must sign this paper in which you withdraw your counterclaims. How did it come about? Well, before the papers were shown to him by the Prefect. I met him walking on the street with all the virile gladness of an unspotted soul. I told him I had overheard the Prefect talking about your counterclaim for 250,000 soles, and I advised him as a friend to do something about it. 'These people are frightfully rich,' I said; 'they spend thousands while you spend only centavos — they'll ruin you, brother Pilón. They'll ruin you.' Well, what could you do? he asked. Then I said I happened to know you and perhaps I could persuade you to drop your counterclaim if he would drop his. 'Anything,' he said, 'anything.' So today we visited the Prefect's office and signed the paper relinquishing his claim. Case closed!"

V

Into the Carabaya Country

W E HAD arrived at a point of decision. Here at the road junction of Juliaca, near the northern end of Lake Titicaca, we could either continue our road research toward Cuzco or we could venture eastward into the mountains of the "verie riche river of the Carabaya." It was Willi Gölz who weighted the scales in favor of the Carabaya.

He was the finest mechanic in the entire southern section of the Peruvian Andes, and since he had spent so many years in remote places, Willi Gölz was an almost legendary figure. During his Odyssean wanderings he had installed electric plants, worked in mines and had been involved in so many different enterprises, all claiming his mechanical skill, that his little wasted figure and his dreadful cough, the result of gassing in World War I, were known to many. Beaten by the passing years, almost as toothless as the day he was born, he had settled in Juliaca, where he owned a garage. Between the intervals of working on our trucks he told us about the world beyond — he was a treasure house of information.

"If you want Inca roads," said Willi Gölz, as he sat on the running board of our truck, "you must go to the Carabaya. There I have seen stone steps going up the mountains *so*" — and he moved his hands in an ascending series of gestures: "up and up, one, two, three thousand steps." And, sensing our almost hypnotic interest, he went on, "Who but Incas would have built like this in the Carabaya? Yes, I have seen these, and when Willi Gölz says such-and-such is there, it is there."

Our notes had given hints that, off to the east of the Lake Titicaca basin, there was evidence of Inca roads which led into these little-known mountains. However, on our field maps these were no more than a line of provocative asterisks. Now we had the confirmation of the existence of such roads.

In the full glare of the sun, we spread out our charts. Looking at these maps, we could see that we would have been wiser to pursue the known route of the Royal Road, moving toward Cuzco. Yet here we were, at the gateway to the mysterious Carabaya and those Inca roads which climbed up thousands of steps into the *puna* like stairways to the moon.

The American Geographical Society map gave us a graphic picture of the topography. The vast Carabaya country lay midway between the environs of Lake Titicaca and that part where the Andes begin their precipitous drop into the jungles. Glacial valleys lay close to snow-bound peaks, which in turn were flanked by still higher peaks. Then the land fell downward into deep valleys and cascading rivers, which rushed on through forest-covered montañas into lowland jungles. This was the Carabaya.

The map showed four large rivers — the San Gaban, the Huari-Huari, the Tambopata and the Inambari — also a bewildering number of smaller ones which apparently cut their way through an utterly wild country. It was a land of extremes. Here and there, dots pin-pointed villages hanging, so it seemed, from the clouds: Ayapáta, Ituáta, Usicayos . . . all held together by stone-laid Inca roads. Willi leaned over the map, "And there is gold there, too, floods of placer gold." He pointed. "See those little marks? Well — these are the places where they found the gold of the highest carat in Peru." That, then, was the reason why the conquistadores called it "the verie riche river of Carabaya."

I glanced at Silvia, who was staring fixedly at the map. She knew what these contours in the map meant. The going would be difficult; there would be bad food and insect-infested sleeping places. . . .

At dawn around Titicaca Lake, it is winter; at about eight o'clock, with the arrival of the sun, it is spring; and when the sun reaches its zenith, it is summer. One passes through the seasons within a few hours.

When we started out from Juliaca the next daybreak after first thawing out the motors, we rode in those first hours with frost thick on the windows. Yet, once we rounded the northern shore of Lake Titicaca, we found ourselves caught in one of the contradictions of this climate. Here at 13,000 feet the shores were alive with bird life. Rose-colored flamingos — birds I have always associated with the tropics — went stalking by, maintaining their balance on the ice in stately fashion; there were ducks in profusion; and sooty-black ibis, and white-winged aerie gulls — all of them seemingly as unperturbed by the freezing winds as if they were only tropic breezes.

The marshland about the lake was as flat as the velds of Africa, and as treeless as the moon; we went snaking around on a raised causeway through a continuous bog. As far as we could see behind us, the land was waterlogged. Once we were out of the swamps, we came onto a plain dotted with what at first glance appeared to be tepee-shaped dwellings. Then, as we drew nearer and had a good look, we saw that they were the twenty-foot high mud houses of the Aymara-speaking lake Indians. Fashioned out of tundra-turf which had been cut like flat adobe blocks, each house was built so that the blocks converged toward the top, leaving an opening which became — in this singular windowless mudhouse — a chimney.

Within, each house was as snugly warm as an oven and as filthy as an abattoir. Untanned cowhides stretched out on the hard baked-mud floor were the beds, the piles of blankets upon them emitting an overpowering stench. In one corner the untended fire consumed cow dung; on the blackened walls hung bright woolen festive clothes, with next to them the carcasses of flayed sheep. On the one hand we had the beauty of the land; on the other, the filth of these human habitations.

Beyond the environs of Titicaca, we continued through villages of monotonous sameness. Presently we had left these behind us and began the climb. All through the day we climbed. In the late afternoon we came to the village of Asillo and a swift-flowing stream which was none other than that "verie riche river of Carabaya," the waterway to the region of the same name.

The village was, or rather had been, a *tampu* station on the Inca road. That the ancient highway had passed through here was attested to not only by the ruins which we could see like jagged scars on the bare hills but by our ever helpful friend and guide, Pedro Cieza de León. At the plaza in Asillo, we stopped to look at our maps and I opened my Cieza: "From Ayaviri, another road goes to Oma-suyu — it passes by the large village of Asillo . . ."

High on the hill that shadowed Asillo in the late afternoon — the natives call it the Hill of Calvary — was the ruin of this same village. Undoubtedly so placed to keep it out of the reach of the lake's periodic overflowing and away from the marshes, it was at once a high-top fortress and the way station.

From the plaza of Asillo, a dirt road traveled toward the northwest in the same direction taken by the Inca road — into the Carabaya country, that region from which the early Spaniards took more than 1,700,000 pesos of gold of "such fineness that it exceeded the standard."

The most surprising feature of Asillo was its church. An imposing structure of carved red stone with a marvelous three-storied façade, it was done in Indian baroque style with a strong Quechua flavor. Likenesses of Indians, guardians of the Sacred Heart, accoutered with feathered headdresses — a detail rarely found in church sculpture — were carved on the doorway. Almost twenty years in the building (1678–1696), it had throughout a strong native accent. We found the Indian name of the architect carved on an immense red ashlar: BARTOLOME SUCARU ZAPANA HUAYLLICCOLLA.

Once the Church of San Jeronimo de Asillo had had a thick grass roof — the contrast between the plaited straw and the rich carving must have been fantastic — but now the roof was of galvanized iron. The interior was equally noteworthy. Enormous canvases of the life and times of San Jeronimo, the church's patron saint, as painted by Indian artists in one of the seventeenth-century ateliers of Cuzco, were hung in enormous barbaric frames with a wealth of gold lead adornment. With its great baroque porticoes and the barbaric wealth of a parvenu, all designed and executed by Indians, it was a bewildering contrast.

We followed the Carabaya River on into the precipitous hills. Not overly wide, the river which was deep and swift, had grooved out a canyon during the millennia of its existence. Now wide and sterile pampas alternated with weird upthrusts of limestone and granite mountains. Atop these crags were more burial *chullpas*, which at Cerro Inampu appeared as ruined medieval battlements offering their mummified dead to the fury of Andean climate.

*   *   *

Into the Carabaya Country

After several hours of slow travel, we suddenly were aware that we were actually paralleling the course of an ancient roadbed which ran above the river level — etched, as it were, into the high banks.

At one of the bends of the road where the river narrowed and was compressed between stone embankments, we came upon a platform cut into the living rock, an outcrop of which had been chipped away to receive the cyclopean stones. The rounded towerlike base terminated in two piers eight feet higher than the ramp, and on these the rope cables of the bridge were suspended. The bastions on the other side of the river were similarly constructed. In a deserted house nearby we found the bridge itself, a skein of rope cables and guy ropes which when unwound became the suspension hangings. The bridge was evidently still used and had only been put away until the onslaught of the rainy season.

As we went on, we found ourselves time and again traveling along a narrow road, the importance of which to the Incas was indicated by the numerous ruins of bridge sites along its route. Again we climbed — this time from the river up into an immense blackness. The twisting and turning of the road took us higher and yet higher, carrying us up to the snowy crests.

Silvia and I led the caravan in the jeep. The slower Power Wagon, carrying a ton or more of equipment, was far behind, growling in low gear. At times we glimpsed it, far, far down, a swatch of red against the gray-black desolation of rock.

It was a tortured grassless land as unliving as the desert. As we wound our way upward, it was like climbing out of a crater's mouth, round and round, out of the blackness into the light.

When we gained the top we found we were on another wide wasteland which stretched away, patterned only here and there by greensward. With scarcely a rock or a tree to break the icy blast, it was a stony nakedness swept by unremitting winds. The only living things other than ourselves were four watchful vicuñas who, standing high on a peaked ridge, curiously observed our coming. When we halted and I climbed out to photograph them, they disappeared in a concerted leap. After they were gone, the shrill warning whistle of the male floated down to us.

Night was coming on. The long shadows fell across the empty way, and we looked at the altimeter. We were close to 15,000 feet up. Our motor was turning sluggishly and we ourselves were experiencing the now familiar onrush of mountain sickness. My own heart pounded as if it would tear loose from its moorings, and my eardrums were closed. We must have presented a strange picture sitting there unmoving like wax images, our faces set, our breathing labored, as stiff as an exhibit in a wax museum. As best I could, I went through the mechanical details of driving.

Where, I wondered desperately, was Macusani, gateway to the Carabaya? As if the compassionate gods had heard me, the land suddenly dipped down, a wide chasm opened up to the left, and there were the small flickering lights of Macusani. Wordlessly we looked at the magnificent sight before us. Out of the dark void already lost in shadow rose the snow mountains of Allin-capac, reflecting the last light of a setting sun which the Indians in their poetic way called "Magnificent [*Allin*] Youth [*capac*]." In its reflected light we skidded down the slippery road into the village.

Macusani was, as Willi Gölz said it would be, both high and cold; but the twentieth century had found it out. Electric lights illuminated the plaza and the stores. They were not the pallid little lights of other mountain villages, where one has to use a match to find the switch in order to turn them off. This was light, Gölz-installed, constant and direct. The village, nearly three miles high and so above the natural range of plant and man, was devoid of most of the other comforts of normal living. The villagers huddled around the open doors of the stores, shivering in their woolen ponchos. The dwellings were low and squat and of mud; the adobe church had a storied tower roofed with straw, and an open belfry. The bronze bell, thick with verdigris, bore the date 1607. Under the belfry was a sound box, a makeshift radio which gave out such raucous music that it drove us out of the plaza to find shelter elsewhere.

A man to whom we applied for rooms welcomed us, opened his door wide, and in we tumbled. Our trucks did not need watching, he said, for within the hour the natives would be either too drunk or too frozen to steal anything. By this time we were too numb to worry. He showed us our quarters. It was a good thing that he was too poor, as he said of himself, to afford electric light. One good look at what we were sleeping in would have driven us out again into the freezing night. If Nature has given us ignorance to act as eyelids for our souls, she certainly here in the Andes had given us night to obscure our surroundings. Although we were famished, none of us had the energy to bother with our supplies. We each had a hot toddy, a barbiturate for sleep, an aspirin for our altitude headaches, and then we all sought oblivion in the sleeping sacks. Across the plaza the radio was blaring out a mambo.

A curse on Willi Gölz and his electric generator, I thought, as I drifted off.

"Your Grace, I have the honor . . ." Dawn had come to Macusani. I opened one eye still heavy with barbiturate-induced sleep, shook my head in an effort to drive away the cobwebs — and there again was the insistent voice: "Your Grace . . ."

I zippered open my mummy sack and came out of it like an insect emerging from its pupa. Standing over me was a man of uncertain age, unshaven and wall-eyed as a pike. He had a thick cob-nose and thinning hair which hung down to his shoulders. His cavernous mouth was filled with ill-set yellow teeth. As he talked, he thoughtfully explored the inner rim of a nostril with a dirty forefinger.

63

The contrast between his appearance and his cultured speech was amazing. His was not the speech of a mountaineer, a broken thread-bare limping speech.

"Your Grace," he said, "your fame, leaping over the Andean crags, has penetrated even these remote regions, which know only the hindquarter of God. Yes, your fame has swept the lofty Andes and you will one day rank . . ."

"The Lord-Inca!" I exclaimed, and turned back into my sleeping sack.

Unmindful, he went on. "Yes, even as the great Raimondi gave us the best days of his years . . ."

From deep down in his sleeping sack in another room, Daugherty groaned. "Whatever it is, ask no questions, shoot it first. What is he saying?"

Dimly I realized that we were being invited somewhere. I sat up quickly. "You were saying . . . ?"

"That I have the honor to explain that my *patrón*, who is, so to speak, the Lord of the Manor of Macusani, sends his greetings and through me begs leave that you consider his house your own and . . ."

Charles Daugherty stood in the doorway clad only in his long red underwear. With his beard and puffed eyes, he could have been a doughty conquistador just recently poured out of his armour. "Well, then . . ."

Our visitor looked from one to the other. As the representative of Macusani's most important official, he could not fathom our jesting about so formal an invitation. So I put matters right. Slipping into my clothes, I put on my fur-lined jacket and my tyrolean hat with its medallions and luxuriant *gamsbart*. I bowed low and asked him to lead the way.

His *patrón* turned out to be a charming person. Don Luis received us from his gleaming metal bed. An imposing sight with his olive skin, black twirled mustache and impudent eyes, he lay propped up by enormous pillows, exhibiting the while pajamas which were cut like a hussar's jacket with silken arabesques encircling the buttons. Above the brass bed was an oleograph of Christ, while within arm's reach was an electric heater and an expensive radio. The room reeked of eau de cologne and sanctity.

The large house with its leaded windows had a neat thatched roof, giving it an air of distant English moors, and also, so Silvia whispered, a real functioning toilet, a small miracle in this region. Don Luis offered a hand on which was displayed a huge aquamarine, and then motioned us toward chairs. Everything here indicated a comparative opulence. Along with vast wealth, which came from his ownership of vast herds of alpacas, the real wool-bearing member of the llamoids, went considerable political power. He had, so we learned from the villagers, fought with the Communists in Spain when it was fashionable to be inclined to the Left. Later he became a Nationalist identifying himself with the Agrarian Party. But now that the turn of the political kaleidoscope had brought on new patterns, he had found it expedient to side with the party in power. He had, however, been extremely politic and had offered himself as candidate for congress in all parties, and had been unanimously elected.

Don Luis had read in the Lima papers, it appeared, of our progress, and he had hoped that we would arrive here on our way to these parts. We had heard of course of the Inca roads in the Carabaya that threaded through the montaña? It was all quite true, he assured us. Moreover, there were ancient cities in the region which no archaeologists had ever seen. Now that we were here, what were our plans and how could he further them? We explained that this was only a reconnaissance and that we had unfortunately a very tight schedule since in our travels we must avoid the rains. Therefore all we could hope to do now was to cover as many of the roads as possible and later return for a specific expedition to further explore the Carabaya. In order not to duplicate our effort, and knowing how difficult it was to arrange horses and pack animals for a large party, Silvia and I had planned to go on alone. We would need only two pack animals and two horses. Meanwhile Lawrence and Charles were to continue their special project, the study and photographing of the alpaca in its native environment. Also while they were here, they would like to photograph and if possible capture a condor alive.

Our host put a fresh cigarette in an extravagantly long holder and, caressing his mustache very delicately, observed that Silvia and I would need at least two riding horses, two pack animals, four Indians and a guide. As for those who wished to catch a condor, they would need a dead animal and they too must have Indians and saddle horses. He pursed his lips while making the calculations; then he clapped his hands. At once, as if he had been shot out of the floor, our friend of the extravagant manners appeared. Our desires and our needs were outlined.

"Remember," said our host, emphasizing each word with a stab of his cigarette holder. "Tomorrow without fail. I do not want our friends to be held up a single moment." Then he turned to us and the interview ended.

We shook the hand with its large aquamarine and departed.

We were following a high Inca road which my altimeter showed was at an elevation of 14,800 feet. As soon as we were out of Macusani, we had picked up this highway which led to the montaña. Built to be only a lateral road to the fabulous gold regions of the Carabaya, it had been as well constructed as the main Royal Road. A low stone wall marked its boundaries, culverts were spanned with small stone bridges, and on the slopes the road was built up and made level with dry-laid masonry. And though thousands of animals had traversed it in four hundred years, kicking paving stones loose with their iron-shod hoofs, the road was still essentially in good condition. And what grandeur! Here we were, traveling over a road constructed some five hundred years earlier, which skirted lakes and clung to mountains. Built for eternity, it had withstood the assaults of nature, and, running like a long wound through the region, it would yet remain visible for centuries.

Presently we came to a glacier under which the road passed. Here the engineers, anticipating the glacier's movement, had raised a retaining wall to catch the cascading rocks and to divert the snows high above the road. Here and there the eternal sweep and retreat of the glacier had sent rock crashing into and destroying a part of the road, but generally speaking it was in a good state of preservation.

At noon we came to our first *apacheta*, one of the stone propitiatory cairns that we were to find at frequent intervals along the way. A pyramid shaped of small rocks ranging in size from small nuggets to those the size of a human hand, these stone piles are to be found on the highest passes of the road. Our Indians as they passed now reverently added their stones. Not to be outdone, we did the same. From now on in the high mountain areas, wherever there was an Inca road or where one had been, we were to find an *apacheta: apa* (burden), *cheta* (depositor). The stone thus became a symbol of the burden, and the placing of a stone an act of homage. An early traveler described these piles of stones, which are built up in every mountain pass and crossroad: "The Indians carry a stone picked up on the trail a little while before arriving; they believe that by adding to that *apacheta*, they leave their tiredness behind and that the gods will give them new strength."

This first cairn marked the continental divide. From this point all the rivers would flow toward the Amazon. We had now entered the "verie riche land of Carabaya." We could see ahead of us chasms cut deep into the mountains, fog poured in from the forests and hundreds of little ice-cold rills tinkled out of marsh and tarn, all Amazon-bound. Even the "air-temper," as the chroniclers called it, changed once we were over the divide, or perhaps it was just that we were becoming acclimated to the high altitudes. Below us in the rift of clouds we could see a wild country, jagged and savage in its violence. I knew that this was a region where we must travel alertly or perish. At best this was hazardous traveling for which there had been no careful ground preparation — we were just riding off into the unknown. We followed the road over mountains and down the precipitous descents to the valleys; we followed it to the edge of lakes and around glaciers.

As we drove, I understood better than ever what the good Cieza felt as he traveled this same route:

> One of the things which I admired most was the way the Indians could have made such grand and admirable roads along such dizzy and frightful abysses that, on looking down, the sight failed one. In some places, to secure the standard road width, it was necessary to hew a path out of the living rock; all of which was alone done with fire and their picks. In other places the ascents were so steep and high that the steps had to be cut from below to enable the ascent to be made, with wider spaces at intervals for resting places. In other parts there were avalanches of snow, which were more to be feared. . . . Where these snows obstructed the way, and where there were forests of trees and loose clods of earth, the road was levelled and, when necessary, paved with stones.

On the third day out of Macusani we dropped down to the Tam billo valley and found that here the road ran along the riverbed We had heard much about the paved roads of the Incas but unti this moment we had not seen any. Now we were riding ove enormous stones. Silvia turned to me in astonishment: "It looks just like the Appian Way!"

The roadbed was constructed of huge paving stones sunk deep into the ground with drains cleverly laid and so well preserved that it could have been yesterday rather than the year 1400 when these were put down. Had there been any lingering doubts about the Incas' right to be known as road builders, they were dispelled by one look at this Tambillo road. Generally the Incas avoided water, and fearing wet earth they placed their roads high above the reach of rivers which here rise with great swiftness. But at this point, for some reason, they had run their road at the river's edge and had paved it with these immense flat stones so that it would be impervious to the rampaging river. Over this pavement we followed a herd of llamas into the village.

We stopped for the night in Tambillo. It lay in a small valley at the base of abruptly rising hills, which in former times had been terraced. The village was Indian, or almost entirely so, and Quechua was its language. Here in the declining light we talked to the villagers, who gathered about us, and from them we chose our Indians for the morrow's trek. One of them, Cutimbo, whose bronze skin was like beaten copper and who spoke broken Spanish and seemed more knowledgeable than the rest, we selected as our head guide.

The present village of Tambillo is but a short distance from the ancient *tampu*, which we could see on a promontory in the opening of another valley. Cutimbo took us there.

That afternoon while the light still held we visited the ruins. They consisted of several structures, all of dry-laid masonry, and a small plaza around which were grouped various buildings, one of which contained a stone table arranged with seats and steps. The road bifurcated here. One section went up a steep hill in a superb sweep of steps called *pata-pata* by the Indians. This was the road to Ituáta connecting the *tampu* stations of Aya-páta and Ollachéa. To the left and east of the path we were to take on the morrow, the road led to an amazing stone bridge such as we had not seen before. It had been made *wholly of stone.* Inca engineers, cutting into the living rock which protruded on both sides of the gorge, had built up the walls and gradually extended the larger rocks into a corbeled arch, and had bridged the gap with four gigantic fourteen-foot lengths of rectangularly cut stone. The approaches on both sides were also of stone. It was a marvelously ingenious piece of construction.

Kara-waya is a Quechuan word, *kara* meaning "wound." And now as we rode along we could see how beautifully expressive the language is. We were in a country marked by gaping abysses, a humid unhealthiness in its rivers and a terrible cold in its heights. We had climbed the Inca step-road out of Tambillo valley — steps that went up, up, up — I counted over one thousand, and then lost count — until we had come out once again on the *puna.* The land was broken and filled with upthrust rock of reddish granite that assumed fantastic forms. Through this we followed the track with our safari of horses, llamas and Indians. As the rising sun touched the tops of the rocks to gold, we came out of a rock passage to find the road running along the side of a terrifying chasm, so deep that we never once glimpsed the river, yet we constantly heard its dull roar, the sound ricocheting against the vertical rock walls. It was easily two thousand feet down. It seemed scarcely credible that workmen had once crawled up that precipice and, with a tenacity which now defies our understanding, had built up agricultural terraces to its very edge. This was the Kara-waya, alternately cold and hot, rain-filled and fever-filled — a forbidding land, entered only to fulfill the wishes of the Lord Inca for the Carabaya's gold. "In

Peru," wrote a sixteenth-century lawyer to his Viceroy, "there are gold mines in many places, as for instance in Carabaya . . . in which the Indians' labor is greater beyond comparison because the air-temper therein is so hurtful they are in the water all the time washing ore . . ."

In time the Carabaya became the graveyard of countless thousands of Indians who labored to pry out the metal which the Incas regarded as the "sweat" of the sun. Yet the terraced plots on the vertical hills overlooking the river gorge indicated long occupation while the carefully constructed roads suggested great movement.

The road along the chasm now became so treacherous that Silvia, preferring to trust her safety to her own two feet, dismounted. Hung over the edge and narrowed now to less than four feet, the trail made a tumble off into space very possible, and very soon I followed her sensible example and together we walked gingerly along that narrow way, hugging the rock wall. Landslides, the result of the torrential rains, had destroyed sections of the road, and every now and then a gap appeared. Picking our way carefully across the disarranged stones, we came to one place where the gorge was most precipitous and the road all but gone. Our guide, Cutimbo, went first holding the rope of the lead horse. Silvia's mount followed with difficulty since some of the large paving stones which once formed the road were perched on end. The vertical wall to the right went straight up, only spined cactus grew in the interstices of the rock, and to our left was the void of the chasm. Next it was the turn of our lead cargo mule. It carried two large boxes and our canvas bags containing our beds and sleeping bags. An intelligent mule, it sniffed at the situation and, not liking it, hesitated for a moment before it moved rapidly across the uncertain road. In the center a rock slipped. Frightened, the beast doubled its hind legs into a leap and so gained our side. The next mule, equally terrified, stepped on the loosened stones, which began to slide. The startled beast leaped toward a narrow edge, but one of the boxes it carried struck against the cliff, throwing it completely off balance. There the poor creature hung for a moment; then with a terrific crash it slid back onto the trail, pushing out a loose section of the road. Both dropped over the edge, to disappear below. It was an awful moment. First there was a dull thud, then the splinter of boxes, followed by the rattle of cooking gear striking the cliffs.

When the dust lifted and the landslide had rolled down and over the gorge, we were amazed to see that where the road had been there was now nothing but a gaping crater. On one side there was the ascending rock; on the other an interval of at least twenty feet which as effectively cut us off from the others as if an impassable river flowed between us. They could not advance — we could not retreat. Aghast, we stood looking across the gap at the Indians gathered on the other side. Recovering somewhat I asked if there was another road.

"Arí, but we must first reach Pukúta. From there another road leads back," said Cutimbo.

"How far is it?"

He did not know. He had not been over this route since he was a boy, but he thought it must be at least six leagues — about eighteen miles. I looked at the sun. We would not have much more daylight for making our way along this narrow trail. I thought sadly of the food which had gone with the mule over the cliff.

"Tell them" — I indicated the Indians who stood stolidly on the other side — "tell them that they are to go back to Tambillo, obtain food and take the other road to Pukúta and meet us there." The message delivered, I wrapped some paper money around a rock, tied it and threw it across to them. As soon as they had disengaged the money from the stones, they turned their llamas around and moved off.

The night shadows thrown by the towering cliffs brought the

first hints of cold. By five in the afternoon, twilight would be on us, and after that we would have to prepare for the night. Camping on a three-foot-wide ledge with no shelter from wind or rain was not a bright prospect. Cutimbo, who had gone on, came running back to tell us that there were some large caves ahead. The sky darkened, rain began to fall, and by now the shadows were so ink-black that I had to use my torch at some spots. During some frightful geologic nightmare, the Andes bubbled into a boiling upthrust and rock bubbles had burst and cooled, leaving enormous caves along the canyon wall. One of them, directly above us, looked large enough to house ourselves and the animals; and while Cutimbo began to make the ascending steps more secure, I tended to such supplies as were left. First we brought up the boxes, a difficult operation, then the sleeping bags, and then, by urging and pulling, we succeeded in getting the animals themselves up to the cave, a sorry substitute for night quarters, which gave out a loathsome odor.

"At least the beds and sleeping sacks were saved," Silvia observed philosophically as we unpacked.

Happily we had some emergency rations — a tin of Nescafé, some bouillon cubes, a canteen of water, the paratrooper stove, a few bars of chocolate — and my cameras. Everything else had gone with the doomed mule. Cutimbo was a godsend. He climbed out on the edge of the nothing that was our world to cut some grass for the horses and the two mules. Next he brought in a few faggots he found. Our supper consisted of a cup of bouillon, black coffee and a piece of chocolate each. Outside it stormed and raged; thunder echoed through the gorge to mingle with the roar of the swollen river. Gusts of wind blew in the cave, making it impossible to keep alight our small candles. The Indian wrapped himself in his poncho and crawled into the sweat-filled mule blankets, while we slid into our sleeping bags and in a moment were snug and warm.

73

We could not help laughing at the irony of the moment. Here we were — lost, cut off from everything and everyone. We had lost most of our food, what small supplies we had now would not last for more than two days, and yet here we were lying in comfort in our luxurious sleeping bags. In the darkness we discussed our prospects.

"What do you suppose is in this deep cave?" Silvia asked, sniffing audibly. "Do you think there are any animals in here?"

For answer I picked up my torch and swung it around the cave. Stalagmites were hanging from the ceiling; there was the steady drip of water and there seemed to be some past evidence of occupation. Then my light froze. In the back of the cave were several mummies. One, its sack broken open and its arms and legs flexed to its body, sat with its hair streaming down from its mummified skull. The head was thrown back as if it was laughing at us with all its might!

Cutimbo left, as prearranged, at daybreak. I brewed some coffee for him over the paratrooper stove, gave him the last of the chocolate and then with such words of cheer as I could muster in Quechua, sent him off down the path. I watched until he disappeared. We had agreed that he should go ahead to see if the road was passable and to ascertain if we could get to Pukúta. If not, then our only way was to go back again to where the avalanche occurred and somehow get over that road. When he had gone we decided to have a look at the mummies which Silvia had now discovered.

Our examination of the pottery fragments which lay about indicated by their design that they were "Cuzco polychrome" and probably had been made about 1450. The mummies were all male and the weavings poor. There were pieces too of some wooden tools

One bronze piece was a sort of metal wedge which could have been used in mining. We had, we suspected, come across a burial cave of Indian miners, some of those who had gone to the Karawaya to get out the gold for the Inca. These were fragments of a long-ago existence — these fragile pieces of cloth which dropped apart at the touch, these remarkably well-preserved skeletons and pieces of pottery.

The valley lay in deep shadow when I went out again to look for Cutimbo. As I was searching the canyon, pebbles rolled noisily down from the cliff. Instinctively I drew back. On a high ridge four guanacos were feeding. I called Silvia. My Remington rifle had never been properly zeroed, I had no telescopic sight, nor had I the means of gauging the wind; and the animals were at least 1000 feet away. The only thing in my favor was that I was in the shadow and could neither be seen nor scented at this distance. I knew that the moment I fired they would all bolt, so I chose the largest of the four and aimed for the shoulder. The sound ricocheted about the canyon. The four guanacos sprang up the side of the steep cliff as easily as if they were running on level ground.

Then suddenly the largest animal slipped, missed a projecting rock, fell half backward, recovered, then began a rapid descent, its sharp hoofs instinctively digging into the soil. It landed on the narrow road only five hundred feet from where we stood. I slipped another shell into the chamber. The guanaco rose unsteadily, wavered. Then, its front knees buckling, it sank to a kneeling position, its head slipped forward and it was dead.

I had already begun to flay the animal when Cutimbo appeared. He had found the way to Pukúta, he said; it was open. Then as he dropped the load of firewood he had been carrying the two of us, impelled by hunger and companionship, fell to work on the still warm guanaco.

*   *   *

Highway of the Sun

A day later we reached the ruins of the ancient mining village of Pukúta. It lay at the junction of two rivers, raised so the rising waters could not reach it. On our second day there, our other Indian who had been cut off by the avalanche arrived with food.

Had they delivered the messages? They had. But in this land of extremes, where everything was an exaggeration, the message, highly embroidered in the telling, was that we had gone over the cliff and were washed down the river. The news reached the local newspapers in Puno, who talked to their office in Arequipa, who talked to Lima, who cabled to New York. As we were to learn weeks later, the *New York Times* carried the following dispatch:

Von Hagens Overdue 3 Days on Inca Highway

Search parties are being organized to go into the jungle to search for Victor von Hagen, leader of the Inca Highway Expedition of the American Geographical Society, and his wife Silvia, who left the Lake Titicaca on May 20 for the desolate interior of Peru to seek the mysterious Inca Highway. They are now three days ovedue at Ayapáta, to which point they were descending after having crossed the 15,000 foot high Cordillera Oriental. Mr. von Hagen . . .

Mr. von Hagen at the moment was neither lost nor missing. He was studying the ruins of Pukúta, trying to discover what that gold-mine village had looked like.

There were twenty-five dwellings, ruins of what were probably miners' houses with typical stone mural niches set in the walls, a telltale characteristic of Inca architecture. There was a small plaza, and one or two rounded storehouses. There was nothing that would indicate that the chief activity had been gold mining, for gold had been taken from the rivers by the panning process or by means of a series of stone riffles laid across the river. Gold in the Carabaya was found in nuggets and, carried down in high water, was deposited in

76

these riffles and later collected in the season of low water. The gold was then taken to wind-furnaces built on the tops of the highest hills. These furnaces built so as to catch the persistent winds blowing from the Amazon and called *huayras,* were circular in shape with the tunnel or mouth of the oven facing the windward side, so that the strong winds produced sufficient draft to obtain the high temperatures from the charcoal fires necessary to melt the gold, which was then shaped into crude bars. These were carried to Cuzco to the Lord Inca.

There were, it seemed, many other gold villages along the road. By careful questioning of the Indians and our recording of the information so obtained on our map of Carabaya, we discovered that there existed a whole system of roads which throughout the region connected the isolated villages that lay between the Andes and the montaña. To the southeast the road went on to Coasa, to Usicayos, to Limbani, and to Sandia, an important village lying low in the montaña at 7500 feet altitude, to terminate at Tambopata. How we longed to pursue these roads into the jungle! Still . . .

Once back at headquarters, leaving Silvia at the house of the *patrón* Don Luis to rest and then to prepare for our continuing trip, I rode out fifteen miles through the great herds of shaggy white alpacas which were being shepherded on the grass-covered *puna,* over the bare frozen hills to the base of Allincapac Mountain. If one could forget the cold, the land had a raw charm and a terrifying beauty. The golden turf ran along unbroken except for outcrops of rock and a peculiarly shaped cactus which in bloom had a canary-yellow blossom later replaced with a grayish beard. Here I found the "condor expedition." In a makeshift blind, Lawrence, blue with cold, sat with camera "at ready," while Charles huddled in his sleeping bag. In front of them in a small hollow of land was the bait. A dead horse, bloated with the juices of organic dissolution, lay on the trap. Below and unseen, lying on thick branches in a trench cut under the dead animal, two Indians waited for the condor to light on the trap. They would then seize the bird by its legs, thus enabling other Indians now hidden behind a large rock to run out and lasso it. As I neared the blind, Charles frantically waved me off my horse. On the flat of my stomach, I wriggled forward to gain the blind's protection.

"What a bore!" Charles had plainly had enough. "These birds have done nothing but sweep down and up. There's one now — sitting on that crag — right under the snow line."

And there was the great bird, its white ruff around his neck as unsullied as Cyrano de Bergerac's white plume, its beak, curved and strong, cruelly sharp.

"We almost had one," Charles went on. "They came down to have a sniff at our bait; but one of our Indians was so drunk that he stuck his hand out too soon — it's a wonder he did not lose it — and, of course, they all took off. They are terrible cowards, those condors. Now we have to wait until their suspicions are quieted. What happened to you?"

I told them.

"What a trip," he said wistfully. "I wish I had elected to go along on that one instead of this . . ."

Dick Lawrence sat motionless, waiting hopefully to get a telescopic shot of the condor the moment it leaped off into space and began its glide.

I told them of a change in plans. We had decided to work our way back to the Royal Road and follow it on north to Cuzco, about one hundred and fifty miles away. They could, if they chose, follow us at their leisure, so long as they arrived by the time of the Inti-raymi, the great Sun Festival. In Cuzco we hoped to find living quarters for the Expedition, and there we would work out a further program of work. We said our good-bys and I wiggled out again and over the rocks to where my horse waited.

It was snowing as Silvia and I made our way down the "verie riche river of Carabaya" on our way toward Cuzco.

Once we had made the high pass at La Raya, we were out of the Lake Titicaca region and almost at once had dropped down into the warmer valley of Vilcanota, where the air was almost benign. We could well understand how the people who became the Incas abandoned their origin place around Titicaca to seek out the warmer climate of this valley.

For some days we followed the Inca road through pleasant villages not much changed since the time when their Inca ruled the land, through the lava fields of San Pedro de Cacha, until we came to the great temple of Kontiki Virachoca. The temple was now in ruins but even so the fragments of high stone and adobe walls and rounded stone pillars spoke of the great architectural genius of the Inca. As we drove, the road was at times clearly revealed and then at other times so thoroughly erased that we could find no trace of it. At Chuqui-cahuana, for example, we found a length of well-preserved road, part of the Royal Road, measuring fifteen feet from wall to wall. On we went northward through hills now purple with the blossom of the potato, past the Lake Urcos which lay like an emerald at the bottom of cultivated hills.

Not far from this we came to ancient stone quarries at the gates, so to speak, of Cuzco. Here was an enormous passageway, with one of its sides faced with carefully fitted red stone, the mark of the Inca stonemason. It was once, so we believed, a control station or sort of toll gate, and the entrance to the road from the south which led through a large pre-Inca city into the immediate valley of Cuzco. From here northward this old Inca road more or less becomes a modern road.

On our way along this, which was once the Appian Way of the Incas, we passed multitudes of people in holiday attire, many of them driving gaily decorated llamas ahead of them, all going toward the Sacred City. Many wore their distinctive regional headgear — the women of Ayaviri their large flat hats trimmed with beautiful upending brocade; those from Sicuani woolen wimples which encased the head nunlike and fell across the shoulders. Groups of Indians trotted along hugging musical instruments, as if they would protect them from the dust of the fast-traveling cars. Some carried harps shaped like ancient rebecs, which they stroked as they walked; others had reed pipes on which they softly fluted.

The crowd increased as it converged on Cuzco. We made our way down the road and entered the square called Rimac-Pampa. This, once the exit place of the great road to the south, was the Speaking Pampa where the people gathered to listen to the harangues of the Inca's officials. It was still the gathering place, crowded now with auto buses and jostling people, noisy with the sound of raucous radios and loud-speakers.

We had arrived over the Royal Road at Cuzco, the capital of the Incas.

V I

Cuzco — the Four Quarters of the World

HERNANDO DE SOTO, so the chronicler said, came first upon Cuzco at sunset.

The sun's great rundle sinking with an enormous burst of reddened glory lighted up the city so that even the poorer buildings took on a burnished golden look. As the retreating sun's rays touched the beaten gold plates that adorned its walls, the pyramided Sun Temple, towering over the lower buildings around it, gleamed as if it were cased in metal.

Cuzco lay in a protected hollow at the northern end of the valley. The hills were bare of sward; no trees except the stunted *molle* grew here. On the northern higher slope of the city stood an enormous stone fortress, a structure so immense that at first sight de Soto and his companion doubted that any army could breach it. Narrow and long "like a puma's tail," Cuzco was made up of narrow streets, its smaller buildings painted yellow and red, the larger buildings constructed of enormous, beautifully laid stonework. In the center was a great square, larger than the Plaza of Saint Mark's in Venice, which, because of the luminous atmosphere, seemed so near that a bolt from a crossbow could have been shot into the center.

Captain Hernando de Soto, from his position on the hill of Karmenka, had good reason to study Cuzco intently. For he, along with two hundred Spaniards in this fateful year of 1533, was engaged in the conquest of an empire five times the size of Europe. De Soto was, according to his chronicler, "a handsome man, dark in complexion, with full beard and dark restless eyes, of cheerful countenance, an endurer of hardships and very valiant." At thirty-five, he was still a considerable distance, in time and space, from his watery grave in the turgid waters at Guachoya on the Mississippi River. At this moment, as a conquistador of Peru, de Soto was in the full tide of his glory. Rather above middle height, graceful on foot and horseback, he rode in the Moorish style and looked well accoutered in buckler and helmet with a straight sword by his side. Now after his four-hundred-and-fifty-mile ride over the Royal Road from Cajamarca to the south where the Inca King was being held for ransom by two hundred Spaniards, de Soto looked down on Cuzco in intent contemplation. He had consented to be escorted to the capital of the Incas by a retinue of Indians with only one other soldier companion, Pedro de Barco, in order to speed the payment of the gold and silver ransom and to make sure of the captured Inca's promise "that he would fill an immense room, once with gold, twice with silver" so as to free himself from his Spanish captors. Knowledge was needed, too, of the size of this strange kingdom, of its roads and its defenses, for the Spaniards had come not only to siphon off a winnowing of Inca gold but to make conquest of the source of all of it.

Earlier three common soldiers had been sent to Cuzco for the purpose of spying out the secrets of the Incas, but they had grown so overbearing what with being carried about in gold-encrusted litters and their reception in Cuzco as gods, that the native officials, hurriedly getting together six hundred llama-loads of gold and silver, quickly ended their excuse for being in Cuzco at all. So that mission ended without their obtaining vital information. Next, Francisco Pizarro, the Spaniard's Captain General, chose the hidalgo de Soto, "a gentleman on all four sides who was neither Jew nor Moor and who had the purity of blood required to enter the order of the Knights of Santiago." So little did de Soto possess of worldly goods that when he landed in Yucatán in 1519, he had only his sword and his buckler. With these, for the next ten years or so he fought his way throughout Central America and in 1532 he was in Nicaragua nursing wounds when the clarion call came from the Pizarros, who sorely needed men to help in this conquest of Peru. With the rank of Captain, Hernando de Soto arrived in Peru in May, 1532.

Hernando de Soto's first sight of Cuzco filled him with amazement:

> Cuzco, grand and stately, must have been built by people of great intelligence. The city is certainly the richest of which we have any knowledge in all the Indies . . . Neither gold nor silver, they tell me, can be taken out of here on the pain of death and there are many goldsmiths here and workers in silver.

De Soto was received as a god. Carried through the city in a gold-plated litter and followed always by a curious throng of women and children, he saw the storehouses for wool tunics and cotton cloth, strange chambers filled with arms and accouterments of war such as quilted-cotton armour, sharp-edged swords, star-shaped halberds, while still more rooms were filled with corn and shellfish and seaweed — all in the form of tax tribute. He was careful to note, for he was primarily an officer making an "estimate of the situation," the fact that out of the great square went "four roads which led to all parts of the empire."

Actually these were the principal highways to the four divisions, the *suyus,* of the empire: the Chinchay-suyu road over which de

Soto had arrived, went northwest to Quito 500 leagues distant; the Cuntu-suyu road to the coast, stretched off to the southwest; the Colla-suyu which, "so the Indians sayeth," went to a great lake, began at the southeast corner; while the road to the jungles began from the northwest, at a small plaza called the "Salt Window," and was called the Anti-suyu road. The sum of these four divisions, the Inca Empire, was known as the Tawantin-suyu, the "Four Quarters of the World."

The people, so de Soto learned, had originated as wanderers and food gatherers around Lake Titicaca. Eventually they migrated northward. By the year 1000 — since "blood and cruelty is the foundation of all good things" — they had disposed of the original inhabitants of this valley and taken possession of the treeless glebe about Cuzco. Their food, their llama husbandry, their architecture, their ceramics, were Andean in pattern. Yet as these people were exposed to dearth and hunger and seasonal droughts, they began to oppose the titanic force of Nature and to attempt to alter it for their benefit.

The centuries passed like the moving arm of a weaver's shuttle. The Incas made repeated conquests and organized the defeated. They developed the formulae that made an Andean empire possible. They became a disciplined people and, within the frame of their mountain glebe, they became a unified empire. It expanded at the expense of its neighbors, absorbing the surrounding lands like an amoeba. It enveloped them, digested them and made them part of itself. What the Incas could not absorb, they killed. About 1200 A.D., the chieftains of the Quechua-speaking peoples announced their official descent from the Sun God. They called themselves "Incas," and as such became the hereditary rulers of the Quechuas.

Under the aggressively active Inca policy of conquest and assimilation, the Inca realm expanded in all the four directions. Roads were built and a *chasqui* courier system was organized. A caste of

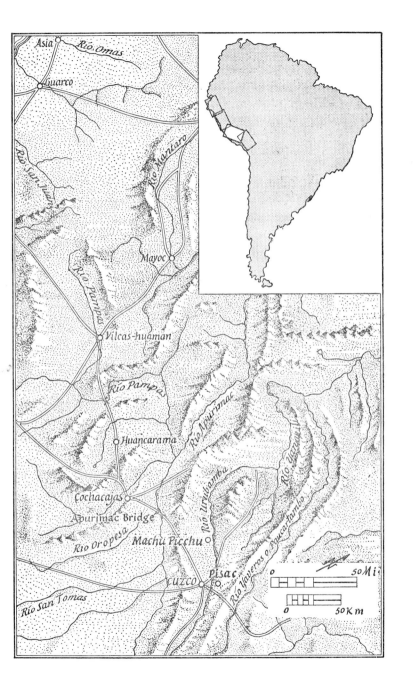

Asia
Rio Omas
Guarco
Rio San Juan
Rio Mantaro
Mayoc
Rio Pampas
Vilcas-huaman
Rio Pampas
Rio Apurimac
Huancarama
Rio Yucay
Rio Urubamba
Cochacajas
Apurimac Bridge
Rio Oropesa
Machu Picchu
Rio Yaveros o Pauca-tambo
Pisac
CUZCO
Rio San Tomas

0   50 Mi
0   50 Km

record-keepers, trained so that they could read the story of the past, invented the *quipu* — a series of colored and knotted strings by means of which records could be kept of grazing lands, gold mines, numbers of people and tribes, tributes and deposits.

Having grown great, the Incas had come to believe that it must have always been thus, and therefore what did not conform to the established idea of the Inca past was eliminated from human memory — and so well that the impression left was that before the Inca there had hovered a void over the Andes.

The Incas ruled their people with an iron but a just hand. Every detail of their life, from womb to tomb, was prescribed. The state was not for the people nor was equality the ideal. It was rather a blending of tribal communism and theocracy, a perilously balanced fusion of two antagonistic systems.

The common people were manipulated like figures on a chessboard. They became part of the decimal system of classification with division all along the social line. An elaborate hierarchy of territorial officials was set up. The highest under the Inca was the Tuc-ri-cuo (He-who-sees-all), the ruler of a division of 10,000 people. And so the categories went down the line to the least common multiple; for every 10,000 in population there were 1331 officials.

Everything was regulated in this welfare state. No one moved on the roads without permission; there was work-service for taxes; there were contributions to state and religion; and each man was automatically a member of an agrarian militia. If a section of the realm was underpopulated, a whole tribe was moved into it. Loyal subjects were settled in a newly conquered land, while the recently conquered tribes were moved out and transferred to a "safe" community where they could be absorbed. Under this policy, most of Andean America was conquered. From Chile to Colombia, a distance of 2320 linear miles, the land was unified, the jungle was invaded, the desert coast pervaded. No tribe, no force, could resist the pressure of this benevolent despotism.

Of this realm Cuzco was the capital. Thoroughly cosmopolitan, the city was inhabited by symbolic groups from the four divisions of empire. Each section of the city was given over to a particular tribal group, each with its own attire, own headdress. If they were *yuncas* of the coast, they went muffled like gypsies; the *collas* (koyas) wore caps shaped like a wooden pump-box; the *canas* wore another kind of cap of greater width; the *cañaris* had crowns of interwoven thick lathes; the *hunancas* had short ropes attached to their hair which hung down to the chin. Cuzco was the microcosm of its empire.

There was only one way by which this community of people could have been held together and that was by the communicating roads. All Indians were obliged to give one third of their time to work service. While each tribal unit must build and maintain the Royal Road running through its section, the direction and master plan were laid down by technicians sent out from Cuzco. These master architects charted the direction the roads would take, planned the way-stops and figured out the distances that the *chasqui* couriers would run and where their platforms would be set up. With these communications completed, nothing could occur in any place in the realm without the officials at Cuzco being made immediately aware of it.

All this and much more did Hernando de Soto see and learn during his stay in Cuzco. The summer of the dry season had come before de Soto quit the city. In that time he gathered much gold, wrote his report, and prepared to move out. Cuzco was now gay with arriving Indians, for it was the time of the Sun Festival, the Inti-raymi, celebrating the time when, as the Indians believed, the Sun God came down to live with them. From all sides Indians were pouring into the city to prepare for the pageantry of the Sun God.

87

What thoughts must Hernando de Soto have had when he turned on the hill of Karmenka and looked back on Cuzco! He was the last European to see it in its pagan state. Soon he was to gather his 300,000 golden pesos of loot, sail to Spain and eventually return to chase the twin phantoms, Youth and Gold — and lose both along with his life in the turgid waters of the Mississippi.

But on that bright June twenty-first, 1533, as this man of "good impulses" rode beside his treasure-laden llamas along the high road to Cajamarca, he moved out from this golden city through throngs of Indians coming to Cuzco for the festival of the Sun God.

Four hundred and twenty-one years to the day that Hernando de Soto quit it, we, searching for the remains of those roads of an empire which he so effectively had helped to destroy, arrived in Cuzco.

The oldest continuously inhabited city in all the Americas — it dates back to about the time that the Battle of Hastings was fought — Cuzco shows little traces of its various epochs. There are the Inca walls — superbly fashioned of stone, laid with an instinctive feeling for the beauty of pattern in stone which impart a feeling of the greatest antiquity. There too is the magnificent architecture of Colonial Spain and in close proximity adobe houses which are without either dignity or grandeur. Between these contrasts are no evidences of growth. Cuzco is like a woman who when born is already old.

Hernando de Soto would have found little in this present-day observance of the Sun Festival to remind him of the city he saw before its rape, even though much of modern Cuzco is built upon the walls and foundations of the Incaic city. What had once been the Curicancha, the Shrine of the Garden of Gold, a structure whose walls were covered with gold as finely beaten as onionskin paper, is now the Santo Domingo Convent. The sanctuary of the Sun Virgins, where chosen women were reared to care for the ritual of the Sun, is, ironically enough, the cloistered nunnery of Santa Catalina; and standing on the site of the Snake Temple, the palace of the last great Inca, is the Church of the Jesuits. Time, man and earthquake have not been kind to Cuzco. Yet the Sun Festival was once again bringing the Indians back into their city, and the streets were enlivened by their gauds.

With difficulty we eased our truck through the press of the crowd to the hotel. The Railroad Hotel, so called because it was over the station and therefore in the rail yards, was the best stopping place for us that the city offered because, since it lay out of the city, it gave us parking space for our trucks, which would soon be piling in from the Carabaya. So, in a dubious bedroom made less dubious by a bath which offered a plentiful supply of hot water to wash off the dust of three hundred miles of Inca road, we relaxed with an enlivening *apéritif*.

Cuzco was, naturally, an important point for us. The four roads of the empire had gone off from the center of the city in the four directions, and around it were the remains of its most imposing structures. In order to make our study we would have to have a base of operations. It would have been ideal if we could have rented, as we did in Puno, some small place outside of the city, but the earthquake of 1949 had leveled much of this area. I remembered, then, that during a previous visit to Cuzco I had seen a place just outside the city which was once an Inca palace. As we made the necessary courtesy calls, it might be well to include the owner of the place.

After we had called upon the Prefect and had been offered and received the city, we sought out the owner of the house I had remembered. We found him in his offices in the richest commercial establishment in Cuzco. The son of the founder of the firm, one who had generously aided other explorers, he readily granted us the loan of his house during our stay in Cuzco. And so, when the long noonday quiet settled on the city, we made our way up to his place.

In Inca times Cuzco was divided into Upper and Lower. To get to Hanan, or upper Cuzco where Kolkam-pata is, you must climb the narrow streets between Inca walls, past colonial doorways marked with the armorial escutcheon of somebody now forgotten, past courtyards of squalor, and on up to the Plaza and Church of San Cristobal. The city at this point lies below. We went along walls spaced with Inca mural niches until we came to an enormous iron gate and there rang the bell. Through the trees we could see the lower bastions of the great fortress of Sacsa-huaman. In front of us lay a chalet of uncertain age and alongside of it was a fragment of a door and wall done in the late Inca style. The best of Inca stone-work, its roughly square stones were skillfully keyed and put together without cement with a precision never equaled elsewhere. A single truncated door led nowhere — that and a fourteen-foot wall were all that was left of what was once one of the finest structures in Cuzco. Yet here was the same beauty with which Greek ruins pridefully conjure up for the beholder some image of what they must once have been.

Kolkam-pata had a special significance for us, since it had been the residence of the last of the direct descendants of the one-time all-powerful Inca. Paulla-Inca had been a willing collaborator of the Spanish conquerors. Adopting the name Cristobal, he had built the church which bears his name and had lived his last years there. Now, searching for the lost horizons of the empire he, also, had had a part in destroying, we were to live in the ruins of his palace.

The other two members of the Expedition had arrived and were already installed at the Railroad Hotel when we returned. They

ere a sorry pair. Dick Lawrence was worn and silent — for once
ll energy was drained from his slight figure. Charles too looked
inched and drawn. To our inquiries as to the success of their ven-
ure, Charles sighed.

"Well," he said wearily, "in the beginning . . ."

They had waited days for the condors to return. Each time one
f the Indians had revealed their presence in the trap, the great
arrion birds took off. Food that I had arranged to be sent to them
ad not been sent; the Indians drank all the brandy; the cold had
een intense. Altogether it was an epic of disorganization.

"The condors came down often, but as the dead horse was lying
1 a veritable refrigerator at 15,600 feet, the flesh did not decom-
ose. Until . . . Yes, until," said Charles bitterly, "the third day
— our last day. We were downwind and we had it all — stench like
he perfume of battlefield dead. The condors came down, pulled a
iece of flesh off the horse, danced about it, nodded to each other as
f they were saying 'After you, my dear carrion-pigeon.' Had our
ndians been less drunk, they could have seized them and we would
ave had our pictures. Instead of which" — he stopped to take a
ong drink — "instead of which it began to snow and snow and
now. Within an hour we were snowbound, not able to see two
ards in front of us. We had had enough . . . and so here we are,
ans pictures, *sans* condor . . ." But they had been given a whole
amb as a gift and it was at this moment sizzling in the hotel's
ven.

And at this point a new Expedition member arrived at the
otel.

Henrik Blohm, tall and blond, a Harvard undergraduate, had
een born in Venezuela of a German family. He was studying to be
zoölogist and so had jumped at the chance to come along on the
xpedition as a volunteer for the three months of his vacation. In
ll the excitement we almost forgot the whole lamb roasting in the

oven. But soon we were all talking, eating, shouting like a group c uninhibited undergraduates.

The Inca Sun-God Inti was kind. The sun shone bright nex morning on the beginning of the Sun Festival and with it came sti more people. First came the opening parade of the various India groups. It moved around the plaza passing in front of the Cathe dral, displaying a variety of costumes and music. There were Ind ans from the jungles; Indians from Titicaca; there were folklo groups dancing with masks, mimicking something long forgotte in history; there were Indians from Pisac with upturned felt hat All in noisy competition marched to music which was, at best, chaos of sound. Occasionally one group would hold up the marc by breaking into a dance.

This festival is only one of many ancient ones. There had bee cults of the Moon and of the Stars, each month with its appropr ate deity and its appropriate festival. There was the Song of th Harvest, with the dances of the small ripening, the great ripenin, and of the young maize; the Festival of Water to welcome the con ing of rain. But of all these, the most mystical was that of the Sur Inti-raymi, for during that period the Indians believed the Sun Gc briefly came down and stayed among them.

As the parade continued, the riot of color became overwhelmin, Indians in flaming red and pink ponchos danced with abandonmen like children, out of rhythm yet with lively unrepressed artless ga ety. At last they disappeared through the inclined streets which le to the main festival-ground at the Sacsa-huaman fortress. As watched them go, dancing and playing their simple instruments, thought of a passage I had once read in which an essayist writing e natural man said: "Oh, let these last sons of nature die out in the mother's lap, do not interrupt with your master's dogmas the childish games, their moonlight dances, their sweet and ephemer natures. . . ."

Fortunately we were swept along with the stress of humanity that poured through the city. Only a few steps down the fortress hill and we were safely inside our retreat.

We began our further journey with the northern route, that same Chinchay-suyu road which de Soto had taken when he quit Cuzco and followed his loot-laden llamas.

Here the Inca road is still made daily use of by Indians arriving with their llamas. At the top of the hill at Karmenka, there once stood Huaca-puncu, the "Holy Gate," the first shrine an Indian found on his journey northward. "One made sacrifices here," wrote Cieza, "so that the Inca road would not collapse or be destroyed." We found beautifully cut stones taken from this shrine embedded in the Church of Santa Aña which now occupies the former site of this sacred place that once guarded the Royal Road.

We leisurely followed the road northward. Tracing its course was little like putting an anagram together. Located on the west side of the narrow valley, the old road crossed the modern highway at times and lost its identity. Then, where the highway curved to make a gradient, the Inca road would emerge again and could be followed, measured and studied, until it entered the environs of a village, where it would again disappear. So with varying success we followed it until we came to the swamps.

Fifteen miles north of Cuzco lies a wide-spreading quagmire. The Incas in the fourteenth century built a long causeway across this, which still is used. More than a meter above the flooded lowland plains, twenty-four feet wide and eight miles long, it was one of the triumphs of Inca engineering. Traversed by all who entered or came from Cuzco, it has, through the centuries, often been described: "a great swamp which could only be crossed with difficulty, had the Inca not built a wide paved causeway . . . with walls on both sides so firm that they will last a long time."

At the northern end of all this, we came to Zurite. Here on the sides of the mountain were the long parallel walls of agricultura terraces ascending the sides of the Andes like a gigantic flight of steps, and here we looked for Xaqui-Xahuana, the lost city of which all the conquistadores spoke, that place which one of the Inca Kings, referring to his flight from the penetrating cold of Cuzco, had called "my refuge."

The village of Zurite dated only from 1570, the site having been given to one of the Spanish conquerors as his fief, and he had, as was then the practice, torn down the ancient buildings and utilized the stone. The modern market, used now by the Indians who still in ancient dress, come down from the hills, was located in front of a large moldering church. Since we could see that the church was constructed of the ancient stonework, we begged its sacristan to open the place for us. As he fumbled with the enormous lock, we were surrounded by hordes of boys shouting for the Peruvian equiv- alent of baksheesh. Once inside the church, the light from our torches revealed crumbling mud walls hung with huge canvases of paintings which had come from the eighteenth-century In- dian ateliers of Cuzco and were in marked contrast to the molder- ing walls broken by Nature's tremors and man's neglect. Nothing here gave us a clue to the ancient city we sought until we reached the richly wrought altar of chased silver fashioned in eighteenth- century baroque style. The date was 1770. Hanging here among the silver flowers and cherubs we found a likeness of the donor, El Cacique D. Juan Quayna Sucnu, attired in flowing cape, knee breeches and silver-buckled shoes. At one side was his younger son wearing the long surcoat of the period. Facing him on the other side was his wife at prayer. Behind her stood another son. The leg- end above this read: DONA ISABEL ESTRADA CON SU HIJO ANDRES

94

UANA-SUCNU. The Quayna-Sucnu family, according to the sacstan, had been owners of the Zurite valley but time — and here e spread out his crippled hands to suggest the cupidity of man — ad robbed them of it. Learning that their descendants still lived ear by, we crossed his wrinkled palm with a piece of silver and ollowing him out of the church and across fields planted in corn ad wheat, we came to a small house of sun-baked adobe. Dogs held s in check until an old man appeared at the door. Shading his eyes om the bright sun, he begged our business in a quavering voice.

Hearing it, he said, "You stand on it — Xaqui-Xahuana" — and, mewhat puzzled as to why foreigners should come to ask about at which time had entombed, he led us up a hill trail along which e saw those characteristic stone walls, always the first evidence of rmer Inca occupation. From the top we looked down, and there fore us were the ruins of the "Lost City," built around a plaza here once large buildings fanned out to form a lunette. This forer pleasure resort of Inca nobles had been the last stop before the ayfarer on the Royal Road had crossed the Anta swamps over the ant stone causeway on the way to Cuzco. "This valley," our roniclers had written, "once contained sumptuous buildings for creation to which the lords and many people from Cuzco came r their diversion," and now we were looking at all that was left these same "sumptuous buildings." While Silvia made a sketch ap of the ruin, I found numerous pottery fragments, the finest e had seen in the Cuzco area.

These plains had seen much history. Here, early in their existence a nation, the Incas were brought to the edge of defeat by the hincha Nation's tribe called the Chancas. Finally victorious, the cas had their enemies' bodies skinned and stuffed in such lifelike titudes "that the human form was made to appear in many posins. Some of them," averred a Spaniard who saw them, "had stom-

achs formed like drums on which they appeared to be playing; ot
ers were set up with flutes in their mouths." The Incas had built
houselike tomb in which these horrid battle trophies were kep
There they remained for two hundred years, or until the Spaniar
entered Cuzco.

Our old guide led us back to his house and there showed us sor
"ancient things," Inca fragments of stone and vases, hand-wroug
nails, Spanish coins which dated from the times of Charles V,
beautifully etched silver partisan, a cruel-tipped lance and a swo
handle, a rusty encrusted sword blade; and then, and most curio
of all, a silver ornament with a unicorn's head crudely stenciled o
it, which bore a bit of sixteenth-century Spanish doggerel, endi
with: "And this belongs to Francisco de Carbajal . . ."

Those who have read the *Conquest of Peru* will recall that wit
cutthroat, Francisco de Carbajal, who, when close to eighty years
age, had come to Peru to become Gonzalo Pizarro's Captain Ge
eral during his bid for the empire of Peru. Our old man had fou
this memento while plowing the same battlefield on which, in 154
Carbajal had met his death. Never was Marius or any Roman ge
eral Carbajal's equal in cruelty, for "in every phase . . .
showed himself a past master; the trees wherefrom he hung his vi
tims, from Quito to Potosí, bear witness to it," wrote Cieza.

It was during the civil war which was fought all over the And
from Potosí to Quito that Carbajal peopled the trees with the bo
ies of his enemies and so earned the sobriquet, "Demon of the A
des." At the end, Carbajal led his men out to Xaquixaguana to o
battle with the King's. Before the battle was joined Carbajal's m
began to desert, and before he himself could take to his heels, he w
captured by his own troops, who hoped, with such a prize, to ma
their peace with the victors. He was roundly abused as he w
taken back to the Viceroy's camp; the soldiers would have had l
head had another not stayed their hands.

"To whom," said Carbajal in haughty jest, "am I indebted for [h]is protection?"

"Do you not know me?" asked his would-be protector. "You have [p]ursued me for five thousand leagues through the Andes all these [y]ears."

"I crave your pardon," retorted Carbajal. "It is so long since I [h]ave seen anything but your fleeting ass that I have fully forgotten [y]our face." On his eighty-fourth birthday Carbajal was led out to [be] beheaded. His executioner, a tailor, had been instructed to quar[te]r his body. "Treat me, dear little brother," Carbajal said, "as one [tai]lor would do the other."

Shortly the four pieces of the body that had been Carbajal were [ha]ng in chains at the four entrances of the Royal Roads into Cuzco.

V I I

Somewhere, Lost Vilcabamba

OUR SEARCH for the ancient road which led to the Anti-suyu sec
tion, the eastern part of the Inca Empire, began in the ruins of P'
sac. The Incas, as I have stressed, called each of their four grea
roads after the region or *suyu* that it traversed. The "Anti" quarte
was a vast and variegated section of their world which included th
limitless jungle and the high forested mountains east of Cuzco.
had one day walked along that east road out of Cuzco beginning a
that part of the city once known as the "Salt Window," and to m
delight found, in talking to some of the natives living in the shado
of San Blas church, that they had actual knowledge of the road an
that the one still used by the natives coming from the valley to th
east was in fact the ancient one. With an elderly man as my guid
I followed a llama caravan out over the stone-laid highway. Th
road, beaten hollow by llama treads, led over the hills above Cuzc
passed through many little villages and made its way toward Pisa
By the time I returned a few days later from my trek, I had mappe
out the program for our first assault on one of the "directions" c
the Empire. We were to go in full force and would begin with th
eastern route. For here, somewhere along these little-known road
lay the lost fortress of Vilcabamba.

The valley of the Vilcanota is a delight. The vehicular dirt high
way circles down from the high hills into a warm fertile area when

the river is still held to an even course by stone embankments raised centuries ago. The greensward of the planted valley lies between a double array of mountains which rise to such heights that they are snow-draped the year around. The village of Pisac lies on the east bank of the river under the shadow of the ruin-studded mountain of the same name. Agricultural terraces, hung on the edge of cliffs, rise to a thousand feet high over the valley. From its situation it seemed apparent that Pisac's ancient fortress must have guarded the valley that led to the jungles perched atop of the oval-shaped mountain. Moreover its size is an indication of its importance in the Inca realm. It is five times larger in extent than any other ruin in Peru and is an amazing complex of forts, tunnels, walls, roads, agricultural terraces.

We left our vehicles in the little village, put our gear upon the backs of sturdy-legged Indians hired for the purpose and then in force started up the mountain. In the hot sun we climbed up terraces like a gigantic flight of steps which, following the contours of the precipices, led us on to the heights through long parallel walls of undressed stone. Had these been determinedly held by the defenders, a few Indians well placed here might well have stayed a whole army.

That Pisac had been built as a sanctuary for the inhabitants of the valley was substantiated by the evidences of its many terraces once planted with potatoes, corn, peppers, *quinua*, in ample supply to sustain the besieged. On the crest of the hill, crowning the summit of the *pucara* and approached by a magnificent flight of steps and stone road, is a gigantic gnomon carved out of the living rock. It is — or better, was — shaped something like a dial. In its center was a projection designed to throw a shadow on the rounded reddish-gray rock. This was Inti-huatana, or Hitching-Place-of-the-Sun. Roughly circular, eighteen feet in diameter, the living rock was further cut out to hold the fitted stones which had been used in the sanctuary. The entrance to it was through a single stone door and encircling the sacred rock curved marvelously wrought walls of stones fitted in perfect succession. The whole site was actually an outcropping of granite into which the Inca masons anchored the base of the fortress itself, a fine example of that principle of which Frank Lloyd Wright says: "It is the nature of an organic building to grow from its site, come out of the ground into the light."

We stayed here a week, sleeping among the ruins at night and in the day tracing out the patterns of the roads. We found the main road that led through the valley, and we took time to study the engineering methods used in tunneling through the living rock. For a detailed inspection of the three-mile long escarpment, crowded with the remains of redoubts, fortresses, control gateways and hanging gardens, we could with advantage have lengthened our stay into months.

As it was we went on down into the Urubamba valley, the "Plain of the Spider," following the traces of our Anti road. This again was a warm and gentle valley, almost desert in its summer heat, brilliant with the Scotch broom's yellow flowers, filling the air with a penetrating mimosalike perfume. Two thousand feet lower than Cuzco, the valley is framed by abruptly rising rock walls which climb until they become glaciers sixteen thousand feet high, eternally crowned in snow. Here the eye travels from snow heights through every color gradation, through every clime from glacier to *puna,* from *puna* to bare rock, and on down the various climatic grades to the gentle flower-filled valley.

At Yucay we came to a spot which was little more than a mass of ruined terraces, Inca works which time and man with equal vigor have destroyed. Alongside the road were rows of adobe houses built one on top of another in tenement style. The rude-limbed *cholos* who frequent this gentle land had only the poorest mass

ets and were afflicted with all sorts of rheums. It seemed
ardly possible that so beautiful a valley could have suffered such
eterioration.

From the plaza we were directed to the edge of the green where
ood a two-storied house of sun-dried brick which would have been
ithout distinction had it not been for its beautiful stone door of
aca architecture. As we sat down in front of it to eat our luncheon,
remembered that it was here in 1548 that one of the last Incas
as poisoned by one of his own clan because it was feared that he
ight reveal to the Spaniards the whereabouts of Vilcabamba, the
gendary city hidden somewhere in the vast emptiness of moun-
ins close by. One of the primary reasons for our presence here was
locate if we could the skein of roads which would lead, so our
e-Expedition research had indicated, to this mysterious sanctu-
y. At this point we could do no more than follow the advice the
ing of Hearts gave Alice: "Begin at the beginning, go until you
me to the end, and then stop."

In 1535, save for unorganized resistance, the whole of the Inca
mpire had fallen to the Spaniards. It was then that Francisco Pi-
arro decided to select a puppet Inca and so rule the defeated realm
rough him. For this purpose he chose a young noble, a direct de-
endant of the last great Inca, who called himself Manco Capac II.
or some time there were no active signs of Indian resistance. The
eople, stunned by the suddenness of events, had not yet been able
comprehend the disaster that had befallen the empire. Then came
e uprooting: Indians were marched off as dray animals to carry
e impedimenta of conquest; the Spaniards took over the commu-
al lands, sending the men in droves to the mines; women were
ken from their homes and from the Sun Temples. The conquer-
s were setting off in all directions with the captive Indians as

cargo-bearers, to explore more lands. One army under the com
mand of Almagro the Blinkard set off for far-distant Chile takin
many of the able-bodied troops with him; others went into the for
ests to the east leaving Cuzco ill-defended. It was then that th
young Inca by a clever ruse eluded the watch set on him and dis
appeared.

On the morning of April 10, 1536, four huge and well-disc
plined native armies converged on Cuzco from the four direction
Within a day, the city was sealed off and put under tight siege. Th
Indians had learned quickly. They dug pits with sharpened stake
to prevent the Spaniards' use of their cavalry, they burned th
houses on the outskirts and slowly forced the Spaniards and thei
Indian mercenaries into the center of the city. By the seventh day
the position of the Spaniards looked hopeless. There remained onl
one hundred and thirty-six of them alive, many of whom wer
wounded. There were fifty horses left and two thousand Cañari In
dians. The revolt was general — even Lima on the coast was be
sieged.

The siege of Cuzco went on month upon month. Manco Capa
forced captured Spaniards into making powder for his forces; th
Indians learned to fire guns; they captured horses; they made re
peated mass attacks. Then the Spaniards found a fatal flaw in th
Indians' war-techniques: the great attacks were launched only a
the appearance of the new moon or once every twenty days. Afte
that the attacks ceased and the Spaniards could move with im
punity. Also the Indian warriors were actually little more than a
agrarian militia, farmers who must constantly disband to plant an
to harvest. So the Spanish horse made occasional forays out c
Cuzco, burning the crops, killing off the women who were essenti
as food preparers. Those Indians caught in battle had their hand
cut off. It was a devastating strategy and suddenly, on the mornin
of the sixteenth of February, 1537, the sixteen-month-old siege wa

ifted and the besiegers melted away. Manco Capac was now in
ight. Many of the Indian nobles fled with him. A holding
ction was fought at Ollantay-tambo, a great fortress down the
Jrubamba River, but in spite of it the Spaniards broke the resist-
nce, capturing many of the nobles including the Inca's small son.
et the main prize, the Inca King with thousands of his followers
nd large herds of llamas loaded with ancestral mummies and gold
– the whole variegated paraphernalia of empire — slipped away to
ake refuge in the fortress-city of distant Vilcabamba.

No matter how desperately they tried in the years that followed,
he Spaniards never located precisely the whereabouts of this sanc-
uary.

The cordillera of Vilcabamba is the culminating range of the
astern Andes. Many snow-covered peaks rise out of this massif
vhich is dominated by the twenty-thousand-foot-high Salcantay,
he "Savage Mountain," the mightiest of all the great peaks that
ut out of the range lying almost in the geological shadow of the
vestern border of the Amazon.

The whole area is marked by towering mountains, by plains and
ascading streams heading for the Amazon. Precipitous cliffs of
ranite and limestone mark a land noted for its uninhabitableness.
o the northwest are high plateaus lying between the Apurimac
iver and the jungle-bound Pampaconas River, high areas where
orn and potatoes can be grown and where there is forage for
amas. At the edge of the Amazon were the friendly jungle-allies,
ringing forest products to balance, as it were, the things of the
eights. And here, not more than three days' distant by secret ways
rom Cuzco, was Vilcabamba where Manco Capac set up his neo-
nca state — which was to endure for fifty years.

The raids began in 1537. Spaniards on the King's business were
aylaid, their cargo stolen; those captured were carried alive into

the fastnesses and put to work for the Inca. These included a barber-surgeon, a powdermaker, a blacksmith, all of whom were force to turn out war material for the Inca's growing army. The attack increased with such intensity that Francisco Pizarro, now a Marquis and Captain General, was eventually forced to build a garriso near to the point of attack. This he did at Huamanga, better know as Avacucho. Then, according to an ancient account, "Pizarro nominated a captain to defeat the Inca and make the roads safe." Th captain, seduced by the fiction that one Spaniard was worth on hundred Indians, set off with "five arquebusers, seven cross-bow men and shield men" to surprise and capture the Inca.

The terrible land with its rise and fall was so rugged that th soldiers by the time they had come upon the Indians were tired an worn. The Inca Lord himself, mounted "on one of the four hors he possessed" with lance in hand, headed the surprise attack. Onl six Spaniards escaped alive. That night, the severed heads wer thrown into the garrison village of Huamanga.

The Indians, safe in an inviolable stronghold, attacked the Span iards at will. Now even those Indian nobles who had at first co laborated with the Spaniards were deserting to the new "kingdom In 1542 six renegade Spaniards whose lives were forfeit sought sanc tuary in the fortress. In 1544 the Viceroy, seeking to end the grow ing power of Manco Capac, published the "New Laws" abolishir the slavery of the Indians and promising the return of their land At the same time he offered the six Spaniards a full pardon if the could persuade the Inca to accept the King's pleasure, come out his mountain fastness and put an end to the revolt. The peace over tures did not get much beyond an exchange of notes. One evenir in a game of bowls an argument grew out of the play, and on Spanish hothead crowned the Inca with a bowling ball, killing hi instantly. That ended not only the Inca but the peace overtur and, naturally, the lives of the six Spaniards.

Somewhere, Lost Vilcabamba

The Peruvians were determined to resist. When Manco Capac's successor suggested a compromise, he was poisoned and so another of the royal blood, Tupac Amaru, became the Inca and with him the new empire grew in power. All attempts by the enemy to reach this mysterious Vilcabamba had failed, all military expeditions were defeated and so, in a desperate move on the twentieth of July, 1571, the "most puissant Lord, Don Francisco de Toledo, Viceroy of these kingdoms of Peru" did send for the Friar Gabriel de Oviedo of Cuzco to consult with him as to how to carry out the King's wish that the Inca, now retired in the province of Vilcabamba, be persuaded to come out in peace . . .

Now, pursuing his mission, armed with a guidance for negotiations and treaties and a Bull of Dispensation, Friar Gabriel went north from Cuzco to the Abancay River, crossed over the suspension bridge, and so came to the rest house of Cocha-Cajas and "arrived at the station of Huampu . . . two days' journey from the province of Vilcabamba."

The drift of my speculations about the existence of this fabled Vilcabamba is now apparent. If we could approximate the region where this mysterious last capital of the Incas lay, we could follow the Inca roads into it. Vilcabamba was not as much our concern as the network of roads leading into it. The question of where Vilcabamba lay, then, might be resolved by a close study of the itinary of Friar Gabriel.

Huampu, a small village near to the Apurimac River sixty miles northeast of Cuzco, was the sallyport of the Inca raids on the Royal Road. A suspension bridge had hung there, but the Friar found that it had been cut and the rope strands of the bridge lay in the water. Since there was no way of his crossing the swift current to the other side where he could resume his journey by the nearest route, he returned to Cuzco to approach the region by the only other route known, by way of the Urubamba, the same route which we were now taking. So journeying, the Friar soon came to the fortress of Ollantay-tambo, lying a few miles downstream from Yucay, and there gained the pass of Panti-calla. He crossed the great suspension bridge that hung across the Urubamba River and, after about three days' march into the Vilcabamba Range, he came to the headwaters of the Pampaconas River where he made contact with the Inca. Yet, although we do know that Friar Gabriel was met at some point near the fortress by the Inca and his mountain warriors, neither he nor any white man after him ever visited or described Vilcabamba, the last capital of the Incas.

Hiram Bingham, the American historian and one-time Senator from Connecticut who discovered Machu Picchu in 1911, did *not*, we know now, find this Vilcabamba, as he believed. He was, it is true, searching for it and in the course of his explorations in the periphery of the region he did find numerous ruined sites including those of Machu Picchu. It is not to be wondered at that the sight of this unknown stone-built city lying in an almost perfect state of preservation atop the verdure-crowned mountains above the Urubamba led him to believe that he had indeed stumbled onto Vilcabamba.

While ferreting out the known parts of the Inca road which led down this valley of the Urubamba, our program for research in this section of the Anti had gradually taken on form. Now we were ready for action. Thus far we had found and traced the Anti-road, the main Inca highway to the jungles. We had stopped when we approached the tangled montaña that lay east of Cuzco past the fortress of Pisac. From now on we would concern ourselves with the vast area of roads and ruins that lay in the escarpment of the massif of Vilcabamba.

*   *   *

Somewhere, Lost Vilcabamba

The Urubamba River east of Cuzco, one of the myriad head-waters of the Amazon, over the centuries has cut through the heart-land of this Vilcabamba Range. In the lower courses of the river, the canyon walls rise abruptly and the warm jungle-air currents wafting up the river have so modified the harsh climate that trees, wood plants and even, at times, lush verdure cap the sharply in-clined rock walls. On the edge of this gorge and for sixty miles in the direction of the jungle, the Inca built his hanging cities. The deep gorge was terraced here as at Pisac with long parallel walls of undressed stones following the contours of the mountains. On these, dwellings were built to house the inhabitants. Machu Picchu is the greatest of these stone cities, but each year others are being found. We knew that all of these must have been bound together by roads — perhaps a single road. This we proposed to find.

There was no vehicular road beyond a certain point and so we decided to load our trucks onto a flatcar belonging to the Cuzco-Santa Railway which operated to the end of the Urubamba Gorge. The Expedition was to separate into two sections. Three of us — Silvia, Charles and myself — would seek out the roads which bound the "hanging cities" together and arrive, we hoped, by this passage overland at Machu Picchu. The other contingent — Lawrence, Henrik Blohm and a Cuzceño named Pepé de Pancorvo — were to take the Power Wagon to the rail terminus at the end of the Uru-bamba Gorge and from that point seek to penetrate the mountain fastness to see if they could find traces of Inca roads that might lead to Vilcabamba. Later, after we had visited Machu Picchu, we would cut behind the valley and seek to find if it was joined by road to the region of Vilcabamba. Such was our program.

To Henrik's question as to whether I thought we could one day find the roads that led to the sanctuary I answered that given time I thought we could. Certainly if the place were found, there would be ample evidence of its identity. Thousands of Indians had once lived there and with them into this sanctuary had gone gold and the mummies of their ancestors. Much, I was certain, still survived.

However, the main object of our search was not Vilcabamba itself but the skein of roads that had been built into this region. We had a quaint eighteenth-century map that gave us detailed directions, and other maps which showed a network of roads and the remains of an Inca bridge that led into Vilcabamba. The time had now come for testing our research.

After the fourth day of travel Silvia, Charles and I had left our mules, since there was no footing for them, to fight our way on foot along a road overhanging the gorge of Urubamba. We had passed through the ruins of several spectacularly located sites and always there was the road, a great folkway six feet wide that moved along the edge of the canyon. This superb example of engineering with its stone paving blocks and its retaining walls of dry masonry literally hung on the edge of a shifting and a terrifying abyss. As I clung to an overhanging branch to swing around a tumbled mass blocking the free-flowing road and bent back to lend Silvia a hand, I wondered just why the Incas had bothered to build these hanging cities. The labor of constructing them must have involved thousands of Indians for an extended length of time. How then explain these ruins perched midway between the jungle and the clouds?

On the fifth day out we came upon Ccuri-huayrachina ("the place where the gold is blown"), a small ruin so covered with trees that the outlines of the buildings could hardly be discerned. At this spot, the road curved to follow the contour of the massif. And at its end, gleaming whitely and little more than five miles away, was Machu Picchu.

Walking was now a dangerous operation. A landslide, started perhaps by an earth-tremor centuries ago, had loosened the upper part of the mountain and in its falling had dragged away a mile or more of the stone roadway, forcing us to crawl in places from one stone to the other, holding on to some rough-barked plant until a foothold was secured. Our Indian guides walked carelessly across the loose stones with what I felt was a too reckless confidence in the Deity — for below them there was a drop of two thousand feet. Swinging their machetes, they cleared the first of the entangling bush. Ahead of us, the sheer cliff on which the road had been once fixed was destroyed and the intervening space yawned out wildly and only a narrow line of remaining stone which had marked the road could be seen. Where the road itself once ran was a pile of disarranged rock.

Three hours later, the bad section crossed, we gained a beautiful stretch of the highway and, after descending a long monumental stairway, entered the formal gateway to Machu Picchu.

The ruins of Machu Picchu — no one knows its original name — lie in a topographical saddle between the peaks of Machu (old) and Huayna Picchu (new). In this saddle is a complex of terraces, gabled stone houses, temples, sacred plazas and residence compounds, and the famous Inti-huatana sundials. In its magnificent position, Machu Picchu is the climax of a series of the terraced cities along the Urubamba Gorge. Essentially a fortified city, its strongly constructed houses were most probably defense units. There was but one gate into the city, which, like most *pucaras,* was a self-sustaining unit whose terraces, following the contours of the mountains like a gigantic flight of steps, were planted to sustain its people. There were buildings of polished and well-fitted granite ashlars presumably designed for chieftains, a large place for the Sun Virgins, cruder clan-houses for the common people, barracks for soldiers, and even a prison. All the buildings had once been thatched with straw while the interiors were Spartan in their severity. The Indian slept on the ground on a woolen poncho; and with the usual tapestry hung over the door to keep out the night breezes, the three-legged pots placed over the fire for cooking, a brazier for warming the house, and a few decorations, the house of one who lived in Machu Picchu was complete.

The Vilcabamba contingent of the Expedition was already on the scene. Exhausted and tired from the long climb, we arrived to discover them comfortably installed in large huts, a bequest from a film company which some months before had been here to film a story as fantastic as it was improbable. The huts, however, were wonderfully useful. Machu Picchu has been so often visited and so completely described by others that we had no great reason for wanting to cover again what was now familiar ground. Although fantastically situated in the mountains, it was of no mystical import to the Incas. But we did hope to find if there had been, as was stated by Hiram Bingham, a direct connection between Machu Picchu and the vast geographical unknown to the north, where Vilcabamba was reported to lie.

We climbed the one-thousand-foot peak of Huayna Picchu on our third day at the ruins. However, the steps which the Inca engineers had carved into the living rock have now been completely cleared, so that any real alpinist would regard it as no more than a mild exercise. Within an hour we were sitting on its top, looking down on the ruins — and then on to the horizon ringed with snow-covered peaks. Below us was a fearful gorge and in the opposite direction was the terrifying range the Spaniard called "El Señorió de Vilcabamba." Somewhere beyond or perhaps in that mass of mountain and foliage and clouds was lost Vilcabamba.

It was obvious, from this height, that Machu Picchu could not have been an inaccessible fortress. Indeed a determined enemy would have found its conquest no great problem. Charles had elected to follow the lone conduit pipe which conducted the water to the city up the precipitous slopes to its source. With a flume only three inches in diameter, this would not have carried, in the dry season, enough water to supply more than a hundred people. A hostile army could have easily disrupted the water supply, which would have necessitated a two-thousand-foot descent from the fortress to the river for water. This could mean only one thing. Machu Picchu was *not*, as Hiram Bingham would have it, the fortress of Vilcabamba where thousands of fierce warriors had for years eluded the Spaniard and had organized a new empire.

Carefully we made our plans. Henrik with Lawrence would leave on the morrow to drive the Power Wagon with all the needed equipment for the search down the roadway to Huadquiña. There they would be met by Pepé de Pancorvo, our Cuzceño friend. A descendant of one of the founders of Cuzco, Pepé lived in a large hacienda on the Rio Vilcabamba which had its origin in that mysterious region where lay the last city of the Incas. His belief in the existence of Vilcabamba was unshakable. The rest of us would wait their return at Machu Picchu and explore it the while, before riding off on our own phase of the exploration.

Three weeks later, in the crisp night air we heard, above the vibrant music of the night cicadas, the high whine of the Dodge Power Wagon toiling up the hills of the Huadquiña hacienda. Even before the light showed along the last stretch of the road we were out to meet them, after first securing the fierce dogs that guarded the place. Our associates were long overdue. We had had no certain word of them and, having finished our own survey of the regions about Machu Picchu, we had been invited to stay at the old eighteenth-century sugar hacienda which lies at the edge of the Urubamba Gorge close to Machu Picchu and in direct line with the valley that we intended to follow when we left to explore the regions between our present stopping place and the Vilcabamba Range.

The Power Wagon was caked with mud, its bright red paint bleached by the tropical sun, the canvas caravan top cut into shreds. Richmond Lawrence, always frail, had thinned to a mere wisp and Henrik, who had reached his majority on this trek, had lost all his youthful bounce. All we could get from them, as they shuffled off toward the beds we had prepared for them, was that they had found "something." In the next days we learned what that "something" was:

> HUADQUIÑA, PERU, SEPTEMBER 19: THE DISCOVERY BY THE EXPEDITION OF AN INCA STONE ROAD LEADING THROUGH THE JUNGLES OF VILCABAMBA, AND OF AN UNREPORTED RUINED INCA VILLAGE, HAS REOPENED THE OLD MYSTERY OF MACHU PICCHU. AFTER SEVERAL WEEKS OF EXPLORATION IN THE HIGHLAND JUNGLES BORDERING THE VILCABAMBA RIVER, HENRIK BLOHM, HARVARD UNDERGRADUATE, AND RICHMOND LAWRENCE, THE CINEMATOGRAPHER OF THE EXPEDITION, ALONG WITH UNITED STATES-EDUCATED PEPÉ DE PANCORVO, RETURNED TO REPORT THE DISCOVERY OF THE RUINS OF PUN-CUYOC AND A SIXTEEN-FOOT-WIDE INCA ROAD THAT RAN INTO THE JUNGLES IN WHAT MAY WELL BE THE DIRECTION TO THE LOST CITY OF VILCABAMBA.

Our ancient map which showed charted rivers and mountains with curious jangling Quechua names could now be given credence. We felt certain that, locked within this montaña and accessible, if one could give the time to find it, was Vilcabamba, last capital of the Incas.

Henrik and Lawrence, following the trail Bingham had taken in 1912, had found, as we had hoped, that Inca roads ran all through he region. There was no doubting their Inca origin. Lack of time had prevented them from following a large one running due west — which would have taken them, so they learned later, to the ruin of Choque-quirao. The one they had followed northeast led to Choque-safra and from there a network of roads had spread over to the mountains. Along these, stone retaining walls and pottery fragments told as much as if the departed Incas had left behind a guide book.

It was after they had worked their way back to the Vilcabamba River and picked up an old Indian as a guide that they discovered Puncuyoc. All day they had climbed up and up. At night they slept on a narrow ledge. The next day they went through large trees covered with gray-green moss which gave the foliage a bearded and venerable look. In the afternoon they came across the first traces of a stone road, the continuing flight of an Inca staircase road eight meters wide. On the third day, 13,000 feet high in hills terraced to the very top where worked-limestone ruins appeared ghostly through thick verdure, they found the ruins of Puncuyoc in a saddle at the crest.

The drawing that Henrik made showed an unusual type of Inca structure. Built upon a raised platform perforated with large niches and stone roof-pegs, there was a thirty-two-foot-long building of two stories, a great rarity in Andean construction. It had a gabled roof and a doorway with two windows on each side. Although the techniques were Inca, the handling of the architecture was Spanish-inspired. The discovery of some Spanish artifacts — a button, broken horseshoes and nails and other pieces of iron — intermixed with late Inca artifacts indicated that at one time Spaniards had lived there, probably Spanish soldiers who willingly or unwillingly had been part of the secret Inca resistance groups. These ruins could only be the ramparts of the main fortress-city of Vilcabamba. Pepé de Pancorvo would not turn back at this point, and since Dick and Henrik could not go on with him because of our time schedule, Pepé was given the necessary equipment and was last seen making off on muleback in search of the lost city.

The next morning, with the snow-clad beacon of Salcantay beckoning to us, Silvia, Charles and I said our farewells to the two just-returned members of the Expedition. We were going on by mule to cut behind the range, hoping to discover the passage of the Inca roads, and would rejoin the others at the Apurimac Canyon. They were to gather up the trucks, go back to Cuzco, gather up the Expedition gear and meet us at this river. That arranged, we mounted, crossed a dubious suspension bridge, found the mule path and were soon swallowed up in an ocean of sugar cane.

Within three hours of upward riding through hills covered with ground orchids and wild strawberries we reached the bridge of Charqui-sactayoc. We were now directly back of Machu Picchu and so, keeping the river to our left, we went forward.

The valley later in the day became a deep V at the bottom of which ran the river. Along its banks we saw the thin ribbon of the road. The "air-temper" had become so tropical that, instead of pressing along to the night station which we had set as a goal, we went slowly, drinking in the scene. We had spent a long time in the treeless *puna* without seeing flowering plants. Now, without dismounting and with only a stretch of arm, I could pluck the wild strawberries that grew in profusion on the road. Silvia gathered pink-white begonias and blue-flowered lupines which grew on the shaded banks and, putting them in the halter of her mule, she soon transformed that recalcitrant beast into a walking flower garden. Ground orchids soon appeared and above us bamboo climbed in a delicate lacy pattern.

That night we camped at the edge of the gorge close to the cascades of the Salcantay River. Sharing the light of a single gasoline lamp, we read ourselves to sleep — Silvia with *Madame Bovary* while I, trying to find some similarity between Roman and Inca roads, read Gibbon's *Decline and Fall* and Charles was lost somewhere in Prescott's *Conquest of Peru*. In the moonlight the hoary head of Salcantay was austerely beautiful.

By the next noontime we had reached an altitude of over two miles on the highroad junction of Ccolpa-chaca. Below, far below, we could see a rustic four-logged bridge covered with rock and earth.

Salcantay's peak disappeared from view on the fourth day. For that entire day we rode among inhospitable crags — a bare and horrible sandstone desolation — until we reached another junction point on the Huay-rac-machay River. On our side, the sun-splashed side of the canyon, it was all jungle; the other side was bare and as dry as an old bone. Although we were now twelve thousand feet high we were still among the flora of the lowland jungles, and immense liana-festooned trees hung perilously on the inclined hills and we still saw the orchids and an occasional begonia. Sudden noise echoed through the thick foliage and we were set on by a raging torrent of cattle which stampeded by, crashing into the bush, tearing down the thick lianas and loosening a shower of branches. Silvia's mule leaped forward terrified and as the rampaging steers came on us, it turned to join the stampede. Somehow I managed to grab Silvia's reins and haul her out of the path of the frenzied cattle. Then just as suddenly as it came, it was over, like a tropical storm which comes out of nothing and goes into nothing, leaving a train of destruction in its path. We stopped briefly to repair the slight damage. Then we once more began to climb.

Now the tropic influence seemed to give way. Almost instantly at another rise of ground, we were among alpine flowers, tough-leafed, brilliantly flowered shrubs and more of the yellow-flowered brooms again mixed with solitary blue lupines. Then another five hundred feet altitude, and these too abruptly disappeared and we were en-

veloped by the cold mist and the voids of the naked uplands. W
were again on the *puna.*

There was nothing here but mist and rock — and cold. It seeme
hardly possible that people could have lived here. Yet just off th
trail we came on a brilliant swatch of green and a house of sorts, it
thatch covered with green mold out of which rose a plant scornin
the need for earth. Dogs set up an awful din.

I peered into the house. Several people, hardly distinguishable i
the dark, wandered about in the smoke-haze and small guinea pig
scurried about the mud floor. Charles leaned over my shoulde
sniffed and said: "I'll sleep outside."

The late afternoon was already frigid. Our guide brought w
wood and Charles made a fire against a rock. Somewhere hidden i
the mist were the mountains which had loomed up so high on m
map. I looked at my altimeter — it read 13,900 feet. Sleeping i
the open would make this one of our coldest nights in Peru.

For dinner we had chicken *à la* Salcantay, and shortly after tha
overcome with an aching weariness, we took to our sleeping bag
Soon after, the mist blew away to reveal the full moon. Just ahea
of us was Salcantay — seemingly so near that we could touch it.
could plainly see the solidly packed snow at its top. With the moon
light playing on it, the great peak had a molten sheen and looked, a
it was named, "savage." Then the mist came up like a theatric
drop-curtain forming more snow-mountains, brilliant in their daz
zling white nudity. It was breath-taking. Wrapped snug in m
double sleeping bag, I watched the unearthly spectacle until th
mist reclaimed the night and the curtain dropped on the magnifi
cent performance.

It was a troubled sleep. All night we were wakened by the nois
of glaciers; a sharp report, like the concussion of heavy artillery
then the rumbling and crackling of tons of snow; and the groun
would shake as in an earth-tremor. It was a transfigured night.

Somewhere, Lost Vilcabamba

The morning sun was life-giving. The cold that had been so intense at dawn had modified by eight o'clock as the sun charged the
earth with promised warmth. It grew even warmer as, mounting
higher, we moved into the sun's path following icy rills toward the
pass of Soiro-cocha. Salcantay was dazzling, reflecting rays of such
fierce intensity that I found that I could not look at it for any
length without becoming blinded. We spoke to each other rarely,
for in this rapturous morning every movement was an effort. The
very act of breathing was labor; even one's brain seemed slowed
down as if it was a great effort for the blood to get through the
blood vessels. Even the mules could scarcely put one hoof in front
of the other. At last we reached the top — a flat sward surrounded
by rocks and snow — and, at the very pinnacle, an enormous *apacheta*. Like automatons we slid off our mules, set them to graze;
then as one man, we sank down on the sparse grass. I took out the
altimeter.

"This is official," I managed to gasp — the first thing I had said
all morning which in itself showed the strain induced by altitude.
"We are now at 5200 meters."

"Which is," calculated Charles with his eyes closed, "seventeen
thousand, one hundred and sixty feet."

Silvia sat up at that. "Why! In Europe I'd be perched on top of
Mont Blanc!"

Later, endowed with new vigor, I planted the flag of the American Geographical Society on the highest *apacheta* in Peru. The blue
flag with the familiar U B I Q U E spread out in the wind.

We had now, so to speak, cut the Salcantay Valley in half and
still there was no evidence of any Inca road that might connect
Machu Picchu with Vilcabamba. We turned toward the Apurimac
River.

An old man, seemingly as old as the earth itself, whom we had
met on the road days before, had told us how *not* to lose our way.

Using the familiar thou — he called Silvia "little child" — he had said, "Thou first will come to the Soray. From it issues a stream This stream flows into an aqueduct. Thou will see this. Keep it always on thy right. It will lead thee into the Hacienda La Estrella.'

Still giddy from altitude sickness, we neared the glacier-topped Soray. From it flowed a stream so milk-white it looked like snow As we rode downward, we saw that it disappeared into an aqueduct Had we not known that this had been built in this century, we would have thought it Inca, so well laid was its stonework. For fifty miles it traveled on through the flume until it reached the hacienda for which we were bound.

The prospect before us did not look too bright. The village of Soray was still some miles distant and Osvaldo, our guide, had lost our food hamper during the encounter with the stampeding cattle At the time I had upbraided him for its loss, quite unjustly, I felt afterwards, for it could have happened to anyone. After that he had been unnaturally silent. Until then he had livened up the difficult way with his merrymaking and, although his humor was often ribald, it was easy and diverting. Now he was all gloom. I thought we should press on more quickly, for the shadows that told of cold and night were already on us and even now the valley was darkened Many times during that afternoon I cut back and urged Osvaldo on with the mules.

We were now in a valley bound by high palisades which, though they threw cold shadows across the road, still caught the light of the departing sun. I dismounted to adjust my spurs. Silvia and Charles had ridden ahead; the cargo mules were, as usual, behind.

I looked up to see Osvaldo slinking toward me, my rifle in his hands. I was unarmed — my pistol was in my knapsack, I could scramble nowhere. As instinctively I put the mule between us, Osvaldo put a finger to his lips and pointed to the top of the palisade

A number of deer peered down at us. I counted nineteen. Os

aldo handed me the rifle. I threw off the safety and wiggled forward. Even so, the movement had been enough to set them off. I aimed for the last one. The bullet caught him in full leap. For an instant he hung in mid-air, then as he rolled over and down, Osvaldo was off up the cliff as if 14,000 feet altitude were ground level.

It snowed that night but we dined ravenously on roast venison and fire-baked potatoes.

The sixth day — and the last — was the longest. The land was baked and dry and the only water we found was the thin trickle that here and there came down from that aqueduct. Following the advice of our old man, we had kept always on the right. We were unprepared for this dryness. Even in the shadow of snow-covered peaks, we were in a parched region where water seemed as rare as on the desert coast. The day went on endlessly. We spoke only of food and water and what we would do about both when we arrived at La Estrella.

Late in the afternoon we came to the first town we had seen since we left Huadquiña, a small village with a large plaza, and what at first glance looked like neatly roofed houses. It was the same Mollepata that was visited eighty-nine years before by the American explorer, Squier. At the time he was on his way, as were we now, to the Apurimac River and the famous suspension bridge that hung across the gorge. Like us, he too had ridden for some days. "We came at nightfall to the village of Mollepata," he wrote. "It is a collection of wretched huts on a high shelf of the mountain, with a tumbled-down church, a drunkard governor who is also the keeper of the hovel called a post-house, and a priest as dissolute as the governor." The church, at least, is not now "tumbled down."

We inquired here the way to La Estrella. No one seemed able to help us. By good luck we again found the aqueduct high in the hill and, still keeping it on our right, we found that presently waterway and roadway were running parallel. Since the former, we suspected carried the water supply that ran the mills of the hacienda, w could not, if we kept to it, miss our goal. In the distance we had brief look at the gorge of the Apurimac. Across it, in this vicinity had once hung a great Inca bridge, known now to the world as th "Bridge of San Luis Rey" which up until the middle of the last cen tury was one of the world's longest suspension bridges. In the dar! we followed the plunging watercourses downward, short-cuttin through the fields toward a spot where lights twinkled among th trees. We were almost there when out of the dark came the dog: but, of one mind to get to those large hacienda gates, we paid littl attention to the beasts.

We pushed open the huge wooden gates and the mules clattere noisily over the cobblestone courtyard. In the center was a foun tain, a life-size cherub clasping a swan from whose mouth gushed clear stream of cold water. We were drinking deeply, unmindful o our mules who shared the water with us, when I heard a step behin me and, turning, we saw David Samenez, owner of the hacienda, a: old friend from Cuzco who had invited us here to see and photo graph what was left of the great bridge.

So, convoyed by our host and the great gray mastiffs that guarde the hacienda, we wearily climbed the steps and entered a charmin patio planted with orange trees hung with ripe fruit.

Too stiff to sit, we took the proffered orange juice standing, an soon came alive to talk about our coming trip to the nearby ruin of the bridge now known to millions, the "Bridge of San Luis Rey.

V I I I

Apurimac: the Bridge of the Great Speaker

THE RIVER below looked like a writhing serpent, twisting between the chasm that was spotted with stands of cactus and blossom-covred spined trees. Its dull roar, the well-known sound of the Apurinac, the "Great Speaker," could be heard even where we stood two thousand feet above it.

We were out that day to take the measure of the giant which has tched out a grand canyon through Peru's heartland and, with David, had ridden out from the hacienda to the river's edge. From this erilous position, we peered over the sandstone abutments down into the vortex of the dreaded river. Water here is everything. If the rainfall is too little, the whole valley even at this high altitude is urned crisp from the heat of the sun; and if too much falls, the urface of the river rises as high as forty feet within a single day nd in minutes the raging torrent washes away, as it did in the autumn of 1953, that which man has spent a lifetime building.

The Apurimac had been the Rubicon of the Incas. For centuries t held their northward movement in check; but once their technology advanced to the point where they could bridge it, they ung a suspension bridge, the greatest in all Peru, across it. At once hey pushed their empire northward at a fearful pace.

Highway of the Sun

It was known as "*the* Bridge," and in the minds of the Spaniards it was coextensive with Peru itself. For the early Spaniards, the crossing of it filled them with fright and terror. Records and letters are filled with their plaints of how the bridge swung in the heavy wind, how deep was the dark abyss, how terrifying the thunder of the roar of the water as the sounds ricocheted against the vertical rock-walls; how their pulses raced, their eyes grew dim, their hearts faint as they hung onto the rope-cables and made a traverse of it. "It is," said one, "no small terror that is caused by seeing what men must pass through in these indies."

The longest continuously used bridge in the Americas, millions of people crossed over it during the six hundred years of its existence. Inca armies of conquest flowed over it; gold for the ransom of Artahualpa made its one-way passage across it; the Spanish fought their civil wars over and around it; and for three centuries colonists moving on the King's business used it. Even in the days of the South American republics this bridge was the only way of crossing the "Great Speaker." Yet it would have been forever forgotten had it not been for two Americans. In 1864 George Squier stopped long enough in his journey through the region to give it, by means of the only authentic illustration ever made of it, a detailed and accurate description; and in 1927 another American, Thornton Wilder, immortalized it in *The Bridge of San Luis Rey*.

David Samenez had insisted on accompanying us out to the bridge site. He was after all, he reminded us with much jesting, the owner of the Bridge of San Luis Rey. Moreover, he had been born at the hacienda of Bellavista, close to where the ancient road made its descent to the bridge.

This hacienda, which drew its water from the weeping glaciers of Soray thirty miles distant, lay on a flat tableland overlooking the gorge of the river. It had been developed by David's father, a man who did not allow his gentle birth to prevent him from working with his hands, an eccentricity which in the last century in Peru was considered a social crime. He had built up his hacienda, had fought against a dictator, holding off a large contingent of troops near to the site of the old bridge and, in 1935, had served his country briefly as President of Peru. All this we learned as, mounted on our borrowed horses, we made our way over the highway.

The mountains were beautiful that day — Salcantay, its hoary head unbelievably high in the cobalt blue of the sky, accompanied as it were in the heavens by Mount Huamantay with its 5000 feet of glistening snow. An undulating greensward planted with lucerne lined the ancient highway, whose roadbed here had been destroyed by the passing caravans of five centuries.

We moved on beyond to where the earth yawned out widely and there began the ride downward. It took us some hours to get to La Blanca, once a way stop on the descent of the Inca road toward the canyon which led to the great bridge. But from La Blanca we could go no farther. The landslides caused by the rampaging Apurimac had destroyed the rock walls of the canyon. The careful stone terracing of the Incas, erected as long ago as 1390, still hung in sections over the abyss, yet there was no longer any way of getting down. Far below our binoculars, following David's pointing finger, picked out the stone steps that led to the bridge ramparts. All else was obscured. To reach the bridge, we would have to cross to the other side of the river and approach it from its northern side.

On our way back we watched the setting sun painting the snow-capped mountains with radiant rainbow colors, and David pointed out to us the snow-covered Yanacocha fifteen miles away. Even as he pointed it out, my powerful binoculars picked up another river plunging down the precipitant slopes to join the Apurimac. About midway between the glacier and the river were the ruins of Choquequirao, the only extensive Inca ruins known in this part of the Vilcabamba Range. They could be reached, he said, in a two days' walk from the village of Inca-huasi. Did David know if the road led to Vilcabamba?

"My great uncle was one of the first to visit the ruins of Choque-quirao. He kept a journal which I have in the house. He once traveled beyond these ruins and he insisted that those roads led to Vilcabamba, in just the region which you pointed out to me on the map."

We knew this to be true, for when Hiram Bingham found his way to the ruins in 1912, he had seen written on the walls the name of JOSÉ BENIGNO SAMENEZ 1861. One day, I knew, we should have another try at this fabulous Vilcabamba, but to go now would be to upset our carefully planned schedule. I felt at this moment like an earthy Pangloss, always interrupting our wishful thinking with "Let us cultivate our garden." But if we could not now go to Vilcabamba, we could at least visit and inspect all that was left of the Bridge of San Luis Rey.

We began early in the day, so as to avoid the excessive heat. Before the peaks were lighted by the ascending sun, we gathered our gear and Indians together and were driven to the left bank on the northwest side of the Apurimac. Here we began the fifteen-hundred-foot descent into the gorge. Encumbered as we were with cameras and guide-ropes, our descent between the stands of fiercely spined cactus over loose gravel-sand was a little like the performance of a slow-paced slalom. The heat at the bottom, even in the morning, was furnace-hot, and the cactus and sharp-spined acacia accented the desertlike look of the place. As we walked along, heat waves danced before our eyes like St. Elmo's fire, and to add to our discomfort the flies gave us no rest. They flew in gyrating circles about our eyes and our ears, and the prick of their proboscises was like a needle's stab.

Apurimac: the Bridge of the Great Speaker

In this September month we found the Apurimac at its dryest, the land slashed with canyons like the wadis of Africa. The dryness was only a temporary state, for the shallow rivulets could rise with callous ease and within a fierce day of rain be raging torrents. The sides of the gorge were a horrible sandstone desolation cloven down in giant cuts, while below was a wide waste landscape. The gorge itself rose abruptly to the *puna* and higher above us, almost as a mirage, were snow-covered mountains.

We were not alone in feeling the heat. Our Indians felt it too. I remembered reading in some history how the "Inca took the Indians from the coastal desert of Nasca to transfer them to the river Apurimac; because that river, where the royal highway goes from Cuzco to Lima, passes through a region so hot that the upland Indians . . . cannot live in its heat. So the Inca, bearing this in mind, took Indians from the coastal regions to settle in these hot regions even though the River Apurimac has only a small place to settle, for, passing through high and rugged mountains, it has very little useful land, and yet the Inca would not have this little bit go to waste but wished it to be used for gardens so as to be able to enjoy at least the abundant good fruit which is raised on the banks of that famous river." But whatever orchards had been here had long since been destroyed by time, and by the high bourne of this river, a headwater of the Amazon, which had its source a hundred miles southwest in the barren mountains of Chumbivilca.

The small biting flies were at their worst when late in the afternoon we came to the rock walls that once sustained the bridge. At this point the Apurimac cuts into a gorge of solid rock walls which rise straight and sheer to considerable height. Confined to a narrow channel, the river roared its disapproval in such deafening tones that we had to communicate by hand signals.

A tunnel through which the road ran lay above us some one thousand feet on the sides of the limestone cliff. Henrik notched up his rucksack, played out the rope and started the climb. He found a narrow ledge and secured himself. Dick Lawrence followed, holding fast to his camera. Next went David and Charles, then Silvia and last, myself. The Indians found their own way. I could see Henrik far up edging toward an overhanging rock that jutted out above the river. It was a slow process. Perspiration pouring down my face attracted the insects and the flies which, since my hands were well occupied, had their suctorial delight. By the time I reached a spot where I could rest and wipe my face, blood freely mingled with the sweat.

One of the most dangerous aspects of the operation was the crumbling stone. A projection which we supposed strong enough to use as a belay turned out under the pull of our ropes to be virtually as shifty as beach sand. Dick Lawrence, who had taken the greater punishment since he would not relinquish either his tripod or camera to anyone, was having trouble overhead. There had been a steady rain of sandstone and now and again a sharp curse, but as I could see little, I was unaware until later how dangerous some of those moments had been. Henrik led us very expertly up and over to the section of the precipice from which the bridge once hung suspended.

We were now standing on what had once been one of the most important of the Inca roads. The celebrated tunnels were ahead of us and from this vantage place we could see now, and for the first time, the place of the bridge. The Inca road coming out of Mollepata, the last *tampu* station on the Cuzco side, had been run over the high-placed pampa to Bellavista near to the edge of the gorge. From that point it had zigzagged down the artificially terraced canyon to the valley fifteen hundred feet below. It had then followed the valley to the gorge, where mounting steps had been cut into the walls of an obelisk-shaped pinnacle. This had been reached by a narrow inclined path, once ingeniously built with retaining

126

walls; and from there the road mounted to a platform cut into rock. The thick suspension cables of the bridge on the Cuzco side had been fastened deep down in the floor of the platform. The cables, suspended from two stone towers, were then carried to the other side where, we were to find later, there was a similar natural platform. From the platform on our side of the river, the road twisted upward until it came to the cliffs which, because they were of extremely friable sandstone, could not be surmounted. Faced with this geological fact, the Inca engineers tunneled through them. The tunnel near which we were now standing was about two hundred yards long and inclined upward as it turned with the cliff. From here the road climbed to the heights of the naked "idol mountain" [1] and then, adapting itself to the topography of the land, it went north to the next *tampu* station.

Lawrence, having taken up a position on an edge overhanging the abyss of the river, set up his camera to film us filing into the blackened mouth of the tunnel. As it was impossible to hear over the reverberations of the "Great Speaker," we waited for his arm signal, then we moved by him and entered the tunnel. Sunlight poured into its darkened throat. I stopped at the first window openings. Then I suddenly realized that Lawrence had not followed us. I turned back in panic, and not seeing him, flung myself on my stomach to look down below into the churning river. He was nowhere to be seen and I was about to rise and go for the others

---

[1] At this point the idol of Apurimac, so wrote one of the conquistadores, was lodged in a much-painted hut and set up on a thick beam, thicker than a very fat man, and this had many pieces hacked out of it. It had a girdle of gold bound around it and soldered so as to resemble lace and on the front of it two large golden teats, like a woman's . . . Along this thick beam there were other idols, in a line, from one side to another, and they occupied the entire length of the room. These were likewise bathed in blood and clothed in golden robes like the large one. Through this largest idol, they say it was, the demon of the river used to speak to them. (Pedro Sancho, in his *Relación.*)

when I saw him struggling just below me within hand-reach in the branches of a tree. He had fallen and had been caught in a tree growing out of the ledge. There he hung, suspended between heaven and hell. Somehow he had managed to hang on to his camera. This he handed up to me, then he climbed up, terribly shaken, to the tunnel-ledge. There was not much more camera work the rest of that afternoon.

The walls of the tunnel, which was two hundred and fifty yards long by actual measurement, were pierced with openings to allow in the light and air. Through these "windows," into which I climbed, I could see the snow-topped peaks of Mt. Marcani beyond us. The tunnel had been fashioned by the Incas much as the Romans mined rock. After a fierce fire had been built against it, water was thrown on the hot rock splitting the friable lime and sandstone. After that the Incas with their knowledge of working stone with stone were presented with no problem. Their daring techniques in engineering were something else. At the end of the tunnel, which had once been connected with a stone stairway cut and built into the living rock, we eased across that dangerous cleft and gaining the circular stairway, we went very slowly down the step-road. Cieza de León back in 1543 had had trouble with these same stairways, even when they were in good repair: "Here the road is so rugged and dangerous, that some horses laden with gold and silver had fallen in and been lost without any chance of saving them." Several hundred feet below, we came to what had been the platform, on which we found the remains of the two enormous stone towers or pillars supporting the cables of the bridge. Two hundred feet directly in front of us, across the stygian gap of the river, we could clearly see the other side of this "bridge of the . . . Apurimac-chaca." Cieza had written that it "was the largest bridge encountered from Cajamarca . . . with the road well built along the sides of the mountains. . . . The Indians who built it must have performed herculean labor. . . ."

No precise data can be given for the bridge's construction. After the year 1300 the Incas expanded their realm to the edge of the Apurimac and about this time, according to their chronicles, Inca Roca, then chieftain, finished the bridge. This would have been *circa* A.D. 1350. The detailed description of its structure is given by the Cuzco-born historian Garcilaso de la Vega, surnamed "The Inca":

> The Apurimac bridge which lies on the royal road from Cuzco to Lima has its pillar support [he called it stirrup] made up of the natural rock on the Cuzco side; on the other side [where we were now standing trying to figure it all out] was the stone tower, made of masonry. Under the platform that held this tower, five or six large wooden-beams were inserted as thick as oxen — they stretched from one side to another. They were placed one higher than the other like steps. Around each of these beams, each of the suspension cables is twisted once so that the bridge will remain taut and not slacken with its own weight, which is very great.

Until nineteenth-century technology ushered in the use of iron chains for suspension cables, this Bridge of San Luis Rey, hanging by enormous rope-cables across the Apurimac, was one of the largest bridges of its type known. The Incas had no knowledge of the arch, nor did any of the preliterate peoples in America. Depending as it does upon the principles of gravity, pressure and weight, the arch is yet earthbound and passive and therefore could not have been used here even had the Incas been familiar with it. Instead, they perfected the principles of the suspension bridge by reversing the arch-curve and giving it wings.

The Bridge of San Luis Rey, as were all suspension bridges on the Royal Road, hung from rope cables hand twisted from the fibers of the maguey plant. Those of this bridge of "the thickness of a man's body," were just laid over the high stone towers for their "suspending" and then buried in the thick masonry on the platform of the towers. From the suspended cables, supports hung down, and to these the bridge platform made of wood planking was attached. Cables attached to the main bridge served as wind bracing.

Although the materials were primitive, the essential nature of the technology of the Inca suspension bridge is, in principle, the same as the best constructed suspension bridges of today. Rope bridges have been built since immemorial times, but few other cultures before the advent of recent times built so well as the Inca. This particular bridge indeed was so well made that it lasted for five hundred years, the cables, of course, being renewed every two years as a part of their work-service by Indians living at the *tampu* of Cura-huasi. This system of maintenance, so efficacious that the Spanish conquerors maintained it throughout the colonial period, disappeared only after the "wheel" conquered the Andes, and the bridge which had served as a highway for foot and mule traffic for a period of six hundred years was allowed to fall into slow decay.

The Incas built for eternity. Permanence was to them, as it was with the Romans, the base of all their construction. If the Inca road system is here occasionally compared with the Roman road system, it is because, until very recent time, there have been no other communication systems that can be compared with either. Other civilizations had, of course, their highways, but until the advent of the Romans none maintained a road system.[2]

However, structurally an Inca road differed greatly from a Roman road. The Romans employed heavy-wheeled carts with rigid

[2] In the times of Diocletian, thirty roads issued from the gates of Rome; maintaining more than three hundred and seventy distinct roads the entire Roman Road system is believed to have totaled 53,568 miles

front axles which necessitated a deep roadbed. The Incas, since their roads were traveled only by those on foot and by llama herds, had no need for the roadbed. But aside from this the two engineering concepts, Roman and Inca, are amazingly similar. While there is no denying Rome's place in civilization's sun, the Incas living on a neolithic cultural horizon tied to stone tools still conceived a communication system that stands extremely high in comparison with the Roman.

The Romans had three thousand years of experience to draw on. The facets of Old World thought and techniques regarding the building of roads are a vast web stretching from the first wagon ruts of ancient India to the stoneways of the Persians. As remote as certain of these areas were, as removed from each other by time and space, the Romans had all these centuries of cultural heritage on which to draw. The Inca had none of these, yet an Inca road is in many aspects superior to a Roman road. Every feature of a Roman road is paralleled in an Inca road except that, for the most part, the Incas built — literally — in the clouds. The Apurimac Bridge, for example, was part of a highway which came from heights the like of which no Roman had ever seen. The passes the Roman conquered were as nothing compared to these in the Andes; Mont Blanc, the highest peak in Europe, is 15,800 feet high; yet here in Peru we have walked over Inca roads *built* at this height. The old Roman roads which crossed the spine of the Italian promontory of the Apennines were no higher than the city of Cuzco, which is 10,200 feet above the sea. Again we turn to our Cieza. As a boy in Spain, he knew the Roman Road. He had walked between Tarragona and Cadiz over the Via Augusta, built in the first century B.C. and rebuilt every quarter of the century by the Caesars. He drove his mules over the Via Argenya, which ran between Mérida and Salamanca — a road which was started by Tiberius, continued by Nero and fully repaired by Caracalla in A.D. 214, so he and others like him knew what they were saying when they wrote of Inca roads that there is "nothing in Christendom that equals the magnificence of the Inca roads."

The remarkable thing is the similarity in approach to the "idea" of roads between the Inca and the Roman. Both civilizations were of the land. Both had land armies, and land armies need roads; and since a road is only a road if one can go back over it, both believed that the road must be well built and well maintained. The Romans, it is true, ruled the straight line into civilization's thinking, whereas the Inca's road *surmounted* obstacles rather than avoided them, and their engineers employed what we call "directional straightness" — that is, between two given points their road ran unerringly straight. Caius Caesar personally laid down vast stretches of road and the Claudian family, when public funds were not available, defrayed expenses for road building out of its own privy purse. In Peru the road-building program was also identified with the rulers and the roads were called after the Inca who built them. For example, one 2500-mile long road that ran to Chile was known as Huayna Capac Ñan, or the Road of Huayna Capac. Often an Inca would order a road to be built for himself wider and larger than that of his predecessor. The Romans put up milestones as markers while the Incas built their *topus* "with the distance between them a Castilian league and a half." Along their road, the Romans placed night quarters or *mansiones;* in Peru, the Incas erected and maintained *tampus* every four to eight miles along the entire route of their roads. Roman couriers had a change of horse-mounts at *mutationes* to hurry up messages along the Imperial Way; the Incas, depending on foot, had their *chasqui* stations every two-and-a-half miles as way stations for the trained runners who carried messages over the most terrifying terrain in the world.

The bridge, "the little brother of the road," was ever an important link in the great Inca road system. How many of them there were along the length and breadth of the Andes, we cannot be sure. But of them all, the Apurimac-chaca, the Bridge of San Luis Rey, was the greatest. Few who passed over it did so without pausing to wonder at this miracle of engineering. As to its length, the Inca historian, Garcilaso de la Vega, guessed it to be 200 paces long — "although I have not measured it, I have asked many in Spain who did." Cieza, that most accurate of observers, thought it was "fifty estados" or about 85 meters (250 feet) in length. Sir Clements Markham, who crossed it in 1855, estimated the Apurimac-chaca at 90 feet and its elevation 300 feet, while Lieutenant Lardner Gibbon, who made a survey of the Amazon for the United States Government in 1857, estimated its length at 324 feet.

When Squier came to the bridge in the summer of 1864, he and his companions lost no time extracting the measuring tapes and sounding lines. They found that the bridge was 148 feet long from end to end and that it was suspended 118 feet above the surging river. That was the first and last time this famous bridge was exactly measured, for although it was still hanging in 1890 it was no longer used and the cables, unreplaced, curved dangerously downward into the gorge and were slowly decaying with time. The explorer Squier also made several daguerreotypes of it, which he used in a somewhat dramatized and heightened version as a woodcut illustration in his book *Peru, Land of the Incas*. Of the bridge, he wrote:

> Between the precipices on either side, looking wonderfully frail and gossamer-like, was the famed bridge of the Apurimac. A steep, narrow path following some distance a natural shelf, formed by the stratification of the rock, for the rest of the way hewn in its face, led up for a hundred feet to a little platform also cut in the rock where were fastened the cables supporting the bridge. On the opposite bank was another and rather larger platform roofed by rock where was the windlass [a feature added by the Spaniards] for making the cables taut and where,

perched like goats on some mountain shelf, lived the custodians of the bridge. . . . It was a memorable incident in my traveling experiences — that crossing of the great swinging bridge of the Apurimac; I shall never forget it.

Later, in the beginning of the present century, Hiram Bingham in speaking of the origins of his interest in Peru said that this illustration of the bridge "was one of the reasons why I decided to go to Peru."

It is known that this dramatic picture of the bridge inspired Prosper Mérimée to use it as a literary device in a fictional piece on Peru, and that Thornton Wilder, later inspired both by the suggestions of the French writer and the great span that crossed the Apurimac, and fascinated by its picturesque remoteness, wrote what is now a literary masterpiece, *The Bridge of San Luis Rey*. With this book in hand I now stood looking down on the hiatus between the walls where the bridge once hung. Later I wrote Thornton Wilder from La Estrella hacienda where we stayed during our assault on the bridge's factual and legendary history. I knew that he regarded the bridge as a literary device, but so well had he described this bridge on the high road between Lima and Cuzco that I felt that he must have seen, perhaps in some old issue of *Harper's Magazine*, a reproduction of Squier's stirring woodcut of this ancient bridge which was in fact the actual hero of his novelette. "It is best, von Hagen," he answered me, "that I make no comment or point of it . . . I wish I were with you and could see the great river and the gorge."

The afternoon wind came up loud and shrill as we were standing on the platform that once held the great suspension cables of the bridge to set the foliage that clung to the rock walls rustling. We knew now that an old adage about the wind and the bridge was true and that when the afternoon winds blew, even the wind-braced cables could not hold the bridge steady and it would swing like a hammock.

It was late afternoon by the time we regained the boulder-strewn shores of the river. The sun was lighting the snow peaks while the shadows of the mountains fell across the canyon. A long shadow falling across the vertical cliffs gave a curious illusion of a hanging bridge. At that moment I must have been very close to the spot where the good Fra Juniper had stood looking upward at the bridge when a "twanging noise filled the air . . . and he saw the bridge divide and fling the five people into the river below."

"Why did this happen to *those* five?" the good Fra asked himself, "if there were any plan in the universe at all, if there were any pattern in a human life, surely it could be discovered mysteriously latent in those lives so suddenly cut off. *Either we live by accident and die by accident* or we live by plan or die by plan." With that soliloquy Wilder began his story. It is an ironic truth that if this tragic story had not been written, this wondrous bridge built in 1350 by the Inca Roca which was to endure for five centuries as one of the greatest tributes to man's domination of wild nature, would have been lost to memory.

With the dying sun now playing fully on the glaciers, the river canyon became as bright as if it were full day. The shadows were gone and, with them, the illusion of the hanging bridge. When I next looked back, there was again only emptiness between the two vertical walls.

I X

The Sanctuary of the Hawk

THE VERDANT LAND that surrounded Andahuaylas was wonderfully inviting after the blank and naked misery of soil that we had endured for the past weeks. For the hundred miles that separated the Bridge of San Luis Rey from this town we had driven over a desolate void and our search across the deep valleys and high treeless ridges had been through country so bleak that it almost robbed us of our sense of beauty. At last from the highest point in the winding vehicular road we saw in the distance a shaft of sunlight warming an immense green plateau. In the center of this on a high ridge was Andahuaylas.

A quick glance at the town told us that it offered us only the sorriest of night quarters, so we doubled back to a farm which we had seen earlier to seek a place to stay. On the way we passed natives working on the dirt road. They doffed their wide-brimmed, llama-felt hats in a cringing and timorous manner, and like so many harvester ants, they went on shoveling the movable earth into their woolen tunics; then, folding over the ends of their ponchos, they hauled it off to the edge of the abyss and dumped it. The same garment was their coat and, at night, their blanket.

The hacienda was of ancient vintage with a grass thatch covered with a mold three fingers deep out of which grew many small plants. It was, like most adobe structures, without grandeur or dignity, moldering and old.

Near the main house were men in shaggy clothing who could have stepped out of a Brueghel canvas. Their pants were of baggy blue homespun, split so deep in front that their genitals had to be held by a sort of cod-piece. The jackets were short. And these with their woolen ponchos were all they possessed with which to cover their shivering bodies. On their heads they wore sodden, shapeless felt hats. All were addicted to the coca-leaf habit and the corners of their mouths were flecked with green spittle. Each carried a goat-skin in his hand and each moved in an obedient line toward a copper tank where the sharp-eyed hacendado stood periodically opening the tap to stive the alcohol in the barrel-skins. Each time he noted down the amount dispensed. This scene, so characteristic of the region, was like a tableau out of the sixteenth century.

The great Inca road through the town long since disappeared under the modern road which has been laid over the old roadbed. Yet in Inca times Andahuaylas had been an important stop on the road, a royal *tampu*, "In the center of the province of Andahuaylas, there were large lodgings and storehouses of the Incas," wrote one Spanish scrivener. There was now, however, nothing left of this *tampu*, no ruined structures, no remains of the road or even memories of it among those we questioned. And so we would have gone on had it not been that here we found ourselves absorbed in the history and the legends of the Chancas. We were to come across their traces for some hundreds of miles until we entered the jungles.

Today the Chancas are only a legend, but to the Incas they were the hierarchy of their enemies. They had once had the audacity to attack sacred Cuzco and had almost succeeded in taking it. So feared were these people that, as has been said in a previous chapter, the Incas, in conquering them, did not treat them with their usual policy of "absorption with honors" into the empire, but slaughtered, flayed and stuffed the skins of Chanca warriors and set them up in tombs in a ridiculous mimicry of life as a perpetual reminder of Inca justice.

> When I entered this province of Andahuaylas [in 1548 — so goes the notation in the record kept by our good friend Cieza] its chief was an Indian named Huasco and its natives were called Chancas. They go around dressed in woolen shirts and mantles; they all wear their hair long, arranged into many small plaits, tied up with some woolen cords. In former times they were so valiant that they not only conquered other lord-ships but extended their dominions near to Cuzco. . . . The chief Hanco-Huallu, so famous in these parts for his great bravery, was a native of this land. They relate that he could not endure to live under the yoke of the Incas and so . . . he penetrated with 8000 of his warriors into the depths of the forest of Moyobamba [in the Amazon].

In the late fourteenth century, this tribe had stood in the way of the Inca's northern expansion, blocking passage across the Apurimac River and fighting so fiercely that Inca engineers found it impossible to go ahead with bridging the river. At last the Chancas were repulsed by the sixth Lord Inca, who completed the bridge and set about absorbing the Chancas into his empire. However, these warriors, chafing under the benevolent despotism of the Incas, attacked Cuzco and burned part of the city. They were finally defeated on the "Plain of Blood." It was sometime after this event that Hanco-Huallu and his army of eight thousand Chancas, including women, escaped to the forests of the upper Marañon. For permitting this to happen, the Inca general, Capca Yupanqui, was executed on his return to Cuzco.

The Incas never forgot the Chancas. In time they conquered all the tribes far down into southern Chile and absorbed others in the upper Amazon. They claimed the mountains to the north up to the borders of what is now Colombia. Yet, masters of all this terrain, they never stopped fearing the Chancas hidden somewhere in the forests of Chachapoyas. Their pursuit of this hated foe plays an important role in the history of the Inca roads, and for more than a year we were to follow its course through the Andes and into the jungle.

We would have liked at this point to walk northward as they must once have walked over the fragments of the Inca road — across the wild sandstone uplands which lay northwest of Anda-huaylas — and so within a few days arrive in the once great Inca center of Vilcas-huaman. We decided instead to make a great arc around the area to be explored, find a place for headquarters and double back to this "geographical center of the Inca Empire." In so doing, we came to Ayacucho.

This venerable colonial city — with its moss-covered sagging roofs, its old moldering churches and the remains of what were once great baronial mansions dropping into slow decay — made us feel as if we were looking at the models for some of Piranesi's heroic copper-plates. It was a delightful change for us, after the weeks of desolation through which we had passed, to come to this self-contained city. Once the third city of Peru, with opulent mansions which rivaled those of Lima, Ayacucho has now but twenty-five thousand inhabitants. Traffic has flowed away from it rather than to it and only once weekly does an airplane put down on its airfield. Its small electric plant, wonderfully uncertain, gives only enough power for a pallid light while its water supply is scarce and highly questionable. But the heavens are always blue; the climate, at its 8500-foot altitude, is benign and soft, with the most gentle "air-tempers" of all Peru; and the people, a high percentage of whom are of pure Spanish blood, reflect the ease of the climate. Without pretense and still preserving their native wonder at the outside world, they are, to use an archaic term, "full of incorruption."

For us, now somewhat worn by our efforts to trace the Inca roads, Ayacucho was a haven. In the last week none of us had escaped the debilitating effects of the anoxic atmosphere of the high altitudes from which both machine and man had taken an awful beating. And so our arrival in this sun-enveloped Ayacucho brought us a temporary surcease.

There were changes too within our organization. Charles had now to return to the States on urgent private matters and it was time for Henrik Blohm to go back to Harvard. So until our two archaeologists arrived, our number was reduced to three.

We would have liked to set up a large rambling headquarters as we did at Puno and Cuzco, but doing that here would mean having to find servants, to worry about food supplies and the care of a house. Instead we moved into an ancient hotel that faced the main plaza. Here, for the time being, we rested and on a large balcony that overlooked the plaza, we prepared the reports on our progress.

Geographically we were in an important area. Although the Inca road did not run immediately through Ayacucho, which was founded as a Spanish colony in 1540 and so was not an ancient Indian site as were most of the other famous cities in Peru, it did pass through the dry valleys a few miles to the east. From that point it went on over a high, level pampas south toward little-known Vilcas-huaman, sometimes spoken of as the "Sanctuary of the Hawk" and, so the natives assert, "the center of the dominions of the Incas. For from Quito in Ecuador to Vilcas is the same distance as from Vilcas to Chile, these being the extreme points on the Inca Empire."

We lazed for some time in the subtle charm of Ayacucho. Each day we sat or walked in the sun, listening at midday to the cries of the street vendors; each evening watching religious processions pass long streets which were a little like an Augean stable in their uncleanliness. On every square was an ancient church and every other house, it seemed, boasted the carved doorway of a once beautiful mansion still offering proud escutcheons to an indifferent world. Ayacucho is Spanish and its people, while they still have some Indian blood and speak the lisping Quechua, are primarily Spanish in character and in dress. The women wear long sweeping crinolines and broad-brimmed hats which are decorated almost as if in perpetual mourning with broad, black silk bands. Near Ayacucho the first battle of the war between the Spaniards in South America, the Battle of the Chupas, was fought in 1532. During our stay we found many records dating back to 1545 which had to do with the colonial life of this town, but of Inca roads and Inca ruins and of records immediately pertinent to our search — nothing.

The road we sought lay northeast along the 13,000-foot-high escarpment of the "Sanctuary of the Hawk." Our task now was to pick up the main route of this road, and follow it back south until we reached fabulous Vilcas-huaman.

This was not a vehicular route. We could go only a little of the way by car; the rest would have to be by mule. As we made ready the food and gear that were to last us a few weeks and arranged our small tents and warm clothes — we would again be journeying over the *puna* — Silvia and I found that we should be making the trek alone. Lawrence, our tough little Lawrence, had succumbed to dysentery. We could not wait for we were hoping to escape the great rains and our itinerary was set. So after I had had my final instructions regarding the operation of the motion picture camera and Silvia had made sure that we had all our provisions, we two set off alone to find that "geographical center of the Inca Empire."

The ride had taken the whole of the day and was going into the night and the horses had been changed for the third time before we began to climb the last of the hills that lowered between us and

Vilcas-huaman. The sky became ominously dark and our guide set up a sort of litany to the effect that that which we sought was "far, far away." I had no sooner ordered him to cover the equipment than the rain began to fall.

Nature created South America on a grand scale. Nothing is moderate. There is no sunset — it is light and it is dark; there is a glut or there is scarcity; it is very dry or it is very wet. Now it was very wet. The rain fell in strings, looking much as one sees it in certain Japanese wood-block prints. We adjusted our rubber ponchos and for as long as we did not lift our heads we were snugly dry. The road, as hard as macadam, was soon transformed into a slithering path and the horses, nervous over the flashes of lightning, found their footing unsure. To add to the unpleasantness it began to hail, ice-stones the size of hazel nuts played a drum beat on my taut rubber poncho. A flash brilliant enough to light up the whole sky showed Silvia just ahead of me. At the next flash she was gone — vanished. I flung myself off my horse, ran to the side of the road and looked into the ink-black darkness. Another flash of lightning — and to my utter horror I saw Silvia and her horse rolling down the hillside. They stopped when the horse struck a thicket; the horse struggled to its feet. Silvia lay unmoving.

This was the first real catastrophe that had come our way. Our medicines were adequate for minor injuries but for one of major dimensions . . . This thought went through my mind as I stumbled down the hillside to her. In a matter of minutes consciousness returned; she was bruised and scratched but otherwise unhurt. Thoroughly soaked, our hands and faces dripping globules of blood from the cactus spines we had plunged through, we remounted and rode on and up for two more hours until we reached the unlighted village which was — supposedly — the geographical center of the world.

All the houses were tightly boarded up. We stopped at one house where a candle burned feebly and asked if there was a place to spend the night.

"*Manan-cancha*," was the answer in the darkness.

At door after door we heard the same Quechuan phrase, "There isn't any"; until at last a door was unbarred and a woman held up an oil lamp to light the night. At the sight of Silvia, mud-splattered and wet, with a thin trickle of blood running down from a cut above her eye, she uttered a compassionate cry and drew us in. We had come to the house of the head man of Vilcas-huaman.

The high Vilcas plateau is horseshoe-shaped. The Vischongo River, far below, cuts around the high massif and as far as the eye can see; Vilcas, more than 11,000 feet above sea level, is master of the heights. This center of the Inca world was in every respect well named *Vilcas-huaman*, "Sanctuary of the Hawk." Here as at Cuzco present-day houses are set within ancient ruins — some at the entranceway to the Sun Temple, others built into its walls; all are fashioned from stones once used in the palaces of the Incas. Vilcas differed from the other villages we had seen in having all its houses of stone. There is a small plaza rimmed with towering eucalyptus. In its center is now a group of cement pedestals supporting sculptures which a local artist has made of Peru's great men. Near the plaza, rising above the whole city, is the only still intact Sun Temple in all Peru. All about it are walls of that superbly laid stone, the mark of the Inca craftsman.

It was the temple that drew us first. We crossed a stinking open sewer which flowed in the middle of a cobblestone street and arrived at the base of a truncated pyramid 150 feet square at the base which rose in five tiers to a small terrace reached by a flight of cyclopean steps. The massive stone doorway which faced the plaza was still standing, and we went through it and slowly mounted the steps which, with their high treads, made a stately and dignified ascent. The immense plaza, still outlined by the foundations of the ancient buildings, had been large enough, so it is said, to hold twenty thousand Indians. The ruined palace with its many wall niches — man's height — was the size of a square city block. We could readily understand the statement made by one of the newly arrived conquistadores that thousands of Indians had been in attendance on the Inca and that five hundred women alone were housed here to do the Lord Inca's weaving. Of this great temple at Vilcas, Cieza wrote: "The Sun Temple, made of very fine fitting stones, had two large doorways with two stairways leading to them with approximately thirty steps each [there were by actual count thirty-two]. Within the temple were the lodgings for the priest and guards for the Sun Virgins. . . . Much treasure was contained here, including a very valuable figure of the Sun God." The golden sun-image had long since been melted down in the crucibles of the conquistadores, but the seat of large stone . . . "where the Lord-Inca sat to view the dances and festivals," is still to be seen. Hewn out of a single piece of stone, it rests where it was first placed, since its weight alone defies movement. It was on this seat "covered with gold plate" that the Inca held court.

The Sun Temple was a fine vantage place from which to view the diorama of the area. From it the strong outlines of the ancient walls, despite the sprinkling of houses, gave an excellent idea of the original shape and size of the plaza. Out from the two southern extremes of the plaza went the roads. At our backs, rising like the crest of Gibraltar, was the rock of Pillucho where we saw the ruins of the seven hundred houses where the Inca had once kept the supplies for his armed forces.

Since the roads of the Inca Empire met in this plaza, we set about in the days that followed making an accurate plan of the ancient town. As often happened, the present-day houses had in many places been built over the Inca walls. In one of these homes we encountered a woman who suffered from a disease the Incas had called *uta* which had eaten away her upper lip and her nose. Similar disfigured faces appear on vases taken from graves on the desert coast of Peru. This woman with the cruel aching years of pain on her face, begged piteously for medicines — I am still haunted by the thought that we could do nothing for her. In another dwelling, adjoining the Sun Temple, we found several darkened rooms. On the beaten mud floor of one were three large stones; under them a fire; on top, blackened earthen jars. This was a kitchen. Tin plates and battered cutlery were placed on boxes; food hung suspended from leather thongs and scraps of food thrown on the bare earth were being fought over by ravenous dogs. Pigs, chickens, children and bright-eyed guinea pigs came and went. In a corner a woman with surprisingly delicate features sat in the dirt and, near her, a dog. Mother and bitch, equally human and equally animal, suckled their young.

We were amazed to discover so many comely women and blue-eyed people in the village, indicating the almost complete dilution of Indian blood. Most of the native population had been killed off in the earlier days of the conquest, and those Spaniards who, surviving the slaughter of the Battle of Chupas in 1542, had come to the remote hills about Vilcas to escape the King's justice, had mated with the natives and so gave them the genes which have survived today. Yet the language spoken is Quechua, and the people live much as bonded peasants lived in the time of Don Quixote.

Once as I photographed a particularly interesting stone niche formed by an ingenious arrangement of cut stone, I looked up to see a man and a cow staring at me in vacant curiosity. The cow, ruminating on its cud, seemed considerably more intelligent than the man ruminating on his coca cud. Wherever we went, whatever we did, we were followed by a horde of boys and men. If, after I had opened a new film, I tossed away the empty box, there was a mad scramble for the possession of it. So we were followed day after day, through the ruins, into houses, over walls, while we studied and measured and drew the ruins of Vilcas.

We found and mapped the massive wall on the south side of the plaza, the same once described as being in "front of the Sun Temple" and "5 stades high." We later came upon the buildings for the keepers of the Sun God, "the place . . . where lived five hundred virgins dedicated to the Sun." Where the village church now stands must once have been the site of the palace of the Inca for around it we found ten-foot high niches, those false doors where golden-plated effigies of Inca gods were once displayed. Everything here — the sculptured stones, many with snakes and totemic animals, the precision of the masonry and the uniformity of the architecture, suggested that Vilcas-huaman had been built late in the empire by master-masons sent from Cuzco to trace the plans and to teach the Indians the method of the laying of stones in the edifices.

Vilcas-huaman dates from around 1440, the time and reign of the Inca Pachacutic, the "Earth-Shaker." He came, he saw and he conquered the Tanquiha, who were the original inhabitants. Then, having depopulated the region by war, he transplanted a whole population of approximately two hundred thousand people. With these new settlers he formed the area into a large province which in time became one of the most important centers outside of Cuzco, and, as the conquests of the Incas continued to extend over the vast regions of South America as far north as Quito and as far south as Chile, the geographical center of their dominions.

As such, Vilcas-huaman took on a mystical character. Accordingly, much attention was lavished on Vilcas and its surrounding areas, and Incas vied with each other in building roads leading to the city and from it, each road bearing the name of the ruling Inca, as did the Roman roads those of the Caesars. The first was known as that of the Inca Yupanqui; a second as the Road of Topa Inca, who reigned 1471–1493; while a third, the Royal Road, was then the Road of the Huayna Capac Inca (1527). "This last, reaching to the River Ancasmayu in the north and to the south beyond what we now call Chile, is so long that, one end to the other, the distance is over one thousand, two hundred leagues."

Vilcas attained its greatest opulence during the reign of Huayna Capac, the last great Inca, who ruled about the time that Christopher Columbus was coasting along the Americas. He was "not of great stature, but well built, good features and much gravity; he was a man of few words but many deeds; a severe judge, he would punish without mercy. Huayna Capac wished to be so feared that the people would dream of him at night . . ."

This man of "few words but many deeds" in that fateful year of 1498 was making ready to visit the kingdoms to the north and so gathered an army of two hundred thousand soldiers to accompany him. First, his soothsayers consulted the oracles, offered up sacrifices to the Sun God, brought out the great chain of gold to encircle the plaza and held therein drinking bouts and dances. Then the captains received their appointments near to the "Stone of War" — and that being accomplished, "the Inca set out from Cuzco with his whole army and journeyed along a road as grand and as wide as we now behold it."

This same Lord Inca "ordered that there should be made a road more royal, more grand and wider than his father's and to extend all the way to Quito, whither he intended to go. . . ." All the storehouses and the *tampus* were by order filled with food for the royal trek, and so he marched north "until he arrived at Vilcashuaman, where he rested . . . in the buildings which had been erected for him near to those of his father." Under construction for more than a half century, these were about completed. Huayna Capac rejoiced to see the Sun Temple was finished, and giving gold and silver ingots to the governor, he ascended the high steps to the beautiful terrace which had been especially prepared for him. Then, greatly pleased with what he saw, he took part in the sacrifices to propitiate the gods. This being done he set out from Vilcas with his army . . ."

Once our work in Vilcas was done, we set off southward to find the road and link it up with the parts we had missed when we had made a roundabout trip by way of the vehicular road. We took the Cuzco road which left from the southeast side of the square. Once the Lord Incas had come this way in panoplied processions of power and magnificence. The scene was now quite different. Villagers coming in heavily laden from the fields doffed their grayish mushroom-shaped hats as we went by. But we were intent on the road, now in an appalling state of disrepair, seeking to avoid the many loosened stones.

On the highest knoll of the now naked land lay the remains of Pillau-ccasi, an ancient control gate and ruins of the garrison guard stations that had once been placed on either side of the road. The common Indian of those days had a limited geographical orbit. His needs were few and the Inca rulers saw to it that he moved on this Royal Road only with permission. These control gates were the check-points to see that the general prohibition was obeyed.

From this point, too, we could make out the course taken by another road, the coast-bound highway which had left from the southwest side of the plaza in Vilcas. Like the Royal Road, it was twenty-four feet wide and marked with a low wall of stones and it, too, had at the same distance from Vilcas a control point and a small garrison house to control travel over the road.

The way continued empty and cold. The halcyon sky had kept its earlier promise of a clear day but the wind, rushing down from some eternally glaciered peak, was as biting as a wintry north wind. At high noon as we rested we were joined by two condors. One of our Indians, stretched out on the roadside trying to catch something of the warmth of the sun, first drew their attention. Ignoring us, the great birds came down with a rush of sound, passed over the horses, startling one of them almost off the road, and made full for the reclining figure. Whether or not they would have attacked is questionable but at the sound of the swishing pinions, the intended victim came to life. Vigorously he waved his hat and the condors, with only the slightest movement of their wings, soared up, riding the wind currents at an astounding speed. They followed us hopefully through a good part of that day.

As our visible road continued to march across the barren *puna* we never ceased to marvel at the audacity of Inca engineering. The section we were now on is no longer used by the muleteers. The dangerous passages over the stone steps, no hazard for foot-traveling Indians and the nimble-footed llamas, is not for horses or mules, whose iron shoes can find no purchase on the stone steps. From here forward was the most perilous part of the road-journey, one we thought best to negotiate during the day.

At the little village of Contay we halted and set up our camp. The mounts were unsaddled, fettered and turned out to graze in the spare greensward and the Indians rolled themselves up in their ponchos and nestled between odoriferous horse blankets. Nearby we set up our tent. With our air mattresses and arctic sleeping bags, we made ready for the arrival at midnight of ice-laden winds blowing at a high velocity. From our supplies we made a tomato bisque from dehydrated tomato flakes and dried milk, then *charqui*, a dish made of sun-dried llama meat diced into rice which we seasoned highly. To top this off, we had a hot buttered rum and we were ready for the night tales of the guide we had brought from Vilcas.

He had ridden these ancient trails since boyhood, had followed them throughout in the frigid area of the province of Soras,[1] and, being of perspicacious curiosity, he had climbed every crag which might hold Inca ruins. He had been, he confessed, a rifler of tombs — and he told of the many ancient pieces he had dug out and the gold that he had found, some of which was now, so he said proudly, in museums outside the country. That is how he knew of the Capac-Ñan road and as he thought back to his wandering through the Soras country, he enumerated for us the villages through which the Road passed.

So he too joined the ranks of those whose travels added greatly to our knowledge of the ancient highway.

In 1533 Pedro Sancho, the official scrivener to the Spanish conquest, in describing the descent that we were now undertaking, made what we considered an understatement of considerable enormity when he wrote: ". . . and although the journey [between Vilcas and Uran-marca] was short, it was laborious since we had to descend a mountain all the way, the road consisting almost entirely of stone steps."

I counted close to a thousand of these descending arpeggios of stone steps before, forced to concentrate on my footing, I lost count. Yet judging each tread to be over a foot in height, our zigzag way went down a drop of two thousand feet. There must have been at least three thousand consecutive stone steps. The distance was, as Don Pedro had said, "short," but it was a truly astonishing

[1] About this Soras — de León said that "the river Vilcas rises in the province of Soras which is very fertile and inhabited by a warlike race. They [Soras] and the people of Lucanas speak one language and go about dressed in woolen cloaks. They possessed large flocks of llamas and in their country are rich mines of gold and silver. The Incas esteemed the Soras and Lucanas so highly that their lands were favored and the sons of their chieftains resided at the court in Cuzco."

piece of engineering. Being all dry masonry, this necessitated elaborate terracing with retaining walls for which the rock had to be carried some distance before it could be faced and worked. It was — in this realm of astonishments — one of the most extraordinary of these amazing roads.

Francisco Pizarro and his small army, bent on the conquest of Cuzco, took this road in 1533, but long before his advent uncounted thousands of Indians had swept back and forth over it. Still to be seen are the turn-outs where the palanquin-bearers carrying their chieftains would rest on the upward or downward inclines of the step-road.

As we circled down into the valley, the heat rising out of the chasm grew furnace-hot and Silvia began to peel off sweater after sweater. The land was desertlike with tall organo-cactus growing out of rock and coarse gravel and thorny mimosalike plants making the air fragrant with their scent. The hot wind came up like a sirocco. Again we experienced the extremes of this extreme land. Wakening in arctic cold and snow, long before high noon we were broiling in the sun. Ahead of us we heard our Indians crying out to their animals as they slid down the royal stairway to the floor of the valley.

In late September at the height of the dry season the Pampas River, now only a stream, meandered all over the wide sandbed, but sheer cliffs and high dark stains fifty feet above the riverbed gave concrete evidence that the Pampas was showing us only one aspect of its character.

At Pucara near to the chasm there was a fortress. Time has claimed it and only a few stones mark it. Below at the river's edge, a bridge once hung suspended, the largest in all Peru after the great one of San Luis Rey.

On our side toward Vilcas we found no sign of this bridge, which the rampaging river has long since destroyed. But at Pariabamba where we forded the Pampas, we came to the remains of the immense towers from which the cables of the bridge had been suspended. "Here," stated Cieza, "the great river called Vilcas [the Pampas] is crossed. On each side of the river there are very large stone pillars made very strong and with very deep foundations. From these pillars a bridge of cables . . . is slung across the river. These cables are so strong, and the bridge is so strong, that horses may pass over with loosened rein as if they were crossing the bridge of Cordova in Spain. The bridge was one hundred and sixty-six paces long when I passed over it."

The conquistador-scrivener Sancho — who had not perhaps the same eye for accuracy — wrote that when the Spaniards passed it, in 1534, it was 360 Spanish feet long and wide enough for two horses to pass abreast on it. There was no doubt that these towers were the remains of that bridge, all that now is left to mark the site.[2]

Uran-marca, the Inca post-stop on the Royal Road which furnished the Indian laborers to maintain the bridge, lay ahead and above us. It was but four miles away, up about 3000 feet, a climb as perpendicular as the one we had just descended. Through my binoculars the rustic stonework of the ruins was plainly visible.

The place was, according to our chroniclers, a village of transplanted people, the result of the Incas' policy of population transference. Wherever there was need for a large labor group to service the road, its *tampus* and its suspension bridges, whose rope cables

[2] The bridge must have survived for at least a century after the conquest in 1599, for Poma de Ayála noted in his record: "Oran-marca; village: royal post, and the largest bridge in all these kingdoms called the 'litter of cables,' built by the Inca Yahuar Huacac."

If this statement is true and the bridge was built by the sixth Inca, it would have been there in the year 1290. This Inca "was very quiet and very cautious and very peaceful," so the legends say. "He always had bad eyes and they were so red that, by exaggeration, his people said that he wept blood, and for this reason they called him Yahuar Huacac, the Bloody Weeper."

were renewed every two years, the Inca simply moved people into the hiatus. So the Inca had said, "Let there be a city," and on a high plateau, devoid of man and plants, there *was* a city.

I was eager to visit Uran-marca but when I made a move in that direction I encountered open rebellion. The animals would not stir; the Indians said flatly they would not go; one guide said equally firmly that he would await our return; and Silvia, who had cheerfully climbed every mountain crag for six months, announced that she would "sit this one out." I looked at the heights, briefly contemplated doing it on foot, and then I too surrendered.

It would take all our energy to go back over the step-road to Vilcas.

Once more back in Vilcas-huaman village we waited for the cessation of the broad loom of the rains which had transformed every rill into a plunging torrent. Meanwhile we rested from our last trek, occupied ourselves by excavating the walls about the Sun Temple and planning our next project, the search for the forgotten ruins of Pomacocha.

On the first clear day as we stood on the Temple of the Sun, glasses in hand, the rays of the morning sun fell full on a small tarn which in the distance lay in what seemed to be the bottom of a volcano. When I pointed the lake out to our guide, he shook his head; there was only *one* Pomacocha, a colonial hacienda which, until their expulsion, was operated by the Jesuits. As for there being an Inca ruin at Pomacocha, he who had ridden everywhere in these mountains would have known it. We would be wasting precious time were we to look for one out there.

Our records were extremely vague at this point. It was only that I remembered reading somewhere that during the civil wars in 1542, when the conquistadores fought over the golden swag of the fallen Inca Empire, one group had "marched to Pomacocha, a strong position." At that time the Spaniards had little time for building and so when they "took over a stronghold," it could only have been an Inca-built redoubt. I looked at Silvia. Having been through the treadmill of these travels, she had earned the right to say whether we should take on additional burdens at the moment. She nodded: "On to Pomacocha."

On our way back down the eroded hill which we had ascended in rainy darkness, we had a look at the country that we had not seen then. Although the hills were bare, the hollows and small valleys had once been well settled. Ruins of chapels scattered about suggested the opulent power of the Jesuits who had once held so much of Peru that they had become, in effect, bankers to the State. Now these chapels, built in the eighteenth-century baroque style, had become nightstalls for wandering burros and cows. Presently we met a horseman coming toward us who — so we discovered after an exchange of irrelevancies — was the manager of the hacienda of Pomacocha. On hearing of our mission, he shook his head dolefully. "There is nothing, gringo, but horrible Indians, horrible women and horrible weather." The hacienda, he said, had been built by the Jesuits in 1737 and had only ruins of their buildings on it. There was nothing Inca there. On that negative interchange we parted company. A bit farther on, we pushed through a flock of sheep to cross a small colonial bridge spanning the river and entered the one-time hacienda of the Jesuits. The approach, arched over by immense trees, shadowed the entrance to an old mill. Within, powered by a water flume, ancient millstones turned ceaselessly grinding the wheat which Indian women poured into the timeworn funnels. Above the door was the legend "AÑO 1750."

The hacienda was eighteenth century, and the buildings reflected the century — squat, massive and thatched with grass. The courtyard was impressive and around it the buildings preserved that air of authority which had made the Jesuit well regarded as a colonist. On the verge of admitting defeat, I bent over an aqueduct which conveyed a rushing stream of water to the well. There I saw the work of the Inca — granite stone, shaped as only the Indian masons shaped it, lined the flume. Next we found a lintel fashioned of the same stone, and then a stairway. Similar stones were embedded in the houses, in the courtyard.

We stayed at the hacienda no longer than decorum allowed and soon we were riding off in the direction of the lake we had seen from Vilcas. We left the path and took off on a little-used trail and so soon left the small houses of the hacienda behind us. Within minutes we found ourselves going up what was left of an ancient road which, unlike any other road we had seen, was at least forty-five feet wide. Impressive even in its ruined state, it seemed to sweep down toward the river in a direct line with the Jesuit hacienda, which we could still see buried under the gloom of trees.

We rode up the broken lip of an upthrust mountain which had evidently once been a volcano, and from the top we looked down on the lake in its hollow. At one end was a dam, the workmanship of which was eighteenth century — probably erected by the Jesuit engineers to provide the water which turned the millstones. Near to the lagoon we set up our camp and then we were off to learn what we could of Pomacocha.

The tarn, a roughly formed figure eight, was quite shallow; cows were wading in its center, munching the tall *totora* grass. Swimming about, completely indifferent to us, were ducks and mud-hens and white herons, while crimson-winged flamingos walked with dignity in the short grasses. At the first sight, there was nothing. Only squat trees covered the shore. Then as we slowly and meticulously moved our binoculars over the terrain, we saw the remains of ancient buildings. We had found the ruins of Pomacocha!

That this had been a sacred lagoon we felt certain by the end of that first day, for here was a sanctuary on which the Inca Kings had evidently lavished much care. Nowhere outside of the Cuzco area had we seen such magnificent stonework nor such precision in fitting together irregularly shaped stones in accordance with their natural contours. Smaller stones combined with large ones were so interlocked that the walls were actually a stone mosaic, a lasting testimonial to the builders' extraordinary feeling for the aesthetic quality of the texture of stone. The amazingly compact palace projecting slightly into the edge of the lake rested on a solid stone base extending below it into the water. Back toward the high cliffs was a series of formal squares. We kept climbing over enormous two-ton ashlars cut in the form of isosceles triangles over six feet in length. These monoliths must indeed have been a part of some unusual structure, for we had not before met with this peculiar type of cut stone. Unfortunately there was nothing left now except an immense desolation of fallen masonry. As we mapped the ruins for the first time — Pomacocha has never been listed in archaeological records — we found another well-preserved wall complete with mural niches and doorways. Our Indians who had followed us curiously from rock to rock were now put to work excavating and sinking test pits.

That Pomacocha had been sacrosanct was further confirmed by our discovery of a twenty-foot high, free-standing rock of equal diameter. The sides, hewn and cut, were formed of stones carefully chamfered into the rock mass and so skillfully that we could not at first distinguish which were man-laid and which living stones. Mounting a stone stairway Silvia found that she was standing on another of those ancient Inti-huatanas sacred as "Hitching-Places-of-the-Sun." The top had been flattened and in the center was the

emains of a meter-high gnomon, much like the one we had seen
arlier at Pisac. These were used by the Inca necromancers to deter-
nine "which days were long and which were short and when the
un departed and returned." There are several of these sun clocks
n Peru but only this one lies outside of the immediate Cuzco area.

The ruins themselves were voiceless. We found at Pomacocha no
"talking stones" such as are found among the Maya ruins where
iieroglyphs have been found on stone stela, on walls, on steps, on
intels, on pieces of shell, on jade and in folder books. Nor was
here here anything to suggest the rebus writing of the Aztec nor
ven the pictographs used so effectively by the North American
'lains Indians. No form of writing, no matter how much scholars
iave strained their imaginations, has ever come to light in the
\ndean area. We have only a verbal history of the Inca, transmitted
y professional "rememberers" with the aid of the knotted *quipu*
ords and these, however, ingenious, were only aids for the memory.
The history of the ancient people of Peru is dependent on chronicles
vritten by the early Spaniards, on the priest-chroniclers who ma-
iipulated the things they heard and saw in the last days of the Inca
Empire to fit their own theology, and on the story told by the Inca
uins. In Vilcas we had found pottery in many places which told
is many things — the styles, what tribes had passed that way and
o on. But at Pomacocha we found not a shard.

At the end of the lagoon where the water formed one of the
ounded circles of the figure eight lay an outjutting of the moun-
ain up which the stone-laid terraces climbed like gigantic stepping-
tones. At its pinnacle was another structure which, like those in
he plaza, was made of the finest stonework. Below, where the can-
ons formed a gully, we came across the ruins of a stone aqueduct
vhich led us to a superbly laid fountain or bath. This structure —
vhich could have held fifteen people at a single time and was, we
udged, the place where the Inca made his ablutions — had been

built around a large rock which had been hewn until squared. The stones had been set into the living rock and in the nature of organic architecture the whole reached upward out of the foundation into the light. It was a delight to see.

When we crossed to the other side of the lake at the waist of the figure eight we found the remains of what must have been the *tampu* or the temporary night-stop for those making the mecca to Pomacocha.

What *was* Pomacocha? And why had so beautiful a ruin not previously been visited or mentioned? There was nothing here to point the way to us, only the mute tale of the broken buildings. Not one of the historical companions of our long journey had ever mentioned it except to say that Pomacocha had a "strong position."

Silvia's protests about being dragged out betimes into the Andean cold just to see the rising sun could have been heard across the quiet tarn. It was still dark as we picked our way across the fallen masonry of Pomacocha. The night had been frigid, a real winter night and the dawning day still held the chill; fog hung over the lagoon and gave the sky a leaden look. This little world at the moment was almost empty of sound and the sudden baleful chirping of some protesting nestlings hidden in the lake-rushes sounded as startling in the silence as would a clarion voice. Silvia's remarks were both loud and pointed. She had worked late on drafting the plans of Pomacocha, she had climbed, measured, carried gear about for days she saw no reason why, just to prove a theory, she should have to rise in the arctic dawn; "we were not Siamese twins"; and so she went on, her outraged words flailing at me until we stood again atop the great rock.

And then the sun . . . We were approaching the time of the autumnal equinox, and as the light of the rising sun fell across the

The Sanctuary of the Hawk

Hitching Place of the Sun the lagoon was bathed in a brilliant golden metallic sheen. This then was what Pomacocha — or more correctly Puman-chochan, Lake of the Lion — really was: a sacred lake which received the sun. As we stood there we felt something of the orphic feeling that all this must have evoked in the Incas. For a brief moment the place seemed to echo to the sound of the Inca walking in measured tread behind his *Amauta*, his Keepers of the Sun, while they, carrying the earth-mysteries in the garments of their ritual, slowly approached the rock.

There was a poignant beauty in these overturned stones and enduring fragments of walls. Was it the symmetry of the stone and its patterns, or was it the balance that made it so beautiful? We could not say why it stirred us. We only knew that it did. I have only a moderate confidence in metaphysical formulae. I believe that we shall never know exactly why a thing is beautiful. But these ruins had a beauty apart from their connection with the vanished people who built them.

Who then had destroyed this beauty? These immense stones did not fall alone by the weight of years. The fact that the Jesuits used some of them in the construction of their own "kingdom of God" pointed the finger of suspicion at them. Many sacred Inca places, such as Pomacocha, survived the conquest, and the native religion which had been worshipped in such shrines did not die — it went underground. The Indians worshipped the hills, the springs, the lakes, the rocks. The failure to Christianize the Indians had led in the seventeenth century to a great witch hunt when the padres, who found some six hundred important idols still being worshipped, destroyed them and burned more than six thousand Indians at the stake.

"Whatever can be burned," said the priests who directed this extirpation of idolatry, "is burned, and what cannot be burned is broken." It was wantonly effective and complete. By 1660 the

Catholicization of the Inca's people had been achieved. But in remote spots the pagan rites lingered, and in such inaccessible places as Pomacocha, the step road built by the Incas in this region was too severe a test for Spanish horses — and so the King's Highway was put elsewhere and the Indians were left long undisturbed to worship the Sun.

Today we know no more than that the Jesuits with their clerico-military organization came here early in the eighteenth century probably destroyed the sacred city around the Lake of the Lion and then used the tumbled stone for their own buildings. The rest, since there are no records, is silence.

It was the dark of another dawn when we mounted the old Inca road and put out toward Ayacucho. We zigzagged up an immense hill on the rim of the crater that held the sacred lake and by the time the sun had again taken command of the earth we were on its very top. The lake seemed now like burnished copper, broken only by the flight of the egrets and flamingos over its surface. As we turned our mounts back onto the Inca road, the ruins were suddenly aflame, and our last look at Pomacocha showed us the sun's rays were again falling across its Hitching Place.

X

The Highway of the Sun

THE Mantaro River is shaped something like a fishhook. Unlike
other rivers which slowly emerge from out of inoffensive trickling
ills and in descending becomes a fury of rushing waters, this one
leaps into being fullborn where it comes out of the ice-fringed
Chinchay [Junin] lake. Drawing the run-off of rain from the plen-
eous *punas* through which it flows, the Mantaro becomes, within
fifty miles, less a river than a gargantuan earth-moving force which
has gouged out a canyon so deep that it does not allow man to harness it for his benefit. It is useless alike to nature and man. So the
Mantaro must, like unreasonable weather, be endured. Yet the Incas refused to endure it — they avoided it. Since they did not have
the wheel and their means of travel were not those of the modern
world, they laid their communication system above it and out of
harm's way.

We however could not escape it. At this point in our journey, we
were — alas — bound to the modern highway which here has been
cut alongside of the canyon-edge of the Mantaro, making it the
most dangerous in all Peru. One hundred and fifty miles out of
Chinchay Lake the river makes a fishhook turn to race east to
join with another turbulent river and so form the upper Amazon. Just at the point where the hook makes the twist and becomes
the sharpened barb on which it pinions nature and man, there were
we, hung quite literally for a few dreadful moments on the edge

of Mantaro. Suspended between safety and disaster, one half of the Power Wagon dangled over the canyon while the other half still rested on the so-called road. Almost everything in the way of Expedition gear we had was in the truck. Charts, maps, notes, plans, photographs, equipment — and our hopes; all the months of climbing and searching recorded in our written reports — all this now hung there on the edge of the abyss.

The mind performs strangely in times of stress. To escape tensions, it ofttimes digs up the most ironical elements of the human comedy. Now I wondered how I would act when the truck finally broke away from its temporary moorings and crashed two hundred feet down into the canyon, carrying to irrevocable destruction all our work. Would I smile at life's foibles, as did Isaac Newton when his dog Diamond upset a candlestick and reduced in a minute all his years of work? Would I say, "Well, let us make another start," as did Thomas Carlyle when his manuscript of *The French Revolution* was mistakenly thrown in the fire? I did not know. As the drowning man is thought to parade all the events of his life before him, with devilish insistence on alternatives and an excoriating examination of the "if's," my mind quickly reviewed my most recent decision regarding the Expedition's route.

Back at the Bridge of Mayoc, for example, should I have taken a mule and followed one of the branches of the forkway where it divided, one part to go up the 3000-foot-high east bank and the other along the west bank? Did I do right by allowing that Lilliputian sized Peruvian, a new addition to our party, to undertake and alone the survey of the east road? Should I not have heeded Silvia's warning that we should delay at Mayoc until the threat of rain had abated over the Mantaro? We had managed to follow the Inca roads to the river's banks. It would have been foolish for us to try to cover both parts of the diverging roads, since to do so would have meant mule rain travel for at least two months — and why not let our young Peruvian win his explorer's spurs? I alone had believed that it would be best to set up headquarters in distant Huancayo and from there work backwards. Yet the Devil is also a logician. The others thought we should not defy the Mantaro, that we should break up our equipment and place some of it in hired trucks rather than risk it all in our own Power Wagon. This I had opposed, believing we should advance intact, like a complete military caravan entering into the country of the enemy.

At first there had been no portent in the sky other than the sun. But we had scarcely passed the guard check-point, where because of the narrow road traffic is regulated, when the sky darkened and it began to rain. Within two hours, so heavy was the downpour that we traveled a road streaming water. Above us were sheer walls of mud and stone rising two thousand feet; below us, two hundred feet down, was the rampaging Mantaro. Had an Inca engineer proposed the building of such a road, his life would have been forfeit. Inca roads were built so as to exclude all water. Water was the determining factor in their every move and knowing that a road along the canyon edge of the Mantaro could not be maintained, the Incas had split their road at Mayoc, where once hung a suspended bridge, and had flung their step road up the opposite sides to the high *puna*. From that point they had built it across the rolling mountains.

Any idea of drainage on the part of those who cut this modern vehicular road was totally lacking. Water poured down from the lowering cliffs onto it, washing immense chunks of it into the river, while wooden bridges that spanned the larger rills were left hanging on hope and air. It was a diurnal nightmare.

In the smaller car ahead, Silvia swung deftly around a fallen avalanche of earth and stone. I, not seeing it in time, threw the truck into low double transmission and plowed like a tank through

163

the obstruction. Ahead I heard a dull roar, like the sound a great tree makes when the ax bites into its heartwood: a splintering, rasping sound. Silvia had just cleared another danger spot when an earth-mass fell into the road and I, torn between taking the brunt of it and avoiding it, turned the wheels quickly toward the embankment. The car lurched to a stop. Lawrence, who rode with me, was out of the Power Wagon with incredible speed. Enmeshed in the gears, I did not find it so easy to free myself. Once we were both out, we quickly lashed the front axle, knowing it would avail little if the weighted truck moved downward. Then we unwound the steel cable of the winch and secured it to an enormous freestanding rock.

Three wheels of the truck were still on the road. The left rear wheel and a good part of the body hung over the cliff. Since the winch was to do the work rather than the wheels, that meant that one of us would have to get back in the truck to start the engine and shift the gears to the winch motor. Lawrence elected to bell the cat. He was lithe and small enough to free himself, so he said, should the truck begin its death-fall. But even the motor conspired against us: it would not start and the roadbed meanwhile kept falling away in chunks. At last Lawrence managed to throw the gear into place and, as he did so, he leaped to safety. The truck lurched dangerously but the cable held and now it was slowly inched forward. I did not breathe. A whole lifetime passed in that five minutes as slowly the truck was pulled forward until all four wheels rested on firm ground. As soon as I was breathing again, I reached into the forward chamber of the truck and took out a bottle of rum. "Splice the main brace," I ordered.

We arrived, days later, at Izcu-chaca, having traveled a distance of but forty-five miles. Where a graceful colonial Spanish bridge curves over the Mantaro gorge, a second river, the Angoyaco, joins it; and here, over a writhing, twisting torrent just below the Spanish bridge, the Inca had once hung another suspension bridge. Here too we found ourselves at last on the Highway of the Sun, the main road of the Inca system.

So we traveled on day after day, our caravan keeping to the modern dirt road until we could find a place to leave the trucks, then we would double back by foot until we found the Inca road again. It was a laborious business — this incessant climbing, this following of and photographing the road.

The wear and tear of these passing months had had its effect on each of us. Silvia had become a seasoned explorer with a sound knowledge of the geography and a firm grasp of the problems of the road that were real factors in our success. She asked as a woman no special consideration; she went everywhere, and her drawings of the architectural features of the road were invaluable. Lawrence made no compromise with geography or altitude; he never allowed his camera out of his hand and though he angered us frequently by his insistence on thoroughness and was a martinet in his lens-world, his film footage grew handsomely with the passing months. In all the time we traveled through one of the most terrifying terrains in this world, he never lost a roll of film nor was one spoiled by injudicious delay.

We were a team now, often working with irritation, but *working*. Every evening when we were not climbing or measuring roads and ruins I was at my reports, and once monthly I sent off my dispatch to the *New York Times*. Often there were the newsletters written to acquaint our colleagues and friends with accounts of our daily progress; and there were always other letters to be answered, reports to be made on each new-found ruin, and the constant irritation of putting down our mounting expenses. The days were so exhaustingly filled that often before the stars completely commanded the heavens we were asleep.

Farther along, the high marching cliffs of the Mantaro dissolved into a valley and we came to the little village of Marcavalle. This was the first village in the Jauja-Huancayo valley area, and it was here that the two Inca roads which had split one hundred miles southward at Mayoc, to take to the *puna* above the Mantaro Canyon, joined and became the wide Highway of the Sun.

We stopped at a wayside inn where Indians came to slake their thirst with *chicha*, a grayish fermented-corn drink. I had hoped that about this time we should have some word of our young Peruvian who was still somewhere in the hills tracing out the east wing of the Inca road, but there was no sign of him. So, after leaving instructions with an old Indian woman who smilingly showed us her single tooth, we again took to the road and in an enveloping gray dust we bore down upon Huancayo.

That night, too exhausted to eat, I fell asleep betimes under the portrait of Andrew Carnegie which hangs in the rooms of the old Carnegie Research Station.

Huancayo is one of the largest cities in Peru. Every Sunday the largest and most colorful markets in all the Andes are held there, strung along the Inca road which here stretches to three times its original width. In this present-day Andean market the Indians, as they had in other times, put up their stalls where the things of their earth are sold. We followed the Indians to the market early one Sunday morning shortly after our arrival, walking along the modern highway which rests on the King's Highway, which in turn stands on the road of the Incas. There is no telling how many come to Huancayo on fair days but at such times the Royal Road of the Incas literally swarms with people.

The Jauja-Huancayo Valley, fifty miles long, is approximately the geographical center of Peru. It is now and always has been an important self-contained valley and a strategic one. On a direct line with Jauja, and scarcely one hundred miles away, lies Pacha-camac on the shore of the Pacific. The mecca for most of ancient Peru and the site of the oracle of the creator-god Pacha-camac, it was one hour's journey from the valley as the condor flies, three days as the Indian walked.

To the east of the valley and relatively close were the montaña and the jungles. The valley, controlled by the Huanca tribes, was once defended on all sides by towering hills topped with fortresses. "Even now," wrote Cieza in 1548, "they appear, to one seeing them from a distance, like towers of Spain."

We reached Jauja within an hour's dusty ride from Huancayo, traveling over the route of the Inca road. Where the Mantaro River leaves the valley to begin its passage through its gorge, there, surrounded by hills covered with moldering ruins, lies old Jauja. The ancient fortresses had once belonged to the Wankas, a fierce little people whose houses, built as "rounded fortresses of stone, were like small castles."

It was this tribe, "field guardians" the Incas called them, that for a time effectively blocked the Incas' northern conquest. Although the Inca sought through his ambassadors to induce them to "embrace his friendship . . . without his having to get it by making war," the Wankas, faced with an offer of absorption or extinction, chose extinction. And in the great battle which followed, the Incas conquered and forthwith adopted the survivors into their kingdom, imposing upon them Inca religion and techniques but permitting them to keep their own customs and language. And so Jauja became the Inca capital of Chinchay-suyu, one of the quarters of the Inca world.

Even though today a modern highway runs through the town and there is a railroad station on the outskirts, the outlines of the original town are still visible. In the rubble is part of an Inca wall and the old church stands on the site of the Sun Temple, once a structure three tiers high of worked stone with stairways and thick straw roofs. Near to it was the Temple of the Virgins.

We walked among the walls, gathering potsherds and trying to reconstruct the ancient city from the piles of amorphous stones. Nowhere was there any sign of the onetime grandeur of this, the first capital of Peru. All we know of it is in the records. On Francisco Pizarro's march southward to Cuzco in November 1534, we found the following notation: "In the city of Santa de Hatun Jauja, this twentieth and ninth day of November, 1534, the very noble lords found the city . . ."

In the valley north of Jauja where the eroded limestone hills command the view, we again found the Royal Road. Built across the flat *puna*, twenty-four feet wide and bound by crumbling walls, it was a joy to follow. For the first time in five hundred miles we were able to make a leisurely tour of the highway without being subjected to an exhausting scaling of the heights. It was only when the road mounted an obstructing hill in broad low-stepped treads — it was always the Incas' way to mount obstacles rather than avoid them — that we had to make a detour in the truck over the vehicular dirt road until we could take to the ancient road again.

Since the modern road turned and twisted to provide the same gradient which the Inca provided by steps, when we came upon it next we were on a higher pampa. My first sight of it from a little distance away showed that the direction had changed radically —

the road now ran northeast rather than northwest as it had when we had left it. This puzzled us for, generally speaking, the Incas built their roads with directional straightness. It was Silvia who gave us the first indication of the truth. When we reached the road, we found it going over a rise in a series of large steps. There was something unusual about this section of the road.

"Look," said Silvia, who was pacing the width in long strides, "this road is forty-five feet wide."

"But how . . ."

"Either the Royal Road became much wider after we last were on it or this is another road. Do you suppose we have found their military road?"

From the top of a hill we had full view of the valley stretched out northward. At the base of the hill was one road and this, since it was the regulation twenty-four feet in width, was without doubt the Royal Road. Following it through our binoculars, we saw that it went along the valley floor frequently passing over bare stone, its rock-balustrades fully marked, its plainly visible steps conforming to the rise and fall of the escarpment until it appeared on the continuing pampa. There we could see the remains of a building and there the road divided. Forming a V junction, the Royal Road kept to its directional straightness while the second road veered a full fifteen degrees to the east. From this distance it seemed twice as wide as the other. We stared fascinated at what we saw. Could this be . . . ?

I thumbed through the sheath of notes we had along until I found a copy of a report on the Inca roads, dated 1543, entitled *The Ordering of the Halting Stations [Tampus]: The distance of one to the other, the methods of the native carriers and the obligation of the respective Spanish overlords of said tambos: done in Cuzco the 31st of May, 1543.* This was the first Spanish report on the Inca highway and the *first* road regulations ever made in all the

Americas. "Due," it read, "to the serious depopulation of natives at said halting-stations called tambos, and the empty untraveled roads both in the mountains and the plains and the excessive cargos the Indians are forced to carry and the large journeys that are forced on them and the bad state of repair into which the highway had fallen . . ." and so on for some fifty pages. A commission sometime earlier had been formed to look into the state of the road and this, its official report, described the direction of the road and mentioned many of the halting places. Then we read: "Now make note that from the tambo of Jauja, there are two roads the one parting here for Huánuco and the city of the frontier, Chachapoyas . . ."

The large maps of the American Geographical Society were unfolded. We traced the Inca road to Huánuco, a hundred miles to the north, then on to the right bank of the Rio Marañon, one of the longest tributaries of the Amazon. Far, far beyond, in the high mountains on its right bank, at the very edge of the deep green of the Upper Amazon jungle and more than four hundred miles away, lay Chachapoyas. Was that where this road led? There was nothing in our records about *this* radial or why the Incas had built a road into this region. What mystery lay here?

This road, if that Spanish report written in 1543 was true, ran east of the Royal Road for a distance of some four hundred miles. Why so great a road? We knew from history that when the Lord Inca was bent on conquest he would hurry as many as one hundred thousand troops over his roads in a single movement and that accompanying the troops were burden-bearers and thousands of llamas serving as dray animals. This army was primarily a land army which moved only over roads, and with the rise of this Andean Empire, new formulae were injected into warfare. The Inca wars were no ritualistic military promenades nor elaborate panoplies to overawe an enemy; they had but a single object — victory! Their roads were built to enable them to overwhelm an enemy with the shock of great force.

A conquest of new territory was begun in this wise: the governors of all the territories through which the army of conquest was to pass were notified. They were to prepare the road, set up communications, build up a supply of weapons and set up and service all of the *tampus* that appeared every four leagues [12 miles] along the road. The roads came first. "I will explain," said Cieza, "the ease with which they were constructed by the Indians without increasing the death rate or causing excessive labor. When the Inca decided to have one of these famous roads constructed, much preparation was unnecessary; it remained but for the Inca to give orders. For then, the overseers went over the ground, made the trace of the road, and the Indians received instructions to construct the road using local labor. Each province completed the section of the road within its own limits; when it reached the end of their boundary, it was taken up by others; when it was urgent, all worked at the same time."

When the road was completed, the Lord Inca in Cuzco gathered his people in the great square of his city and took his place before the Stone of War "in the shape of a sugarloaf, well enclosed with gold" and dedicated the conquest to the gods. The functional aristocracy planned the campaign and led it. Battle leaders were chosen and each, carrying his own heraldic device, took his place at the head of his warriors armed with lances, sling-throwers and war-headed clubs. All the great storehouses along the road were made ready and the tribes along the route of the road alerted so that the road and the bridges were in the best condition. "All necessary things having been done, the Lord Inca now set out from Cuzco with his whole army and journeyed along a road as grand and wide as we now behold it . . ."

The Inca himself was conveyed along the road in a golden-plated litter carried by sturdy Rucana tribesmen clad in pale blue livery. The Inca Sun God dressed as did the others, only more elaborately. He wore the breechclout, a split-neck poncho made of silklike vicuña wool; his hair was cut in bangs; enormous golden earplugs studded with diadems were plugged into punctured ear lobes; and he wore the royal "fringe," a multi-colored braid four inches wide from which dangled red tassels hanging from little gold tubes. In his hand like a medieval knight he carried a mace. Thus arrayed and preceded by his entire army, "all of them brown and noisy," they proceeded along the Royal Road until they reached Jauja "where the Wanka tribes prepared a solemn reception." The Lord Inca rested here while he had the various reports on the road which led toward Chachapoyas.

Was it possible that we were now looking at the very road over which these great Inca armies had passed on their campaign of conquest? Northward lay our route. At the top of a high pass, close to 14,000 feet, at a spot referred to as Inka-Katana [seat of the Inca] by a little old man whose house we came upon at the side of the road, we reached the wide road. Ahead of us it stretched out for miles across the naked plain, while to the south there was a cascade of stone-tread steps. We calculated that we were seeing at least thirty miles of continuous, wonderfully preserved road, precisely what we had been hoping to find: a stretch of road long enough to permit us to study techniques of road construction, determine the Inca concept of topography, and details, if such could be found, of their extraordinary system of communications, and . . .

That night we put up the large command tent in a raging snow-storm. Silvia had insisted that the place I chose for the campsite was in too exposed a position, but I wanted it to be right at the edge of the Inca road. As we struggled in the night wind with the tent, I remembered that old Arabian saw, "A woman's opinion is of small value, but a man would be a fool to disregard it." At long last the tent was up and Lawrence, after long struggle, started the generator. Before long we had bedded down in our sleeping bags.

At dawn, with the temperature at freezing, we were awakened by the arrival of our Indian-laborers. I had arranged for their coming the day before by offering double the sum they generally received and as an added incentive, a generous portion of coca leaf. They were a sorry lot. Shapeless felt hats were pulled down over their heads; some had scraggly beards, an indication of Spanish blood; their rainbow-patched trousers and the ponchos which hung over their shoulders were all that clothed their nakedness from this bitter cold — reason enough for the rheums that racked their bodies. While our meager breakfast was being prepared, I lined up the men and passed out the portions of coca leaves. This they at once proceeded to munch into compact balls which, lodged inside of their mouths, made their cheeks look very like a lemming's food pouch. What a Spaniard said of coca in 1550 was equally true today: "If coca did not exist, neither would Peru."

All work in the Andes is geared to the coca leaf. It is quite impossible to obtain workmen unless they are given their daily rations. Millions of people — Indians, *cholos*, even whites — are addicted to the habit throughout not only Peru but Bolivia, Chile, Argentina and as far north as Columbia. For centuries coca chewing has been the subject of prolonged controversy.

Among the Incas, the use of the coca leaf was limited to the priestly hierarchy, to those who worked in the mines and to the very old. But with the conquest the habit became general. "So pleasant is coca to the Indians," said a Spaniard, "that they prefer it to gold or silver or precious stones." As to the effect of it, "they merely savor the fragrance and swallow the juice . . . and the Indians that chew it show themselves stronger and more apt for labor . . . they work the whole day without eating." That, however, is part of the folklore of coca. Actually it does not take the place of food. If an Indian consumes fifty grams of coca leaf daily — and he does — he is getting about forty centigrams of cocaine, an amount which is certainly enough to narcotize the misery of the present. If it cannot be said to give a "lift" to his daily life, it at least does blunt the edge of the cold and allays the effect of thirst and hunger.

The coca leaf ceremony over, our men shouldered their mattocks and moved to appointed tasks. What I wanted to see was just how these roads were built, and when the turf was removed and the dislodged stones replaced I would then have a chance to examine the equivalent of an original section of the mountain highway. The day was only a thin solution of the fog-bound night. In this voiceless region without a tree or a bush to break the monotony of the flatness, it seemed as if we were on another planet. We had dressed as we would for the arctic, for the winds were sharp and snow still covered the *puna*. Yet by the time the men had started their task of cleaning the turf and the sun commanded the temperature, it was warm enough to melt the snow.

A cleansed section of the ancient road revealed the first surprise. It was not, as we had supposed, paved. The hard *puna* had offered a natural surface for such wayfarers who had only to worry about the scuff of the foot and the tread of llamas. While there were, we found, many sections of paved roads in the ancient system, they were not all stone-laid. Construction changed with the terrain and circumstances. If the road passed over a marsh, it was raised on a causeway; if it traversed a region of constant rainfall, it was paved. But generally on the hard *puna* — and we were to find this true also on the coastal pampa — the road surface was the earth. But no matter what material the surface, the mark of the Inca road was always to be found in the stone boundary walls. Here the wall of dry masonry stood two and a half feet high, its purpose to mark the boundaries of the road, to contain it, and to keep soldiers and llamas to a defined path. Wherever the road ascended a gradient, it was laid with stone steps at intervals of twenty feet, and between each ran a stone-laid drainage which effectively drained water off the earth-surfaced roads. That it had served its purpose could be easily seen, for where the stones had been dislodged the road was cicatrized with a small eroded gully.

It is all very well for us, having grown used to our various systems of communication, to pass over their significance and, in our preoccupation with the here and now, to forget Man's long tortuous road of cultural growth. Democritus worried over atoms and atomic structure as early as 450 B.C., and flight by Man was envisioned long before Icarus made his fatal plunge into the Aegean. Man's technical progress has been slow; he has progressed only by the pressure of his needs. But to get back to the Inca roads. In lifting the turf off a road built more than five hundred years ago in this inhospitable land, where in four days we had been subjected to hail, snow and freezing winds at an altitude higher than that of most European peaks, and in examining the revealed techniques of road construction, we found an index to the marvels wrought by the Inca civilization before it was destroyed centuries ago.

While the work of excavation went on, Silvia and I decided to walk out over the highway to see what we could discover of its other features. We started off down the great road early one morning while the fog still hung over the *puna*, armed with cameras, compass and measuring tape. For a while we shared the wide highway with a herd of llamas being driven out by two small girls to graze in the distant hills.

In the weeks past we had not had much time for leisurely talk together of the death of kings and ruins of empire. As often as not in our search for the road, we had had to climb breathlessly to a roadbed which was most accurately described in literal terms as the "highway" — and on arrival we were at once too involved in making measurements, or else in worrying about each step we took on the perilous hanging road, to be given the luxury of speculation. Now it was different. Although we were thousands of feet high, we were walking along a flat *puna*. This road, we had decided after studying it and our too brief notes on its history, had been built fairly late, probably about the year 1470. Why had it been built? If it was a military road, against whom or what was it directed? At that time the Inca was concerned with his conquest to the north where he planned to overwhelm his rival, the fabulous Kingdom of Chimor, on the coast. At the same time a second column of conquest pushed slowly on toward Quito. The main highway, the Royal Road, swarmed with workers laboring like an endless stream of ants to project that overwhelming road across the sterile land. Then why *this* road?

The Chancas again! In the lives of people as well as in the lives of nations there is often a single, a traditional, enemy. Time and the alchemy of time changes that enemy, makes him less real; the physical threat is gone, the enmity has lost its potency, yet remembrance of the hated one remains. The Incas had such a traditional enemy in the Chancas. We had met the ghosts of this tribe, of which only Cieza de León has written, many times along our way. At the site of the Plain of Blood battlefield, we had seen where they had been defeated and where the Inca erected his macabre museum of stuffed Chanca warriors. We had met them again at Andahuaylas, their traditional tribal home before they were forced out of it by their conquerors. And now along this road. After the defeat inflicted upon them by the Incas, the tribal survivors, under Hanco-huallu, the Chanca leader, had successfully resisted the usual process of absorption into the new order and had escaped to the eastern Andes. This the Incas never forgot. This road, so we now believed, had been built to make a final conquest of the hated tribe.

The Highway of the Sun

Within an hour's walking time we came upon two *chasqui* stations.

It was not the first time we had seen ruins of these courier stations, way stops for the native runners who carried the Inca's messages throughout the Inca Empire, but this was the first time that we found them in succeeding order. These raised platforms lying close to the road on which were circular houses, each large enough for two Indians, have often been described by the early Spaniards, who thought the *chasqui* system one of the marvels of the "newe founde worlde."

With the discovery of two such ruined stations we proceeded more carefully, setting our pedometers so as to have a relative idea of the distance between the stations. On the top of a hill near Mesapata we found our third *chasqui* station, an even more elaborate one with raised platforms on either side of the road and large night quarters for the runners. That day we found seven such stations at intervals of a little less than two miles apart. We decided to give an empirical twist to our explorations by actually making test runs between the stations.

From the beginning, Man has sought to establish some form of inter-communication. He has — in time — shouted, used fire, wigwagged flags; he has beaten drums, used horses, relay runners, carrier pigeons and cannons. Alexander the Great perfected smoke signals to high degree, but until the telegraph was invented to consider "what hath God wrought," the Incas, a preliterate people, maintained the speediest system of communications. A message sent by relay runner from Quito could reach Cuzco over a route of one thousand, two hundred and thirty miles in five days. From Cuzco the same message could be sent to the far end of Lake Titicaca in three days. On the coast, where altitude was not a delaying factor, relay runners carried messages from Lima to Quito, often over thousand-foot-high altitudes, in three days. And in his palace at Cuzco the Inca dined off fresh fish delivered from Chala on the coast, a distance of two hundred miles over the highest Andes, in two days.

The Spanish conquistadores, accustomed to a world where sixty days was considered to be a normal lapse of time in which to secure communication with nearby countries, were incredulous. Of this system one later reported:

> The Incas invented a system of posts which was the best that could be thought of or imagined . . . and so well was this running performed, that in a short time they knew, at a distance of three hundred, five hundred, or even eight hundred leagues, what had passed. . . . the roads passed over rugged mountains, over snow-covered heights, over stony wildernesses . . . and it may be taken as certain that the news could not have been conveyed with greater speed on swift horses.

Still — one thousand, two hundred and thirty miles in five days! That would mean that the *chasqui* relay was run at an average of 246 miles a day over a terrain which averaged more than 10,000 feet elevation and through passes which often were 15,000 feet. Even the Romans were fortunate indeed if their mounted courier could cover a hundred miles a day. There are no figures on the transmission of news from Rome, but in the age of Cicero forty-seven days was considered normal traveling time for a letter to be delivered one thousand miles from Rome, and when Cicero was in exile at Cybistra he spoke of receiving a letter in "good time," or fifty days after it left Rome. So the idea of five hundred leagues — twelve hundred miles — being traveled in five days was understandably startling to the newly arrived Europeans.

We made our preparations for the test. The road beyond Jauja repaired and cleaned of any obstruction for more than ten miles was more or less as it had been in the times of the Lord Incas. We selected six young *cholo* men used to the high altitudes and for these Silvia made copies of the original Indian *chasqui* tunics. We went through the final details of our test. The distance having been measured between each *chasqui* station, we carefully reread the details of the run as reported by Cieza:

> The chasqui stations were built from half league to half league [Ours were on an average of a mile and a half to two miles apart]. . . . The roads were lined with these small houses at regular intervals. In each house the order read that there should be two Indians stationed there with provisions. The *chasqui* then ran with great speed, without stopping, *each one for his half league.*

Our young men were not trained runners, while the ancient *chasquis* had been "chosen from among the most active and swiftest of all their tribesmen," and their bodies had been taught to function under such conditions as they would encounter at heights of 10,000 to 15,000 feet. Due to the rare atmospheres in which they live, all Andean people have developed enormous lung capacity. This and this alone allows life at these great altitudes. So even though our runners were not trained, we hoped at least by establishing an arbitrary handicap to make a fair test of the *chasqui* system. Dr. Roger Bannister had not yet made his historical run of the four-minute mile. We later learned that he had trained deliberately, slowing down his heart action and building up his chest expansion to give him generous supplies of oxygen for conquering anoxemia or shortness of breath. Thus by artificial means he had induced a physical condition which the Indians, inured to these high altitudes, had acquired through environment.

Our *cholos* did at least look like the ancient *chasquis* and with their knit caps pulled down over their ears, their tunic-like ponchos extending to their knees and their feet shod in leather sandals, they looked as if they really were about to run on the Inca's business. At each of the seven stations strung along the Inca road we had assistants with stop watches, and at each we had an Indian *chasqui* poised to run. The starter of the relay held a *quipu*, the knotted pendant of cord by which figures and even concrete ideas were transmitted to trained readers. This *quipu* was to be handed from one runner to another, along with a simple oral message as each new man started off toward the next station.

Lawrence stationed himself at the start to film the various stages of the run. At the signal, a short bow-legged runner started off with a burst of speed. I watched him running smoothly down the wide road — he looked incredibly small on that expanse of man-made highway.

I saw him reach the next station and through my binoculars I could see the two runners exchanging the *quipu* while still in motion. Then the new runner burst away to make his run to the next two-mile station. As this figure disappeared over a knoll and I walked down to join Silvia, I remembered a passage out of Cieza — it was like the quotation borrowed from the Greeks which adorn the New York Post Office:

> With such secrecy did the runners keep their messages . . . that neither entreaty or menace could ever extort it from them. . . . And it must be understood that neither storm nor anything else prevented the due service of the posts in the wildest parts — as soon as one started another arrived to wait in his place.

It snowed again that night. Our six *chasquis*, utterly exhausted by the day's run, were now wrapped snugly in their ponchos. They had gone the course many times so that we might check our ow figures and so that Lawrence's Bolex might catch numerous angles of flying feet and the exchange of the *quipu* for the film documentary. Now, after a hot meal, they had succumbed. We were busy over the figures. We had computed the exact time it took for them to run between stations and the overall figure of the thirteen-mile relay run. Our untrained *chasquis,* performing at about 14,000 feet altitude, had run an average six-and-a-half minute mile! On this basis they had run the approximate six stations — or eleven miles — in fifty-nine minutes. Therefore, the 246 miles they would have had to run in a twenty-four-hour day to complete the Quito-Cuzco relay could have been accomplished.

We were now in a position to confirm Cieza's report and those of other earlier chroniclers that the *chasqui* system could accomplish the run between Cuzco and Quito in five days; that from Lima to Cuzco in three days, and from the coast to Cuzco in two days. And so the Lord Inca *could* have been served daily with fresh fish from the sea.

That night I dreamed of a *chasqui* running up the road with an out-sized fish — it seemed to be having trouble breathing in the high altitude.

Late November found us traveling through the snowbound antiplano. Silvia maintained she could no longer remember a time when she had been really warm. Only at rare moments did the sun give respite from the unrelenting cold and rain, hail and snow, swept down in succession and with no pattern.

Through it all we followed that continuing road, stretching endless miles across the flat snow-swept plains, climbing the rock mass of mountains, crossing on stone causeways over some bottomless bog. But all this was no longer a cause for wonder on our part. We had reached a point where the best we could do was to record the unusual, make out our reports, film some remarkable engineering feature, set our compass and move on. Once Silvia was sure she was suffering from the *surumpi* (snow-blindness) or that she had the beginnings of hallucinations, for as she stood on the road stamping circulation into her frozen feet, she thought she saw a line of black-winged flamingos walking in front of her. . . . It was no illusion. Flamingos *had* walked by. We had come by way of the Inca road to Lake Junin.

All the rest of that day we kept to the east side of what is Peru's second largest lake. It was high and cold — and deserted. The little villages at the edge of its thirty-six-mile shore lie at an altitude of 13,000 feet with no protecting hill to break the blast of the ice-laden winds. Junin was once called Chinchay-cocha (Lake of the Lynx). The original inhabitants, famed for their warlike spirit, when attacked would take to island-fortresses in the lake's center and to conquer them the Lord Inca had to send to the coast for balsa-reed boats with which to assault their island strongholds. Once they were subdued, however, they became loyal vassals of the Inca, and the region of such importance that it became "one of the directions of empire." The northern route of the highway itself was called the Chinchay Road.

Our caravan continued on along the Inca road stopping only long enough to take compass bearings and mark the route down on an overlay of the Peruvian military map. At the northern end of the lake, the land became an immense bog and we lost our way constantly in the thick fog and, to make matters more complicated, it began to snow heavily. By the end of the second day's travel we had no idea where we were. Mud dwellings had appeared here and there but when we approached them the people were too frightened to answer our questions. We were looking for Bonbón, where, according to our research, lay a large Inca site and where three roads were said to have met. By nightfall we could only inch along literally feeling our way. About us was a horrid desolation. It was so cold now that we had to take turns riding in the Power Wagon which alone of our cars had a heating system. It was impossible to prepare food outside, so we munched on the last of our chocolate and found some consolation in drinking coffee. A primitive bridge which we crossed in darkness indicated that we had gone over the only river which drains this lake. We were puzzled to see that this flowed due north, while our maps showed that the river we sought flowed south.

Should we stop and make camp in the snow or empty out the Power Wagon and sleep in it? Should we keep on searching for that illusive Inca site or should we drive on? We were considering these alternatives when, above the throb of the motors, we heard the roar of falling water. It grew louder as we went slowly on, until it was deafening. Then, as the road turned, we saw the twinkling of electric lights. Soon we had pulled up in front of a wooden house. Almost at once we were around a pot-bellied iron stove which gave out a wonderful glowing heat. After so many days and nights on the antiplano, we were now to have heat and the comfort of a bed. Gratefully we allowed ourselves to be provided with hot food before we dropped into oblivion.

In the morning we could hardly believe our eyes. The Inca site of Bonbón, which for a century had thwarted historians' attempts to pin-point it on the map, lay before us. This was a somewhat embarrassing situation for an explorer! The whereabouts of this town — the hub site of three radical roads, so it was reported by the early chroniclers — was actually no mystery at all. Close by was a modern dam which held back the Mantaro River as it flowed out of Lake Junin. This had been built by the Cerro de Pasco Mining Corporation, whose engineers had torn down much of the ancient village to get the stones for the dam. But there was no doubt about its origin. On the banks in the backed-up waters we could see the remains of an Inca suspension bridge. A causeway led from the bridge up to a wide stone staircase and entered northwest along the walls of what once were large stone buildings and extended toward the immense plaza. We had seen nothing like it in size since we had explored Vilcas-huaman. The trapizoidal-shaped plaza proved, when accurately measured, to be over a thousand feet long. In the center stood a Sun Temple, and from its approximate sides went radial roads — one to the coast which an Indian could reach in three days of walking on the Inca road, another to the north which went over the *puna* to the highways of the snow-capped mountains of the white cordillera, and yet another, the Royal Road, which led to the northeast and the stone city of Huánuco the Old. There must have been five hundred stone structures within Bonbón and those which had not been entirely denuded still revealed their original form.

Eager to learn something more of the history of this place, we began to gather such potsherds as we came across. Silvia found a large cache of broken pottery on the stone-terraced banks of the river, and soon we were scrounging in the debris of centuries. In a few hours we had a large collection of fragments of broken pottery, spindles, spindle whorls, pieces of figurines and ax clubheads. They were, as we could see by the design, shape and structure, all Inca artifacts and the type of polychromic ware used when the Incas had reached their peak. Therefore, since these fragments were many and lay close to the surface of the earth, we felt we could safely assume that the Incas had built Bonbón. It is well known that the history of preliterate people is mainly written in such artifacts. There was little doubt that this was the same Bonbón to which Hernando Pizarro had come in March 11, 1533, "when he marched into Pompo where he stayed for the day he arrived and one day more."

The scrivener's description of it fits the place exactly; he wrote that the river [the Mantaro] which originated in the lake flowed by Bonbón "very clear and deep" and that it "connected with the Royal Road" as it did by means of the bridge. We found the remains of three cable stone towers which by some miracle had survived time, weather, and immersion in the Mantaro when its watercourse was high. It was this bridge or fragment of bridge which Poma de Ayála, chronicler of Inca events, in his guide to the roads and tambos on the road, mentions cryptically: *bonbon tambo rreal puente de crisnexas del inga topa ynga yupanqui.* Translated this indicated that Bonbón, a royal way station with a suspension bridge, had been built by the Lord Topa Inca. That placed it close to A.D. 1450.

It was well that we had not delayed in our examination of the ruins of Bonbón, for two days later, the sky grew dark, snow began to fall, and soon the ruins were blotted out of sight.

X I

The Road to Chachapoyas

IN A WIDE FLAT PLAIN lay Huánuco. The ground was strewn with beautifully worked stone and we entered the plaza from the Inca road by means of a formal entrance of steps and guardhouses. It was immense. Ruins of dwellings, many and thickly placed, filled the plain outside the plaza and a low hill to the northwest. In the center of the Gargantuan square was what had doubtless been the Sun Temple. At the western end of the square stood the palace. Here we found six continuing stone gateways, the finest, I would say, in all Peru, and over each portal crouching animal figures which resembled lizards. Through these I entered a series of immense rooms which led into an architectural complex where there was a sunken bath fed by two water flumes, "one for cold water, the other for hot," said our guide. He was unable to explain how the hot water reached Huánuco from Baños some ten miles distant.

Huánuco is so gigantic — the whole of Incaic Cuzco would have fitted into it — that we found it difficult to grasp the immensity of the human effort expended to build it. Something of its size can be gathered from a Spaniard who passed there in 1548:

> Huánuco has a fine royal palace . . . the chief palace in this province of Huamalies with near it a Temple of the Sun with many virgins and priests. It was so grand a place in the

time of the Incas that more than 30,000 Indians were set apart solely for its service.

In 1539 the Spaniards seized this Inca stronghold which was so "grand a place" and which offered so many captives as potential burden-bearers for their future conquests. For two years they sought to maintain a settlement at the 12,000-foot altitude. Then, unable to bear the secular winds, they betook themselves northeast to a warmer climate and there they built Huánuco the New. Yet life in the old Huánuco survived the conquest, for in 1608 when a padre traveled that way he found the "tambo with a few Indians to run it for the accommodation of travelers since it is on the King's [i.e., the Inca's] highway."

To us Huánuco was important because it was the principal stronghold from which conquests were launched in several directions along the roads of conquest leading out from it. Like Dr. Johnson's Rasselas, I could say that "my curiosity does not very strongly lead me merely to survey piles of stones or mounds of earth, my business is with man." But for the story of those who had once lived in Huánuco we turned later to documents in the National Archives in Lima, where we found a sixteenth-century Spanish manuscript on the city, the most complete report of its kind in Peru.

After the conquest of Peru, the newly installed Viceroy gave much thought to Old Huánuco. Why had a once so greatly populated place suddenly ceased to yield tribute to the crown? What had happened to the more than thirty thousand natives who were there at the time of the conquest and what of the city which was so bright a jewel in the Inca Empire? Accordingly, he dispatched Don Inigo de Zuñiga to look into these matters. He arrived there in 1562. With interpreters and Indian caciques at his elbow to pry out information from the inhabitants, he passed from house to house compiling the statistics which resulted in the most detailed census ever made of the ancient Peruvians.[1] The following is a sample of the information de Zuñiga carried back to his Viceroy:

HOUSE 35

In this house is an Indian named Ana Colque who is a widow around 70 years old, without sons or daughters; her tribute every four months is a ball of spun wool thread and a chicken every year with some eggs.

Throughout the whole district the Indians were questioned in detail on their origins and how they had paid their tribute for the thirty years previous to the then reigning Inca. Some of the old men, trained *quipu* readers, by consulting their "talking strings" were able to relate much about Huánuco.

The original inhabitants of Huánuco, the *Yachas*, were conquered by the Topa Inca in 1462 and the building of the fortress of Huánuco was then begun. To secure the land from uprising, the Inca transferred whole populations from Cuzco to this area. These *mitmaes quichuas*, transferred people of Quechua speech, were the Inca's own — in short, people he trusted to hold the land and insure its allegiance and "to guard the fortresses which the Inca made during the conquest."

The Yachas, adopted by their conquerors, were in turn settled in villages northwest of Huánuco, and the new arrivals along with the "great-eared Incas" were placed to the southwest. Tribute was levied on everyone within the jurisdiction of Huánuco. From the warmer regions, the Indians brought cotton, peppers, coca leaf, fish, corn and gold; from the cold zone, potatoes, salt, cabuya fibers and a tuber called *quinoa*. All this tribute was marked down by one of the conquerors, who had an official counter make a note of it. Of

[1] "Information on estates and agents. Visit for the allotment of Indians of Gomez Arias Davila, native of Huánuco," a report written by I. Ortiz de Zuñiga, 1562.

hose at Huánuco, only the warriors who guarded the fortresses and those who guarded the bridges did not pay tribute. The corn harvested from the communal fields of the Yachas was carried to Huánuco, to Bonbón and to Cuzco. They were also ordered to send men to garrison the fortresses.

Two roads entered Huánuco, two roads left Huánuco. One, the Royal Road, descending in a sharp flight of stairs, made its exit at the northwest end of the elevated plaza and moved straight to the Vizcarro River, where it crossed a primitive bridge made of several tree lengths laid over an Inca stone foundation. "Half league from Huánuco, where there is a bridge over a torrential river made of three thick logs and where there are guards who collect a toll as is customary among these Indians," one of the Pizarros in 1533 had crossed this highway, which, we knew from our previous exploration, was the Royal Road which led to Cajamarca and north to Quito and beyond.

The other road which debouched from the northeast side of Huánuco, I felt certain, was the same forty-five-foot-wide conquest road we had just seen near Jauja. It had broken off there from the Royal Road to take its separate way until it once again rejoined the main road at Huánuco. Since this had been the great military station for the conquest of Chachapoyas, it seemed most probable that this highway was that built by the Incas for their conquest of the Chancas.

Silvia was not overjoyed at the prospect of a horseback ride over some three hundred miles. It would be an arduous journey but at last she gave in, being as unable as I to leave the mystery of the Road of Conquest unsolved. Lawrence and the others elected to remain at Huánuco to work on his documentary film and to further explore the ruins. He would then drive on to the coast, for he knew we could not long remain here with the rains already falling. So it was arranged. We gathered our guides, pack animals, horses, se-

lected the equipment designed for just this sort of travel — and
then rode off into the twilight which shrouds the undiscovered.

"Is it not as I explained to you, Señor? There is the Marañon, far
below, like a great silver snake, and here is the road. You will find
that I, Francisco Ocampo . . ."

We had certainly found out plenty about Francisco Ocampo. He
was the only one among us with enough energy to talk and that
talk was mostly about Francisco Ocampo. Born on the road to
Chachapoyas, orphaned at childhood with his numerous brothers
and sisters, he had managed somehow to live by his wits. By his
bearded face and saturnine manner one would have taken him for
a mere picaro, one who sees the seamy side of life. Yet none was
more ardent than he in searching for the illusive Inca road, no one
more dedicated — an unusual thing in itself, for here the people
have not much enthusiasm for any active enterprise. But Francisco
has ridden often about this desolate country corraling supply mule
trains for isolated gold mines, and so he knew the land.

In the first two weeks of our journey in search of the conquest
road, we had to cross and recross the Marañon, take trucks when
we could, going by horse and mule at other times. When we
reached Cuntur-marca, the "heights of the condor," we were geographically at the halfway mark between Huánuco and Chachapoyas [2] and finally able to travel a continuous road. The upper
Marañon through which we now trekked is the least known region

[2] To give a detailed itinerary, the Inca road to Chachapoyas left the
great square at Huánuco, moved northeast, crossed the Marañon to
Quivilla (on the east bank) continued on high ground to Chavin de
Pariacra, continued at about 10,000 feet to Acrotambo; then to the large
ancient holding called Haucrachucro; from there to Tayapampa, then
to Parcoy and to Pataz, where the Marañon can be seen for the first time
snaking through the high hills of the Upper Marañon; Cuntur-marca lies
ten miles north of Pataz.

n all Peru. While the jungle areas have been thoroughly traversed
by both natives and whites and other remote sections of Peru are
mapped in detail, of the upper Marañon little is on record. Our
maps merely placed the names of widely separated villages in their
relative position and that was all. Geographically the region belongs
to the Central Andes, but the Marañon River has etched out a deep
canyon isolating it from the Mother Andes, and sandwiched between it and the Huallaga River, cut off from Central Peru, lies
this towering land roughly two hundred miles in length and thirty
at its greatest depth.

But the great conquest road was no longer to be guessed at. We
were riding it over rolling hills, treeless and cold, and as we rode,
Silvia and I talked of this road and its history. At first we had been
so engaged in crossing rivers on shaky contrivances, finding places
to sleep, so absorbed with the mere mechanics of moving, that we
had had little time for talk. Now we were again in the open with the
wind blowing in unobstructed from the Amazon jungles which lay
not too far away to set the *ichu* grass, as tall as sugar cane, in motion. The whole heavens curved about us.

Hate and fear had built this road. Perhaps therefore this was a
good time to consider the creative qualities of hate. Even after his
realm had been enlarged to include a lordly section of South America, the Incas had felt impelled, as we have said, to seek out and destroy that small defiant and much hated colony of Chancas living
in the eastern Andes. That this tribe was beyond the reach of their
searching Argus-eyed Sun King worried the Inca to distraction.

In an earlier time, when the Incas were battering their way
through stubborn resistence, the Chancas, eight thousand strong,
had been sent on the road as part of the Inca army of conquest,
the Inca believing so to rid themselves of the remainder of this
tribe. It was then that the Chancas with "their women and Hanco-

huallu and eight thousand warriors, marched secretly away through
the provinces of Huánuco and Chachapoyas into the forests of th
low-lying Andes . . . where they established their kingdom an
multiplied . . ." The Inca Empire at the height of its power gav
chase and attacked, yet apparently without their usual elaborat
preparations, and the Chancas "fought with such fury that th
Incas fled before them."

The answer to this was the road of conquest over which we wer
now riding. Only by staggering human effort and endurance coul
this road have been built. Since there were no rocky outcrop
nearby, the large stone slabs which made up the paved road had t
be carried to it over a distance and the deep canyons — and ther
were many — were miracles of construction with their step roa
and mountain switchbacks, all wonderfully arranged with ston
supports.

By the time we reached Cuntur-marca, where we came to ou
first recognizable Inca *tampu,* Silvia was properly exhausted. Ou
food along the way had been meager and the altitudes at times wer
so high that she had gone through agonizing moments of shortnes
of breath, racing pulse and all the other symptoms of *soroche.* Bu
in ruins though it was, the *tampu* still was the best stopping plac
we had seen in a full week. We were on the top of the *jalka,* a bar
treeless region like the *punas* over which we had traveled so long
except that we were now experiencing cyclonic winds that blew u
from the Amazon.

Our camp that night was set up in the Inca's *tambo,* of stone an
without windows. The roof, replaced frequently throughout th
centuries, was of gabled wooden beams thatched with *ichu* grass
Only a portion of it, a small room scarcely larger than a cell, wa
habitable. Silvia stretched out on a blanket on the ground using he
saddle as a headrest while we busied ourselves with putting th

place in order. Francisco, gay as ever, chased about looking for some pieces of wood. On a rude bed of dry grass, where someone had evidently once stored potatoes, I unrolled our down-filled sleeping bags. While Silvia made herself comfortable on them, I prepared our food over our gasoline-operated paratrooper stove and Francisco, in a corner where the draft could not reach it, soon had a stew of dried llama meat and potatoes going. Then, to the accompaniment of the howling winds, Francisco continued his life's story as he had night after night, a sort of bowdlerized version of the night tales of Scheherazade. He had reached midway in the telling of how he had found a mountain of gold when the blanket which hung as a door between the night and ourselves was pushed aside and out went our candle. Sputtering a whole litany of curses on whoever had let in the wind, I finally located a match and lit the candle. We were confronted by two lean and unkempt-looking visitors. Francisco, looking oddly shaken, hurriedly did the honors of our hovel, offering cigarettes and coffee. The two, roughly dressed and unshaven, said they had seen the light in the *tambo* and so had come to investigate. They plied us with so many questions that finally, our quota of patience used up, we bade them a curt goodnight.

Francisco awakened me a few hours later. In a hoarse whisper he told me that our saddled animals were waiting outside, that we must leave at once, for the two men were bandits and it would be wise for us to move on. I doubted this at first, for few lands in the world are safer for the traveler than Peru. Yet since Francisco insisted he knew what he was talking about, we silently stole out to the frigid night, mounted, put on our heavy woolen ponchos and were on our way north before the rising of the Dog Star.

Three hours later, when the sun had warmed the earth, we stopped for coffee under the protection of the walls of some ruins near a lake at the edge of the road. As we were about to mount,

Francisco spoke excitedly: "They come!" Through my binoculars I could see our erstwhile guests riding toward us. Each carried a shotgun. They were perhaps a half-mile away, traveling along the edge of the lake and pushing their horses to a gallop. I had not, as yet, been much concerned with Francisco's fears, but perhaps just a shot across the bow . . .

I found a good position and aimed well ahead of them. In the preternatural stillness, my big-calibered rifle sounded like the slam of a cannon, the lake pushed up a small geyser of water some distance in front of them and a horse shied. I fired again, this time closer; they reined in their horses, turned and galloped away.

As we moved northward people and houses began to appear with some frequency. The dwellings, mostly constructed from worked stone taken from the ancient ruins, were rough and roofed with grass thatch. The people, although swarthy in complexion, were not Indian and did not speak the Quechua language. Yet they lived in hovels far worse, I judge, than did the natives in the time of the Inca. The entire household slept in one room, generally in one bed made of untanned cattle hides. As a stove there was only a pile of stones laid on the ground. Yet these people could not be called poor. It was not unusual for a man to own as much as three hundred head of sheep, five hundred cattle, horses and pigs. In Europe if a man had so much livestock he would have been considered well off. Nevertheless they lived wretchedly, and I was happy to exchange medicines for such food as they could give us without making inroads into their not too plentiful supplies.

We were now in the third week of travel from Huánuco, riding down the slopes of a long valley covered with tufts of grass so high that at times I could only see the top of Silvia's head. The sky was leaden, the wind blew icily, bending double the tall grass. We rode by immense boulders hoary with moss, sections of eroded rock which had fallen off with the passing of centuries like the leaves of a geological calendar marking the years of the sun.

And so we came in due course to the valley of Atwen. From a natural lake, artificially widened and artificially bound by hand-reared rock walls, flowed the headwater stream of the Uctubamba River, which emptied into the jungles one hundred miles to the northeast. Here we came upon the remains of what was once a gigantic Inca barracks. Although all the surrounding present-day dwellings were built of the stone taken from the ancient structure, enough of it remained for us to study it and to prepare a ground plan. Surface excavations yielded pottery, mace-heads, bronze knives — all of which bore eloquent testimony to the fact that once the Incas had passed this way. This was the first sizable Inca ruin we had found along the road to Chachapoyas and it might well have been the rallying place of the soldiers before they assaulted the enemy fortresses that lay ahead.

The path over which we traveled was now confined to the narrow valley of the Upper Uctubamba and passed through what had formerly been a heavily defended area. Almost every peak was topped by the ruins of a defense point and below these ran the Inca road. Five hundred years of indiscriminate passage by the Spanish settlers had reduced this section of the highway to a mass of scattered stone and where the road had disappeared, it had become a quagmire. No one since the time of the Incas had given thought to repairing the road and the heavy rains plus the constant passage of mule-trains had almost completely destroyed it.

That night we slept in an old house which lay under the shadow of Torre Pukro, the highest peak in the valley. I had been watching it for most of the day as we rode and as we drew close I saw through my binoculars the terraced hills and on the silhouetted pinnacle the ruins of a massive fortress.

Oddly we found a large mirror in the house and so for the first time in many weeks we had a good look at ourselves. Among ourselves we had been perhaps unduly critical of the appearance of those we met on the way. The women, we said, looked like old crones and the men as if they had never bathed or shaved. Now we saw what the land had done to us. Silvia's face was raw from the wind and darkly tanned; her eyes were bloodshot from the camp fire smoke and her hair a pallid ash color from the dirt of the trail. As for me, what with my beard, the dirt and the tan, mine was a visage which would have competed on equal terms with any we had passed on the way. That three weeks should have been so wearing on us!

In the morning I began to climb to the hilltop fortress of Torr Pukro. The first thousand feet was easy and within an hour I was perched high on the cliff looking down on the narrow river. Clearly seen from this height was the scar of the Inca road. My guide, carrying the cameras, eased ahead, found an ancient path that zig zagged up the second thousand feet, and soon we were climbing over the tumbled remains of agricultural terraces. I marveled at the immense human effort that went into building these walls on the edge of nothing for the one purpose of salvaging so little soil. In this vast land which was Peru, arable land was so scarce and man so pressed by necessity that he had had to resort to terracing the clouds.

Above ten thousand feet the going was difficult; I would climb fifty feet, rest five minutes, climb again, rest. In two hours I had reached the top. The ruins of the fortress, massively built of stone, extended all along the topographical saddle of the mountain, much as did Machu Picchu near to Cuzco, offering a fine vantage point for looking down the throat, so to speak, of the valley. At one time this had been an advantageous lookout station for the protection of the Inca road which could be seen running as a thin line three thou and feet below. The conquest of this strongly-placed fortress must indeed have cost the Inca's troops a considerable expenditure of blood capital. From this spot I could see that there were similar fortresses on many of the other hilltops. When I had surveyed the ruins and collected numerous potsherds, I made my way wearily down through a sudden hailstorm.

The climb to that mountain citadel had done me in. In the morning, for the first time in a year's exploration, I had to beg off from a proposed climb to another ruin reported to be on this side of the valley and buried in the gloom of a forest. We were still up 9000 feet and though there had been no change in the barometer nor in the thermometer, which kept to a mean of forty-five degrees, yet the valleys and portions of these hills were as thickly forested as a jungle. An old woman who had come to our camp to ask for medicines while I was inspecting the fortress had told Silvia that at Choquillo up in the wooded hills "there was buried a stone city built by the savages." Many times had we, responding to such rumors, climbed some wearisome hill only to find nothing. Too often time and energy had been spent chasing these shadows. Now here was another tale of another "stone city buried in the trees" lying at the end of an archaeological rainbow. Even Francisco with all his tricks of raillery could not move me. Silvia and the two guides could go without me if they so desired.

When they had gone I lay back in immense tiredness. I wanted only to be allowed the utter luxury of being motionless.

"Señor!"

I wakened to find one of our guides beside me, pulling my sleeve. "Dona Silvia has sent me, you are to come. She has found the stone city."

That was quite enough to shake off my weariness and in no time

I was up and following him through the scrub brush in the hollow past a ruin or two, and on through a deep canyon. Then we were in the forest of Choquillo, where we were swallowed up at once in growth so thick that the boy had to use his machete to cut the encumbering vines. An occasional palm tree showed its head, liana-like massive ship cables bound tree to tree, aërial plants clung t trees, orchids hung in profusion from the highest limbs and bird silently fluttered among the growth. I could not have been mor surprised at finding this jungle in the Andes if I had been trans ported to a magic forest.

Here and there sections of massive man-made white stone wall covered with thick verdure, were just visible through the under growth. Ahead I heard the sound of a machete and the crash c trees — and in a clearing in front of a round towerlike stone build ing was Silvia, directing the cutting of the vegetation that ham pered the view. Excitedly she came to meet me. *It was true.* Th whole stretch of forest was filled with stone buildings!

Great trees had embraced the walls of the ancient site, just as had seen them at the Maya ruins at Yucatán. We would see at firs a patch of white. Then, upon coming close, we would discover th patch to be a rounded wall, part of a circular structure. These wer set in clusters of three and were connected with beautifully lai ashlars forming stone steps. The dual walls were high and roofles but apart from such stones as had been uprooted by the trees, mos of the buildings were well preserved. Here the jungle had acted a a protecting screen from the elements and, lying unseen, the cit had been spared the usual ravages of time.

We cleared the vegetation from what we judged to have been th largest structure. And there it was — a dwelling set on an enor mous oval-shaped stone base. From out the jungle growth, a wel made wall of dry masonry rose up twenty-five feet, its axis ove seventy feet long, with not a stone out of place. On top of this ova base, set back in a recess, was another similarly designed structure differing only in that this one had a door and square windows and the suggestion of a fret design in a mosaic of stones running about its top. Before its sharply pitched roof made of grass thatch had fallen in, the building must have had an overall height of sixty feet! Francisco cleared the stone stairways and we, following him between the two houselike ruins, found ourselves on a balcony edge. We walked around it toward the doorway on a thick moss carpet which covered the stones. This we rolled back, and under it we found well-laid masonry as glowing white as it must have been when it was first laid down. Under the moss, too, we discovered large carved stone heads sculptured on tenons which were part of the architecture. As the unrolling of the moss-carpet progressed, we found five such heads.

In the exact center on the circular wall was the doorway much like the doorways I had seen in Mayan structures. The terrace which had been made of wood had succumbed to the elements and had fallen, dislodging a few stones. This was the only defect — otherwise the walls were in perfect state. Stepping inside the circular building, we passed into a dense growth of trees covered with flowering orchids. The quiet of this forest and the mysterious jungle-covered ruins made me think of John Lloyd Stephens, the New York lawyer who, during his travel through the Honduran jungle in 1839, first discovered the Maya culture. "I am entering abruptly upon new ground," he said. Just so were we.

On the outside walls a fret design with large Greek-key motif ran around the entire edge of the building. This, too, was a type of wall decoration very similar in design and technique to those found in the Maya ruins of Ucmal in Yucatán.

The roof was gone, but all else was in place — window spaces for ventilation; square mural niches in which the images of local gods had been set; a deer antler lodged in the wall and probably used as a tunic hanger; a large stone on the floor for grinding corn, intact with stone roller; and, as our excavation progressed, a floor laid with flat flagstones. Then to our surprise and delight we came across evidences of Inca occupation. The structure, which we were by this time convinced was not Inca in origin, had undoubtedly been contemporaneous with the Inca Empire, and now the finding of Inca-designed pottery and a copper knife and stone celts indicated that this, too, had been a city conquered and used by the Inca's troops.

If only there had been some writing, some hieroglyphic scorings such as one finds in the ruins of the Old World! But there were only these silent circular stone buildings standing in a jungle. Was this one of the cities and the forts on the hills which belonged to the sought-after Chancas of whom de la Vega had noted: "The Topa Inca went to conquer Chachapoyas; they [the Chancas] had built many fortifications and he had to take them one by one . . . the first was near the town of Pias . . . then he had to go through a mountain pass called Chirmaccassa and from here southward he had to conquer all the towns for eight leagues." Or were these the remains of another culture without name or history which stood in the way of the Inca in their frantic search for the illusive Chanca tribes?

The mountain ramparts along the Lower Uctubamba Valley are filled with ruins of ancient fortresses, cities and burial *chullpas* some of which have been explored for more than a century. High on the east of the Uctubamba Valley are the ruins of the great fortress of Kuelape, similar in construction to these we found about Choquillo; and very high in the frigid *jalka*, there are other similar structures. At Jalka Grande we were to find round structures identical to those we found in our "city in the forest." But in following this Inca road from Huánuco northward into a little-known region we had opened a whole new region of archaeological incognita.

*   *   *

The Road to Chachapoyas

For the next several days we walked through an amazing luxuriant jungle. On both sides was a double array of towering limestone cliffs and in the center of the jungle was the plunging Tambillo River, along which ran the all-weather paved road of conquest, its massive rock slabs quarried from the nearby cliffs still surviving after five centuries.

Frequently now we met people moving along the road — pallid-looking people racked with intermittent onslaughts of tertiary fevers. The women wore large brimmed panamas and crinoline cotton skirts and walked barefooted. The men, usually driving oxen which did double duty as pack animals, were sallow-faced and unshaven. They were a kindly people, asking politely about us, admiring Silvia's youthful good looks, incredulous that we should make so long a journey merely to walk the Inca road.

It rained heavily as we journeyed across the mountains of Puma Okra and the gusts of wind blew with such violence that the tired mules could hardly keep their footing. The storm, coming in unchecked from the direction of the eastern jungles which lay only a score of miles eastward and downward, capriciously alternated with sudden gleams of sunlight, and the cloud shapes floating over the treeless *jalka* hung down into the unseen jungle.

The red earth was steaming under the rays of the triumphant sun as we rode into Levanto. The compact little stone-built village stood at the end of the plain. Back of it rose abrupt hills, tangled in trees and the broken masonry of ancient buildings. In the neat and quiet little plaza, dominated by its old church, we were met by four men carrying the silver-headed sticks of village officials. They doffed their gray llama-felt hats and in a strangely lisping Spanish bade us welcome to Levanto . . .

In much the same way had Alonzo de Alvarado been welcomed when in November 1535 he arrived with his men to take over the rich province of Chachapoyas, his reward for his defeat of the Inca.

Only then he had been met by Inca and Chachapoyas chieftains attired in long woolen tunics, their heads festooned with golden ornaments. So confused were the Inca nobles at Levanto by all that had happened — the capture and the death of their Inca and the official orders to place themselves at the command of the white man — that they had offered little organized resistance. The conquistadores found these Indians the "most fair and good looking of any . . . seen in the Indies and their women so beautiful that many of them are worthy to be wives of the Incas . . . Exceedingly beautiful, fair and well formed, they go about dressed in woolen clothes, like their husbands, and on their heads they wear a certain fringe." So Alvarado accepted the homage of the Indians "and founded the city of the frontier in a strong place called Levantu."

Now four hundred and twenty years later here around us were the ruins of this first Spanish settlement whose walls were now hidden in thick brush. Back in the hills were other immense ruins and five hours from here, deep in the valley, was Chachapoyas — which the Spaniards later sought out as a refuge from the ice-laden winds

The village elders, following us with a pompous show of their ornately decorated silver-topped staffs of office, directed us to the village school at the edge of the small grass plaza and there we took refuge from the rain. A little lady, so small that she appeared to be only a miniature of a human being, offered us a gentle welcome shared with us her evening meal of beans and rice and gave Silvi. the only bed. She poured out her last drop of kerosene to give u light when the house was whipped by the sudden storm. On thi exposed height the winds, roaring up from the jungles which lay fifty miles distant and six thousand feet below us, blew shrill a screaming banshees about us and the rain poured down on the frai house as in a deluge. The rats and the bats kept up an awful din but we were too exhausted to worry much about it. Tomorrow w were to take yet another ride — this time to the airfield at Chachapoyas. But at long last we would be on our way to the coast.

Before sleep claimed us Silvia had the last word. "At least the desert will be warm. I haven't been warm in so long I don't know how it will feel."

Only the squeal of the rats answered her.

X I I

The Unliving Desert

THE LAND cannot be said to be dead, for that would imply that it once lived — it is unliving. There is no water, no tree, no grass, "nor any created thing," said a wandering Spaniard, "except birds, which by the gift of wings wander wherever they list." This coastal desert begins at Tumbes near the equatorial line to the north and continues southward for over two thousand miles, the entire length of Peru and on into the northern part of Chile, its arid, waterless desolation varying in width from one to a hundred miles, bound by the sea and the bare Andes which intrude their unclothed ribs into it. The mist which hangs here often dulling the glamour of the stars is not rain but moisture in mist-clouds like unshed tears. If this balance is destroyed, as sometimes happens, the flood gates open and the flimsy mud houses of the dwellers in the valleys are dissolved as a child's sand castle is melted in an onrushing wave.

When the desert day dawns mistless, it is so hot that it is noontide within the hour. No tree, no cactus, nor even canker-weed grows in this desiccating heat, nothing that "would exalt one in desolation above Idumea." Blue sky curves to meet blue sea and no showers refresh this desert which like split Syrian gourds is left withering in the sun and beneath a torrid sky the land lies cracked as by a timeless drought, its one distinctive note uninhabitableness. "Have mercy upon me," its wailing spirit seems to say, "and send

The Unliving Desert

Lazarus that he may dip the tip of his finger in water and cool my tongue for I am tormented by this heat."

Yet Man lived and prospered here for thousands of years, shaping a desert civilization as Man has elsewhere done in the world's aridity. Along the entire length of the desert coast, the score of rivers — some constant, others capricious — which break through the rock-hard Andes to flow to the ocean have made valleys which, under centuries of irrigation, have become oases in the desert. When as early as 3000 B.C. Man first appeared in these valleys, he found the land in the river valleys enriched by alluvium, the arid void without disease and the offshore waters well supplied with fish. Water was then, as now, the key to life. Man learned the techniques of irrigation and with long experience perfected them. He sought out streams high in the valleys, built elaborate aqueducts and channeled them to the coast and so widened the natural valleys and increased the areas of fertility. In time, the desert oases blossomed and thus early Man became the human catalyst of the desert.

Each of these valley oases along the thousand-mile coast is separated by stretches of desolation. Isolation creates distinct cultures; and so each valley had its variant in its customs, style, and application, even though all shared the desert environment. All coastal tribes had the same husbandry: corn, beans, squash, tomatoes, peppers, yucca — useful for making bread and liquor when there was a want of maize — sweet potatoes, avocados, guavas, pineapples, star-apples, iron-hard algaroba-trees with a fruit "somewhat long and narrow and not so thick as the pods of beans," and pepinos "of very pleasant smell and taste." Eventually the larger tribes which came into being in the better populated valleys dominated the rest without, however, altogether changing their basic cultures.

The Incas, arriving late, conquered these coastal cultures after fierce and often prolonged wars, swarming down from their mountains to lay siege and eventually engulf these coastal cultures into their devouring maw. The Chimu, the greatest of these and the last to fall, was overwhelmed in 1465, a generation before the myrmidons of Francisco Pizarro fell upon the entire region. After that conquest, the Incas built "a wide road through these coast valleys with a strong wall on each side" which drew the widely separated oasis-cultures together.

So at the height of Carnival time we came down from the bareness of life on the mountains to the bareness of life on the *yunga*-desert to find, if we could, that "wide road through the coast valleys."

It began with a tour by air. The whole Expedition, including our newly arrived archaeologists, Fritz and Dorothy Riddell from the University of California, crowded into the single-motor Stinson and took to the air over the grayish void of land to gain a first comprehensive look at the terrain. After covering some three hundred miles during which time we filmed many of the obscure sections, we returned to the Lima airport and prepared for an immediate ground survey.

With our caravan of vehicles now increased by one more for the personal use of the Riddells, we began the southern exploration of the coastal road at the rim of the city of Lima. The airport had once been the site of a way station on the highway which passed through what is now the landing field for international airlines.

Close on Lima, Morro Solar, a Gibraltar-like rock, rises from the edge of the sea. At its base on the Royal Road is the Arma-tambo [purification bath] where Indians making the pilgrimage to the sacred place of Pachacamac, a few miles distant, made their ablutions before going on to the holy place. Here we lingered long enough for the Riddells to "take their first archaeological scent," then we passed on southward.

The Unliving Desert

Pachacamac, known today as the home place of thousands of sea birds, was once the dwelling place of the Creator God. The largest man-made pyramid in all the Americas, constructed of millions of sun-baked bricks cemented over and frescoed with paintings of birds, it had been revered as the most hallowed spot on the entire coast. Now it is in full decay showing only an occasional trace of ancient murals with here and there ruins of the houses, streets and walls which surrounded it. But at the time the coastal tribes flourished, Pachacamac bore so great a fame that even the Incas when they conquered the coast dared not change it nor the observance of its rituals. So Pachacamac was adopted into their pantheon of gods.

We walked the sand-bound streets between the moldering walls of the buildings which had housed the priests who attended this great oracle, trying to imagine the life of that era. The site was not germane to our study of the Inca roads. Yet because the road did skirt the old shrine and the Riddells were anxious to poke their archaeological noses into this famous place, we stopped briefly in this Inca town to which the Spaniards had sent their emissaries immediately after the Inca was captured and held for ransom. They had arrived, twenty steel-clad conquistadores, on January 30, 1533, to claim and take away ransom monies in Inca gold to the sum of ninety thousand pesos — the equivalent of two hundred thousand dollars. "And the Lord of Pachacamac and the principal men came out to receive them."

On the road south into the desert, we passed through several fertile valley spots which in recent times had been so thoroughly cultivated that all evidence of the ancient past had been erased. Turning westward toward the mountains which rose up like dry bones, we eased our trucks over the sand until we came to the little village of Asia. This too had been an ancient stop on the coastal road. Now the little wattle-and-daub houses surrounded by gardens which had been painstakingly cared for in the midst of this terrible dryness had little to suggest that it had once been a famous Inca *tambo*. We found a small square, a few stores, an ocean of sand and many naked children as serious as gnomes, but nothing else to indicate that the Inca road had "marched along with a wall on each side." But as we were leaving, we encountered an old man and his mule who offered to show us where the old road had been. Seated on the fender of our Power Wagon, he guided us out of the oasis. He was an odd sight, this man, half as old as time, as from his perch he guided us through the desert wadis, while his sad-eyed mule ran behind us loudly braying his fear that we were carrying his master off. And so we came to the edge of the ancient pathway, and there our old friend, happily clutching a bottle of rum and the few empty cans he begged for his wife, rode off toward the village.

The sun sank leaving a vast glory of fiery hanging clouds behind it. A sharp breeze came up with the night, strong enough to blow away such insect pests as had survived the day, and we moved the trucks into a holllow square, set up the awnings and prepared our camp.

Night on the desert has a quality all its own. During the day when the desert is a furnace, a breeze, if there is one, brings only increased discomfort. But with the coming of night, the cool breeze comes up from the Pacific, there are no insects to inflict their torment and luckily in the center of the desert there are no hungry dogs to be driven away from the food. With the distant western sky still reddened with the last of the sunset, we sat about talking of our next week's program. Lawrence had started the tape recorder and in the clear night, emptied of sound, we listened to Mozart's "Eine Kleine Nachtmusik."

What we hoped to find in this low-lying area was a continuous stretch of road and a succession of wayside *tambos*. We did not believe that we could find such a station in a pristine state, since constant gravedigging over the years had left nothing in an unrifled state. In the mountains we had had little success in finding such a road and its stations. But here on the coast such a chance did exist, for the coastal Inca road, like the salients of the caravans of the Middle East, moved toward water; and the passes with their halting stops were determined by nearness to water while the inequality of the distances between the *tambos* was conditioned by the location of each oasis.

Just how had the Incas after the conquest absorbed the superior coastal cultures into their empire? What part of the people they conquered had remained? And who among them built the coastal road? The evidence lay buried in the structures of those dead cities now overwhelmed by sand. Only their graves and skeletal remains would reveal these clues and these bones would have to be fleshed, breathed into and given life. Since, as I had said, the story of a pre-literate people is determined largely by their artifacts and the changes in these artifacts, we would find careful stratigraphical ex-cavation a necessity. But first to find that continuing road . . .

The days went by. We traveled in sand, we slept in sand, we ate sand. Yet we were finding, in our constant coursing of the desert to the south, that the coastal plain was not wholly sand. Although the immediate shore is a great sand strip and the prevailing offshore wind has, over the years, formed dunes as high as two thousand feet, there is also a pampas of hard grayish soil filled with bits of harsh gravel near where the foothills come to the desert's edge. On his the early Peruvians built their road. Where the ancient highway was not covered by sand drifts, we were able to follow the walls and so came in time to the valley of Cañete, one hundred miles outh of Lima, at a point where the valley spreads like a fan out of he narrow canyons of its upper reaches. Here the vegetation starts abruptly; first the desert, then a green valley made fertile by life-giving water from complex irrigation ditches. Much as the coast people lived centuries ago, the valley people live now and their houses, woven of reeds and indifferently roofed, are placed on the edge of the desert to enable them to utilize every available fertile strip of land.

We were greeted courteously as we entered by a pleasant-faced woman of copper brown with marked Negroid features, surrounded by several naked children who peeked at us in open-eyed curiosity as they clung to her widespreading cotton skirts. Life on the coast is casual and easy. As it is never cold, the need for clothing is negligible. Fish can be had from the sea and that opiate the coca leaf, which the mountain Indian chews to numb hunger and existence, is not used here. The yearly crops of corn, squash, beans and peppers are plentiful, and if one is fortunate enough to own and irrigate a small piece of loam land in the sand, it can be made to yield an annual crop of cotton. Here on the coast we found the people much more approachable than those we had met in the interior.

The valley, now in spring's full tide, was planted chiefly with cotton but later after the cotton harvest, the fields would be planted with corn and beans. Although modern irrigation methods have made the valley much larger than it was originally, the ancient Peruvians in their time had thoroughly mastered the art of irrigation. And it *is* an art. A canal system demands careful design, for the working level of the water determined by hydrographic conditions must be so regulated that it will flow down only a slight incline. If too fast, the water will erode the mud banks; if too gradual, the canal will be choked with weeds and the sluices and the embankments will need constant repair. As we drove along, we saw irrigation channels laid along the edges of mountain escarpment where it seemed scarcely possible that water could be conveyed.

At the spot where the canyon wall of the valley met that of the river we saw the way by which the Incas had entered the valley. To our right was the river and along it ran the modern vehicular road. To our left was an aqueduct, and forty feet above it, built into the natural rock, was the Inca road. Superbly engineered and curving with the canyon wall, it connected the Royal Road of the Andes with the coastal road. In many of the larger valleys, too, we found these lateral roads always built against canyon walls high above the river.

For the first time the Riddells were actually seeing one of these ancient roads, and though Dorothy had spent months on the research for this trip and knew the history and the location of the roads even better than we did, the reality was a constant source of wonder to her.

Fifteen miles inland on the road we found the ruins of Inca-Huasi, once the largest Inca settlement on the coast. It stood on the sloping dry hills where the twisting river cut through the valley; a marked contrast with the surrounding desolation, its site covered at least five square miles. There were the usual houses of the Virgins of the Sun perched high on the hills so as to be beyond reach of the soldiers. There was a complex of habitat-buildings with large columns and a gigantic storage center five hundred feet square with two hundred and forty-eight cubicles arranged with the precision of beehive cells, with drying yards and guardian chambers as part of the storage system. What had evidently been the residence of the chieftains was adjacent to an enormous formal plaza six hundred feet long and shaped like a keystone with an altar in its center.

In the middle of the fifteenth century the Incas began their massive conquest of the southern coast and so the roads were extended down from the mountains. Some of the lesser valleys yielded after a short struggle but not so this valley. Chuquimancu, chieftain of the Chanca Confederation, in order to block the Inca advance from the south, threw up a stout defense which prevented the Topa Inca from coming into the lower fertile plains. The war lengthened into four years and the Indians who survived it were still talking about it when the Spaniards arrived: "It was," they said, "a protracted war and though the Inca King himself retired to the mountains during the summer on account of the heat, his troops continued the fighting." It was due to the length of this siege that the Inca built Huasi, a city conceived on so elaborate a scale that it was called "New Cuzco."

It took us some time in our continuing southward journey to cross the Pampa de Jaguay. Once more we traveled over an interval of desolation which separated valley from valley, isolating one from the other, forming them into individualized cultures. The desert was empty except for the path of the road with its standard gauge of twenty-four feet and a stone balustrade two feet high running straight across the sand-void. For us this was more than a road. It was an imperishable illustration of the stubbornness of Man, who in ages past "refused to accept his milieu as fixed and so began to oppose rather than endure."

During the day the Expedition members traveled separately. Silvia and I pushed ahead in the smaller car, feeling out the road, stopping frequently to measure it, while behind us the Riddells made their observations and Lawrence, the untiring Lawrence, went out ahead to photograph our progress across the waste. Each night we met again, arranged our trucks in a hollow square and did our small jobs. The sand filtered into everything. Each night the cameras had to be cleaned and a close check was made on gasoline and water, for we were now on severe rations. So we were as delighted as a pilgrim seeing the towers of Mecca when we came to the wide green valley of the Chinchas. Like the others, it was planted with cotton, the principal crop — which today is as important as it was under the ancient rulers.

This was the land of the ancient tribe of Chinchas whose traces through the valley we had seen in the many pyramids. Near the Hacienda de Laran, a very old holding, we found ourselves on a high-walled road which because of its twelve-foot mud wall we knew to be pre-Inca. This might well have been built by the Chinchas, as a dividing line between the holdings of one tribal chieftain and another. Between double mud walls, our road ran a distance of ten miles from the sea to the mountains.

These ancient Chinchas, warriors so formidable that "all of the neighboring valleys sought friendship and alliance with them, considering it a great honor and advantage," roamed far and wide into the mountains, conquering many of the people they encountered. Then, returning to their coastal paradise loaded down with spoils, they "gave themselves up to their pleasures and amusements with many women . . ." Not much is known of the Chinchas, except that after a stubborn resistance they, like all the rest, were rolled over by the Incaic juggernaut. As usual the conquerors followed their well-known policy of allowing their captives their own rulers and their own customs but insisting upon the worship of the Sun as the official religion. One of the last tribal lords was still alive when Don Pedro journeyed down this same road in 1548: "He related much about the wars of conquest of the Incas. For an Indian, he was a man of ability and good understanding."

Beyond the walls of the road we were now traveling, adobe-block pyramids honeycombed the fertile land, rising up gray and strange out of green fields to dominate the valley. The irrigation ditches now encircle them, while at their base the growing cotton spreads out like a green carpet. After we had spent a good part of two days climbing around on these massive mud structures, we came to the conclusion that they must have always had cultivated land at

213

their base and that these had been shrines or agricultural *huacas* belonging to a period which regarded the cultivation of the lands holy, and so the rituals connected with it were embodied in the pyramid shrine.

Propitiatory shrines are found among many distinct cultures, for there was widespread belief that the aid of the supernatural forces was necessary for prosperity. In Mesopotamia, farmers built structures very like these, and the Tigris Delta is spotted with shrines where the first fruits of harvest were stored. The gigantic tier-stepped Pachacamac near Lima is a *huaca*, as is the stone-built pyramid in Mexico at Teotihuacan. In the New World such structures are representative of the "most persuasive, primitive, fundamental and enduring religious idea," a combination of enchantment, magic and holy place, "a primordial synthesis" which reaches into every sphere of an Indian's life.

Shortly after we left the Chinchas valley, Silvia noticed that the road for some time had been curving to the east. And now on our way to the next valley we stopped to examine the compass and found the road was east-southeast and by more than 15 degrees off a straight course. We were by now accustomed to the "directional straightness" of the Inca highway; this deviation from the straight line puzzled us. In front of us was the Pisco valley and, beyond, the thin ribbon of green from the mountain foothills to the sea was a solid wall of sand with immense dunes as high as one thousand feet. Through my binoculars I could see the wind blowing up the sand like seaspray. We had our answer — to avoid an impassable waste land of sand, the Inca had laid his road to the east.

Tambo Colorado, a few miles up the Pisco River, was like a painted caravan stop. Even though we had seen it from the air, we were amazed to find this ancient site so well preserved. The modern dirt highway that followed the winding valley river had burst through its thick adobe walls into the now familiar triangular plaza whose architecture left us in no doubt about its origin. The rectangular, precision-shaped adobe blocks laid in thick walls and plastered over with mud and the niche, always the hallmark of the Incas, were prevalent throughout.

Tambo Colorado, the "Colored Tambo," takes its name from the reds, greens and whites painted in wide undulating strips still to be seen on its walls. On the southern side of the plaza, limited by the banks of the river, were quarters which, because the rooms are larger and built of cruder style, might well have been barracks for the troops; on the northern side of the plaza was a spacious opening, a wide entrance leading into an open area suggesting a corral or a meer used for the llamas. About this lay a complex of rooms. Here the window openings had a stepped pattern which, out of key with the less ornate features of Inca architecture, suggested that the conquered coastal masons might have added a local touch. Mural decorations are still found on top of the parapets, a frieze of adobe runs about the top, and some of the rooms are so well preserved that they need only be roofed. I know of no other site, save Machu Picchu, where Inca architecture can be so profitably studied. We found also the remains of a stone Inca ritual bath with a stone conduit running into it. This, however, was not the royal *tampu*. That was a little below at a site whose original name was Cangallo, while Tambo Colorado with its connecting fortresses was actually a check point effectively blocking the canyon, and the principal route to the mountain Royal Road toward Vilcas-Huaman.

Here the valley road, the radial artery of the road system, hugged the north bank of the canyon walls and though varying between three and six feet, was wide enough for soldiers, llamas and litter bearers. Fifty miles farther along the valley the road climbed eight thousand feet to Huaytara.

As for the southern route of the road itself, I know with certainty that it had passed here and that the river had been crossed near Tambo Colorado by a balsa pontoon bridge. During our air survey, when our plane had circled the southern side of the slender valley and flown over its bald mountains, I had seen the road very clearly as it came out of the pass near Tambo Colorado and went on southward across the fierce windswept desert in the direction of the next oasis ahead.

Once we had regained the Pan American Highway we understood why the Incas had chosen to go back up the valley in order to go around and avoid the fierce Pisco Desert. It was afternoon and the wind blew like a hurricane sending white sand whipping across the modern asphalt road and through the truck windows. In the corner a small mound gathered, grain upon grain, as if it were an hourglass telling the time. No man unprotected could have endured such exposure for long. Every afternoon this wind, known as the paraca, the exact opposite of the sirocco with its sensual languor, blows in from the sea.

It was blowing now and continued to do so as we limped the forty miles into the oasis of Ica.

XIII

The Marked Desert

IT WAS the season of the grape when we arrived in Ica. Along the sand-bound paths shaded by strangler fig trees little boys rode the chines of their burros, balancing wicker baskets filled to overflowing with white grapes. Ica was giving itself over to a grape orgy and there was scarcely a soul who was not involved in some fashion and the dusty roads looked as if Bacchus had passed. Munching happily at the coolly sweet grape, they were all hurrying the fruit from the vineyards to the presses, for the season for pressing was short.

In the smaller wickerwork houses off the sand road were the ancient wine presses made from the twisted trunks of the guarango tree, a desert-growing mimosa. The vineyards date back almost to Ica's founding and the region's special pride has long been its brandy known as "Pisco."

A charming oasis forty miles from the sea, Ica is bounded on three sides by desert and on the fourth by the towering foothills of the Andes. In the city itself, the streets are shaded by fig trees and the buildings facing the plaza are modern. The finest cotton is grown here and, like everything that grows — the riotous gardens of flowers, the figs, grapes, the small produce farms — it is watered by irrigation ditches and artesian wells. A river which is not a river flows through Ica one week out of the year. For the other fifty-one weeks, children and burros romp on the dry riverbed.

In the nature of things, Ica would seem the most unlikely place to live. Precisely when Man arrived in this valley we yet do not know but indications are that his presence goes back as far as 2000 B.C. Centuries ago this valley oasis was the home of what is now spoken of as the "Ica-Nasca culture" and within this desert-strip one hundred and fifty miles long, lying between the Pisco and Nasca (modern Nazca) Valleys, are some of the most fascinating unsolved mysteries of Peru. Ica, or Villa de Valverde de Ica, to give it its sonorous ancient name, lies at the center of these mysteries and directly on the path of the Inca road.

Here, in a vine-sheltered house close to a cotton gin, we established our coastal headquarters. Our need for such a place was great, for it was high time that we stopped to tabulate the findings of our explorations. My notes were now piled high. Every characteristic road feature that we had seen had its individual report. The techniques of road engineering and geography of each region were to be indexed, and the data compared, before we should have the overall picture of the Inca highway; photographs taken as sort of a pictorial notebook had to be developed, and prints attached to each sheet; dispatches and reports months in arrears had to be written; Silvia's collection of costumes and textiles had to be listed, prepared and made safe against the expected onslaught of insects. In a military sense, then, we were eager to "consolidate our position."

In a section of an old building once a repair station for a wood-burning locomotive which ran from inland Ica to Pisco, its coastal port, Lawrence (who was soon to discover that he shared his quarters with termites) set up his film laboratory. For over a year he had filmed blindly, unable to see what he had taken, and although he made repeated tests on his cameras, he never really knew how much of what he had filmed was being recorded. He spent his nights thereafter surrounded by and peering at literally miles of printed film footage. The Riddells, preparing for their special dig, took the whole yard in which to spread out the specialized tools they would use on the ruins designated for detailed excavation.

There hovered over all of us an air of expectancy. The pressure remained, yet for the first time it was a leisurely pressure. In the Andes, we had seemed always to be engaged in a struggle — against the cold, the food scarcity, the terrible roads with destruction yawning ahead at every turn. We never really relaxed — it was tension from the first ray of sun until its last. On the coast there was none of this. One could drive along the desert without having to concentrate on every foot of the road, and its beauty could be seen and absorbed. Silvia and I had leisure to tour the old Spanish estates which had been set over ancient ruins. Sand and irrigation ditches were the dominating motifs. Here again all that grew depended on the water supply; a foot beyond the area watered by an aqueduct, the world was lifeless. Narrow and meandering sandroads were, in effect, causeways that moved between sunken gardens fed by an intricate system of canals controlled by sluicegates. Woven-reed dwellings were half hidden under masses of climbing grapes, while less fortunate small villages were exposed to the broiling sun. The larger estates, rambling and imposing with their tall windows barred with wrought-iron window guards, stood in the cool shelter offered by the groves of fig trees.

Somewhere hereabouts, in this immense latifundium of private holdings, we were sure was the original site of prehispanic Ica, that place mentioned by Pedro Cieza, where "the Incas ordered palaces and other buildings built in the valley." All that we had so far discovered of old Ica or Tacaráca was a sandy waste and the scattered remains of small pyramids. It was essential that we find the original Ica, for we had again lost the Inca road. Yet we knew, from the records, that Ica had been an important place on the road.

Once again, as we had done in the case of Huánuco in the Andes, we turned to the National Archives in Lima where, in ordered piles gathering dust and termites, is an almost complete account of the history of Peru dating back to its founding in 1533. Every piece of land taken from the Indians and given to a deserving Spaniard is marked by recorded legal transactions; the purchase of a house or a slave, a contract, a lawsuit — all these have been duly attested by a notary. Somehow, though threatened by civil wars, earthquakes, pirates, termites and fire, all, or almost all, of these records have been preserved. Fortunately our good genie, Don Felipe Marquez, for thirty years the caretaker of these holographs, knew where the documents we sought were, or at least should be. While we searched the desert, he searched the National Archives. Would he find in those early documents a description of the original Ica? And if so, where did it lie?

In time we acquired a single but important bit of information. A Spaniard named Juan de Barrios had been given the Ica Valley in fief in 1534, during the height of the Spanish conquest. At that time "Xapana, Chieftain of the Yungas in the land called Ica, turned over thirteen hundred Indian vassals to this new Spanish lord and the valley was split into two sections — Hanan [upper] and Urin, called Ica." The records show how the lands originally given to Juan de Barrios filtered down to his widow; how she, badly pressed for money, sold the land. They told of Indians, disputes, jailing, lawsuits. Gradually out of these papers we were able to form a picture of colonial Ica and the story of the extinction of the Indians, and through them we found the exact location of old Ica.

The bright red Piper Cub plane with its United States Army insignia arrived on time and, flying low over our headquarters, it swooped down to attract our attention before heading for the air-

ield. The Expedition was fortunate at this time in receiving aid
where it was most needed — air reconnaissance — and the Inter-
American Geodetic Survey of the Corps of Engineers of the United
States Army, co-operating with the Peruvian Government in the
preparation of an accurate ground map of all of Peru, had graciously consented to give us the occasional use of their plane.

I found Captain Henry Leighton servicing his small plane when
we arrived at the sand-bound airport. Once a paratrooper and a
career Army man, Leighton had been attached to the Army Engineers, was commissioned on the field of battle in Korea, and in
time was transferred to the United States Army Engineers Air
Corps and sent to Peru. The history of the road and the paradox of
a primitive people who had developed a highway system which
eclipsed in its length and engineering those of other highly civilized
nations had greatly intrigued Leighton. Once he joined in the
search, he became one of the ablest of our collaborators. That the
view from the air could not be omniscient, Leighton and I agreed
as we set off to explore the roads by plane. Yet it would give us,
who were by necessity landbound, a different perspective and so
save us much valuable time.

This was a day of an extraordinary air luminosity — making the
bulking sand dunes, the sky, and the blue sea with its fringe of
breakers plainly visible. Every abrasion in the desert was apparent,
and the straight line of the ancient roadbed, except when it was
completely erased, was clearly defined. In a moment, seemingly, we
were over the Bay of Paracas, fifty miles northwest of Ica. We
looked down at the extending peninsula shaped like a broken ax-
head jutting out into an agitated sea ruffled by the paraca.

Almost at once we saw the gigantic symbol of Tres Cruces.
Etched into the inclining sandhill on the cliffs of the bay, it stood
out clearly and enigmatically, six hundred and two feet high. A
naturalist would say that the strange device looked like a giant

candelabra cactus: an archaeologist would recognize it as the "tree of life" symbol, which appears with amazing frequency in Peruvian designs; while to a religionist interested in anthropomorphic explanations for every natural phenomena, this impressive design is the Three Crosses.

Leighton, who held the plane directly above it, shouted over the howl of the wind that the symbol seemed to point directly north-south and that it oddly resembled the elaborate north symbol on a compass. Made by Indians who scooped out the sand to a depth of four feet, "Tres Cruces" lies against the slanting face of a cliff pitched at a sixty-degree angle, and faces the Bay of Paracas. Over the years the action of the salt-laden sea has hardened the sand, and this, in turn, the wind action has constantly blown in and out of the deeply eroded ditch which is, so we were told, upwards of two thousand years old.

What purpose did this symbol serve? Why did it face the sea and why directly north-south? Was it to guide seaborne balsa rafts to this, the richest bay in sea fauna in all the area, or was it for some other purpose?

Over and back of this inclining cliff toward which Leighton directed the plane was the colored sandhill of Cerro Colorado. There, in deep stone-lined caverns, four hundred and twenty-seven mummy bundles were found by a Peruvian archaeologist — which, when freed from their swathing clothes, yielded the most startling fantastic weavings ever found in all the Americas. The mummified bodies topped by false heads had been dressed at burial in simple tunics, and then clothed with embroidered mantles, ponchos, shirts and turbans, all decorated with multicolored embroidery. Even as we now glided over the sand with our small plane casting a shadow like the outstretched pinions of a condor, we could see a macabre scattering of human bones left behind by the grave robbers who had ravished the dehydrated dead of their rich robes.

The Marked Desert

Not much is known of the people of this necropolis. Had they come from Pisco, Ica or Nasca? The elaborately stylized designs were characteristic of the Nasca Valley peoples, but where then had been the production center from which such embroidered mantles had come? There are no remains of their dwellings, only evidence that they lived temporarily on the Bay of Paracas, subsisting on fish and seaweed while they prepared their dead. In what way is the Tree of Life symbol etched into the sand related to them? Was it a guide to those who brought the dead from the sea?

The amazing similarity between the mummification of the ancient Peruvian dead and the Egyptians shows clearly that similar environments will nurture similar cultural patterns. For both cultures, death was an exact replica of life and the continuance of life after death depended on the well-being of the corpse. The dead were believed to carry off the living to comfort their loneliness and therefore, being hostile to the living, they had to be propitiated; and the things of their lives — food, animals, servants, even wives — had to be buried with them. So were the dead appeased. Occasionally they were revisited, as in the case of the caverns of Paracas, where archaeological evidence shows that the mummies were frequently disinterred and perhaps redressed in those gorgeous embroidered mantles.

Had the Incas, knowing of these people, run a lateral road to the Bay of Paracas? Were the rich caverns of the Paracas dead known to them? If so, the desert beaten by the fierce offshore paraca wind gave little evidence.

Suddenly Leighton shouted: "Look! Is that a road down there?" Looking down, I saw that the plane was flying above a parallel line in the desert. We went down until when the plane leveled off, we were little more than two hundred feet above it. There was no doubt that it was a road. "A people," wrote a Frenchman, "is like a

223

man. When he has disappeared, nothing is left of him unless he has taken the precaution to leave his imprint on the stones of the road." Was this an "imprint," this road that moved directly between the necropolis of Cerro Colorado southeast toward the valley of Ica, fifty miles distant? We were now flying directly over the road. We could even make out the ruins of some sort of small buildings by the roadside. In our travels we had seen thousands of miles of ancient roads, Inca and pre-Inca, and by this time I knew the salient features. Leighton cleverly flew his plane so that the shadow of the wings overlapped the road, and having the exact measurement of the wingspread, we estimated that the road was not much more than twelve feet wide. This was *not* Inca construction. What, then, was it? Had this been the road over which the people, at some time in the first century, carried their dead for burial in the desiccating sands about the Bay of Paracas? If this *was* the pre-Inca Paracas road, it would definitely tie these people of mystery to those widely spaced valleys of Pisco, Ica and Nasca.

The road continued. It climbed a hill marked on my map as Cerro Burros Muertos, "Mountain of the Dead Mules," then grew faint in the ubiquitous sand and, within ten miles of the green oasis of the Valley of Ica, it disappeared completely. Days later we sought it on the ground but we never again found the mysterious road that led toward the caverns of Paracas.

At high noon, with the plane pitching in the hot air of the desert like a small boat in an upwelling sea, we were again flying directly over the Inca road. Now, south of Ica, we saw below us the utter desolation of the desert-pampas of Hualluri. The grayish-white wastelands had nothing of life except an occasional writhing mark where water, thousands of years ago in some curious reversal of Peru's arid nature, had coursed down from the mountains. Across this, moving in a southeast direction at precisely 165 degrees, the Inca coastal road moved along with not a variation of a degree. We surmised that the water marks had been there long before the road was laid down.

How had I known where to look for the road? Leighton asked this as we flew over the newly found road. I explained how experience had shown us that, while the Inca highway was not always unalterably straight, it *did* have what was called a directional straightness. In other words, it always ran in a straight line between two given cities or way stops. Four centuries of intense civilization had obliterated the road here in the Valley of Ica, but by our searching of the early documents we had managed to locate the original site of the Inca city. We also knew that the next stop on the road south of Ica had been the place called by the Spaniards La Venta or La Ventilla — which meant the Little Roadside Inn. This had been a small stop, midway between Ica and a wide expanse of desert. Also the next stop on the road mentioned in the old chronicles was "Huayuri," or *"Huayuri pueblo tambo rreal,"* as the sixteenth century Poma de Ayála described it. That this had been a *tampu* on the missing road was confirmed by yet another chronicler who noted: "Fourteen leagues [fifty miles] south of Ica is the Huayuri Valley small and sandy." These localities we had found on the Peruvian military maps which we used, so, by drawing a straight line on the map between La Venta and Huayuri, and then taking our bearings, we had determined that the road we were now flying over was the Inca road.

"Well, I'll be damned!" Leighton's astonished voice came back to me over the intercom when I finished my explanation.

Now the Inca road and the Pan American Highway ran along parallel to each other for some miles, but when the modern highway bore due east so as to take a gradient over a mountain ahead, the Inca road kept going straight on. It was a wonderful thing to see, more wonderful from the air than it would have been had we been crawling along the stifling desert sand. Death must have often walked that highway. "Up to the Huayuri Valley is all sandy desert," wrote a padre who had traveled over it by mule, "and the Indians usually start out in the evening to cross during the night, for the great heat during the day is apt to kill many of the animals and one has to be a very good driver or expert in the following of the route or take a guide for it often happens that people get lost in these sandy wastes . . ."

We traced the road to a thin line of green and a cluster of modern buildings that stood just above it. Where the escarpments of the mountain range began were the ruins of what had been the *tampu* of Huayuri. Just ahead of us loomed jagged mountains, towering four thousand feet high, looking as if a piece of kraft paper had been taken and crumbled up, and in these we looked for the pass the road might have taken.

Suddenly I tapped Leighton's shoulder and pointed. We both gazed in excited wonder. Below us, a lifeless city of sizable houses with stone walls and small chambered divisions lay in a hidden valley a mile or more distant to the oasis. There were at least five hundred such houses, clustered about the dry valley, along with the remains of formal plazas and hills terraced as if crops had grown there; and on the mountaintops were still more buildings. Even from this height I surmised — and I later confirmed by excavation — that we were looking down on *the only known intact city of the Ica-Nasca cultures*, whose people had preceded the Inca on this coast.

How had any people lived in this wilderness of desolation so dry that it would not even support cactus or lichens in the bare rock? By the number of houses, a thousand or more people must once have lived here. Where had the water been drawn from and where in this barren height had been the soil to grow their crops?

The Marked Desert

We found the pass which must, in a later time, also have been used as an Inca route through the mountains. Then in a matter of minutes our plane had passed over the mountainous upthrust, and without prelude we burst upon a vividly green valley. I had just located the ruins of what certainly was the ancient halting station on the road, when Leighton spoke excitedly over the headphones: "Ahead, on that flat pampa, look at the lines . . ."

Below us stretching out in all directions on the flat gray plain of flint rock was a vast network of drawn lines. A series of rectangles as wide as airfields and long straight lines — some originating from a single complex, others from no source at all — went off in every variant of the compass to fade away at the end into nothing. There were lines, triangles, circles of all sizes appearing at frequent intervals.

As we looked down fascinated at the bewildering maze spread beneath us, we realized that we were looking at yet another of the great mysteries of the southern Peruvian deserts, this time at the so-called "Lines of Nasca."

Unknown until recently and not easily seen from the ground, it was not until airlines began to fly over this route that they were first noticed. There are several theories concerning their origin, all contradictory. One — the popular one — was that they led to buried Nasca treasures, another that they had to do with the riddle of the mummies of the Bay of Paracas. But when the lines were traced and measured by Fraulein Maria Reiche, who has made a searching study of the phenomena, it was found that they led neither to treasures, nor to mummies nor to forgotten cities. Instead, the theory gradually being substantiated is that they are connected with ancient magico-calendaric ceremonies, and were the handiwork of the people of the Nasca cultures.

Somewhere between A.D. 500–900, an Andean people of the Tiahuanaco Empire, which centered about Lake Titicaca, invaded the coastal areas as the Incas were to do hundreds of years later and greatly influenced the cultures of the Nasca peoples by their interest in astrology, including the development of a solar calendar and the determining of the solstices. It is said that one of the Tiahuanacan chieftains "who lived in continual melancholy, without anyone seeing him laugh in all his reign . . . called a great assembly of his wise men and astrologers . . . and they studied the solstices with care." They also perfected a shadow clock "by which they knew which days were long and which were short and when the sun went to and returned from the tropics." It is not altogether impossible that this sort of interest in the heavens was transplanted to the desert coastal people who for some unknown purpose laid out the mysterious "Lines of Nasca."

But it was not until Leighton brought his bright red Piper down to an altitude of five hundred feet that we first saw the animal designs, those amazing traceries which could not be distinguished from high altitudes. They were so extraordinary a sight that I began then and there to write my next dispatch to the *New York Times:*

PRE-INCAS WERE FIRST IN MODERNIST ART

Gigantic Drawings They Made of Animals in Peru
Discovered from Plane

Ingenio, Nasca Valley, Peru, March 24, 1954 — We followed the pre-historic Inca road over the Nasca Valley, and it led us to a modern art exhibit.

The figures we saw from our plane etched in the valley's *pampa colorado* could have been the tortured drawings of a Salvador Dali. But they were as much as 500 feet in length and the "canvas" of the ancients was the desert's coarse sand. Moreover the drawings were upward of 1,500 years old.

The mysterious lines in the Nasca Valley have puzzled everyone — especially the archaeologists, who offer no precise explanation. . . . There are also gigantic figures of animals, birds and insects along with abstract figures of geometrical pattern.

Over the communications system Captain Leighton asked me if I had ever seen anything like it. It suggested to me America's Ohio Valley and Southwest.

For an hour above the desert we attended this ancient-modern art show. We counted more than fourteen gigantic drawings. There was one immense figure, at least 200 feet long, of a whale drawn in extreme naturalism. A harpoon went through its eye.

Long roads of varying widths radiated in all directions about it. Then we came across a bird (was it an eagle or a humming-bird?) more than 500 feet long. With wings spread, it seemed to be diving.

Near it were other figures — abstractions, symmetrical and geometrical patterns. Then, farther on, "Spider" came the word over the microphone. There was no doubt about it; eight legs (one of which became a road); the rounded body; it had been drawn with boldness and simplicity.

It was a weird afternoon, flying around drawings which primitives had etched into the desert many hundreds of years ago, which they themselves never fully saw. . . . How could they have? The lines, yes, for they move along for miles; but the animals' figures — no. Only by hovering at 1000 feet directly above them could they be seen clearly.

Then what purpose did they serve, and what are they? Whatever they are — and one woman, Fraulein Maria Reiche, has given five years of her time tracing them out without coming to any definitive conclusions — they are part of the gigantic series of mysteries of the Nasca Desert.

Yet these lines and figures must have meant little to Inca conquerors. They, who had ruled the straight line into Peruvian thought, paying no more attention to these symbols than they would to a flight of birds had laid their twenty-four-foot wide coastal road right through the lines and the figures.

*   *   *

Days later the Expedition drove on toward the ruins of Acari in the valley of the same name on the southern coast. The Riddells and I had made a careful study of the aerial pictures showing sections of the Inca road as it entered the site of Acari and emerged again to crawl over immensely high sand dunes to the next valley. My aerial reconnaissance has shown that there were at least four Inca halting stations in succession, all of which had been mentioned by early Spanish chroniclers, and that they were joined by the highway which was plainly visible at many sections. The Power Wagon was packed to overflowing with what the Riddells needed for their proposed stay in the desert — tents and generator, food and gasoline, water drums and camping equipment. Fritz Riddell, an accomplished archaeological-draughtsman, stowed away all the technical equipment he would need to map their search into the past, while Dorothy, who was also a specialist in pottery and pottery techniques, arranged all the paraphernalia necessary for a thorough study of the lives of those who had peopled an Inca *tampu*.

So down we went to the south, following the Inca road through the first valleys of La Nasca, whose gemlike strips of green were sandwiched between the desolate dry hills. We passed through groves of guarangos. An early priestly wayfarer wrote of those groves of trees, "On the Nasca road there are five leagues of these woods, so thick that the Inca's highway is the only way to get through them, and one sees nothing but trees and the sky . . ."

After we had traveled two hundred and fifty miles, through alternating deserts and narrow valleys, in the course of which we located and identified every successive halting station on the coastal southern road,[1] and still following the Inca road with its rock-wall

[1] The first, just outside of Ica, was La Venta, now a hacienda; the next, twenty-seven miles across the desert, was Huayuri, a hacienda with ruins of the ancient *tampu* above its modern houses. Over the mountains we found the ruins of Chillo; and at the edge of the third Valley of Nasca at Ingenio, the Sugar Mill, a large and formal *tampu* and administrative

balustrade and smooth even surface, we came at last to the high Cerros of Chocovento. Below this in a narrow valley held by high walls of white sand was Acari.

On the dry desert edge of the irrigated land of Acari, herds of cattle whose ribs were as plainly visible as the keys of a xylophone stood about a pool of noisome water looking thin and hungry. The mules which we had passed in large herds seemed contrariwise to thrive on the meager rim of land, their bodies were sleek and shiny. A handful of men, standing by their mounts, watched the mating of a pair of mules with much ribaldry.

An elderly man mounted on a roan stallion volunteered to lead us to the ruins we had sighted off on the descending road directly in line with Acari. We drove along asking many questions of our guide which he answered with a soft Negro labial which we could not quite place, but his face was that of a full-blooded Negro. As our trucks, in grinding low gear tried to stay with the slow pace of the cantering horse, his specious tales seasoned with old saws of Inca gold, mysterious subterranean chambers, and underground roads, gave us some pleasant entertainment. Arrived at the great mounds of raped stone with the fallen adobes, he raised his hat with simple dignity, wished us a happy sojourn among the ghosts of the past and rode off, leaving us to follow the Inca road into the formal plaza.

Acari had been well chosen for its position. It stood on a high bluff overlooking the river with below it the town, the valley and

---

center which was anciently called Tambo de Collao. Fifteen miles south of this station was the principal Valley of Nasca and on the south bank of the river were the gigantic remains of the formal Inca city now called Paredones, "but then known as Cassamarca." It was not only a station on the coastal road, but was also used as a supply point on the much-used lateral road which connected the coastal highway with the Royal Road of the Andes.

the river, and beyond this the high-rising dunes with the Inca road still visible zigzagging up the sand to the other valley. All around the town, the land was in cultivation and the people, now as then, were growing cotton, corn, beans, squash, tomatoes and peppers in much the same place and manner as they had done centuries ago.

The Riddells selected the highest pyramid upon which to put their camp. The constant wind from the sea eighteen miles away would blow away the mosquitoes and in addition they had a fine panorama of the ruins below. The whole day was used to set up their headquarters. Curious villagers of a variety of skin hues gave us a willing hand and soon the tent and equipment were rolled into place and water procured in barrels from the river. Although most of the buildings were in ruins, the Riddells were eager to begin putting their puzzle together. The ruined buildings, the ancient kitchen middens, the shards of broken ceramics that littered the ground above and below the surface would provide them with the necessary pieces but they would have to work with speed, for even as they established themselves, men were pulling down the ruins to obtain the adobe. Amazing as it may seem, after five hundred years the rectangular sun-dried bricks were still in such perfect condition that townspeople found it easier to take them from the ruins than to make new adobe blocks.

Peru has little protection for its ancient structures and the time is not too far distant when nothing will be left of ancient man above the ground. The good padre Vasquez de Espinosa, who came from Spain to the village of Acari in 1618 and whose writings we now consulted regularly, would not recognize Acari today, so complete is its destruction. "Acari," he wrote then, "is a village of one hundred Indians and forty Spaniards who live here together."

A Carmelite traveling on the Bishop's business, Vasquez, like our other friends of the road, kept a journal. He had visited Ecuador and Mexico and in 1617 arrived in Peru where he set off, sometimes walking, sometimes riding an outsized mule, along the way of the Inca. It might be said of this journal — which has only recently been published — that it gives details of the last audible breath of the Inca. Wayfaring along this same sand-bound road we were now traveling, he came into Acari and there he found "many curious buildings of the ancients and they should always remain the same because it never rains. . . ." The good padre had forgotten about Man the Destroyer.

This one sentence of Vasquez de Espinosa's was all that the Riddells had of Acari's history. The rest they would have to find in the things of the graves.

As we climbed the hill to continue our southward journey, the Riddells raised the blue ensign of the American Geographical Society. We looked back to see the motto U B I Q U E spread out on the breeze.

X I V

Chala: the Fourth Quarter

THE GREAT ROAD of the Incas passed through all these valleys," wrote Cieza during a rare moment's pause in his flight from the furnace heat of the desert, "and in some parts of the desert, signs may be seen to indicate the road that should be taken."

That, however, was in the time of the Incas. Now there is no such thing as a sign and we had to find the remains of the road as best we could by careful inquiry and search. The term "coastal road" here is only a relative term, for the Inca road, in order to avoid the terrifying desert, had been built inland and over the mountains. From Acari it passed over a 3000-foot mountain of sand and rock called Cerro de Mendoza after the Conqueror of Acari, one Pedro de Mendoza. Across the Mountain of Mendoza, the road after fifteen miles drops down into the Jaqui valley. A more frightful desolation we had never seen. Canyons were slashed by dry river-beds like the wadis of Africa, and sand dunes 3000 feet high were so dazzling in the sun that we could not look at them with the naked eye.

It was simple animal economy that made the Inca engineers put their road inland. The coast here at the Desert of Tanaca has a perpetual wind which blows so fiercely that the sand dunes form and disappear almost as one watches. For fifteen miles the sand builds up in monstrous waves and back as far as ten miles from the sea at the foothills, the dunes climb up to peaks of three thousand feet. No living thing can withstand this desert. Even the modern road is eternally besieged by sand and a work crew is kept on duty night and day to keep it open.

A few miles south of Acari between the modern Pan American Highway and the sea, a distance roughly three miles, we saw how the intervening land in a series of ancient agricultural terraces descended as by a flight of giant steps to the sea.

We had come to the "Hills of Atiquipa," the only place in the entire two thousand, five hundred miles of coast where plants grow without irrigation and where it rains with seasonal regularity. It was well known to the early Spaniard that "at the very end of the valley by the sea rise the Atiquipa lomas where there is good grazing, the best in the kingdom."

On looking back, we could see the agricultural terraces continuing for miles southward between the modern road and the sea. We passed herds of fine-looking cattle and, at the Hacienda Parcoy where, in the midst of incredible squalor, people were flaying a still half-living sheep, we inquired the way to the ancient stronghold we had sighted on the highest hill.

The "hill" turned out to be a mountain 4720 feet high, but the heated climb to the ruins of Cahua Marca was counterbalanced in measure — a small miracle — by the fact that the hills were actually shaded by trees.

Why does the rain fall here at this pin-point on the map and nowhere else on the entire coast of Chile and Peru? Silvia asked our guide this question and he smiled toothlessly as he answered that it was because it rained only in God's domain — which was a good enough answer for one whose religion is his only pastime. Above that he did not know. But he did say that rains came from the direction of the mountain from August to October, and from the sea

during January and February. What was there about these hills o
Atiquipa that made them the one exception to the fact that it neve
rains on this two thousand mile long coast? The answer seems to li
in the fact that the entire coast is bathed by a cool 58° ocean cur
rent which, beginning in the Antarctic and owing its origin chiefl
to the prevailing westerly winds and the meteorological whirl o
the eastern South Pacific, moves in a stream one hundred and fift
miles wide for a distance of three thousand miles. The cold curren
lowers the temperature of the air that moves across it, and since it
capacity for heat exceeds the air, rain never falls, or almost neve
Yet at the Atiquipa lomas — as one can see from the trees, the gras
and the long stretches of agricultural terraces — it rains throug
every season. Whatever the reason, the Incas took full advantag
of it.

Cahua Marca itself covered the rounded top of the mountair
Here the houses were strung in orderly fashion along the narro
streets and there was a formal plaza with a ruined Sun Temple an
dwellings with gable roofs and those typical Inca trapezoid
niches. The buildings, although crude and rustic, were much th
same as those at Machu Picchu — with rounded storage bins, un
derground water wells and outside of the city proper, a larg
rounded burial *chullpa*, a catacomb of femurs and skulls. Sti
known by its original name, Cahua Marca [View Town] is only
little less than 5000 feet above sea level and is the highest point o
the entire three hundred mile coastal road south of Lima. From th
vantage spot, fire signals and smoke signals could have been see
for many miles in every direction. To complete the strategic pic
ture, I could see the Inca road plainly through my binoculars as
passed through the canyons, climbed the eroded hills of El Ataj
and moved toward us. Silvia and I stood on the edge of the ruin
Below was the desert of the Arenal de Tanaca where nothing th

ived could have endured the day, but here on the height the breeze
was bracing and, when the sun was obscured, actually cold. For
what purpose then had Cahua Marca served?

"Why not as a reconditioning center for the llamas?" asked
Silvia.

And why not? It was a question which if answered might explain
the existence of this stone-built city. We knew that llamas were
extensively used for coastal traffic from the evidence of the mummified llamas decorated with such "dated" trappings as the scarlet
fringe that Indians hung over their eyes to keep out the sun glare
and from the use of the llama as decorative motifs on ceramics
which pre-date the Incas by a thousand years.

The llama is the most stylized, the most preposterous animal in
Nature's book. It has a camel's head and large eyes, a split nose, a
hare lip, two-toed feet which look cloven but are not. Its usual gait
is as leisurely as that of a *grande dame* entering a salon, but it can
also leap like a deer and, when stampeded, will run as fast as a
train — an Andean train. Along with the camel, to which it is related, the llama has an amazing history. As the camel was used on
the ancient Chinese Silk Roads as a beast of burden, so the llama
was used on the Inca roads.

The earliest ancestor of the llama and the camel belonged to a
primitive proto-cameloid stock of North America, fossils of which
are found only in North America. Yet where the camel was a
rarity in the deserts of Africa until the fifth century, by that time
the llama was well established in Peru as an animal inured to the
heights as well as the desert. Wherever the Indian moved, there
the llama went. Beyond the confines of the Inca realm, it did not go.

To the native, the llama offers a means of transportation, for although weighing only three hundred pounds, it can carry as much
as one hundred and twenty-five pounds for a distance of six to ten

miles a day. In addition, its wool is made into blankets, the coarse hair into *charqui,* the equivalent of our western "jerky"; *taqui,* its dung, is used for fuel; and, if legend be credited, there has been and still is a zoöphilous relation between llama and man.

Although the llama never equals the camel's weight of a full ton nor its ability to carry fifteen hundred pounds, it has the same tenacity to withstand the diversity of climate extremes. The llama can live above the perpetual snow line and it will also live, although it will not reproduce, in Peru's desert. And that they once were very common on the coast we know from the llama bones found in Indian graves. When young, they make delightful pets — charming, inquisitive and affectionate; and, when traveling in a herd, their necks moving with each step, their hindquarters all rising as if on a single note, there is a contrapuntal balance of tension that ties them together as in a fugue. That they suffered horribly in the desert heat, where their thick wool and their inability to sweat frequently turned a desert trip into a death march, there is evidence enough. In the furnace-hot valley of Jaqui just over the ridge on which we were sitting, hundreds of mummified llamas had been found dead for want of fresh fodder and breath with which to combat the hot wind.

So Cahua Marca, with its high altitude, its invigorating cold and its grass, was doubtless, as Silvia observed, a reconditioning center for multitudes of pasturing llamas. Here their foot pads, worked to a quick from the journey across the empty way of the desert, could be restored and their bodies fattened. Even the character of the ruins made this seem probable. Although on the Inca road, Cahua Marca had neither the formal plaza nor the architectural polish of other administration centers. There were no elaborate Sun Temples, and such pottery as we found was utilitarian, the kind a woman uses in her cooking. The clothing suggested natives of a humble social order; the burials were communal; the number of storage chambers (out of proportion to the population) suggested that food was stored for wayfarers on the road or else for transport to the mountains; the dwellings were rustic and utilitarian in style and had doubtless been occupied by a people from the mountains who knew llama husbandry.

So here was another link in the pattern we searched for, one which indicated that in this oddly isolated city with its familiar agricultural terraces, we had traced the Inca civilization down from the heights to the coastal area.

Some miles ahead over the boulder-strewn land and hard upon the coast, we walked along a magnificent section of the road. The sea breeze of the Pacific less than a mile away cooled the day-heat and where a dry canyon slashed the plain, the road swept down to it in a magnificent flight of stone steps so well preserved that an Indian need only employ a broom to clean off five centuries of sanddrift. In a stretch of ten miles we found every engineering characteristic of the road — terraced walls, stone stairways, rock-fill to even the way, remains of *chasqui* stations, a tomb-shaped stone marker or *topo* of distance — all important features on the Inca road system.

One of the most fascinating aspects in any journey of exploration is the element of discovery involved. Not the accidental kind such as an ant employs when some instinct of formic memory causes it to plod tirelessly back and forth until, by sheer elimination of space, it stumbles across an object it is searching for. But discovery which has been arrived at by the use of such foreknowledge and experience as makes it probable that in a specific spot there is this or that to be found. Such revelation is the pabulum of an explorer. When all is said and done, what is archaeology but a tremendous mystery?

Given the scale — here the whole of South America — we had our plot: how had these people arrived; in what, where and when and who eliminated whom? We had the exposition: the styles of pottery, architecture, utensils, figures on the desert, gold-spangled mummies. And for stage setting: the scenery — the overwhelming Andes, the jungles, the desert coast, the strange radiating lines in the desert and giant symbols carved into sides of sand-cliffs. And last, we had suspense . . .

Such was the pattern of our thinking as we stood looking out across the Acari valley. On the other side of the canyon, the road turned a well-engineered curve of forty-five degrees and moved due east up the dry canyon. We were by now too well acquainted with Inca psychology not to know that when they built other than on a straight line it was for good purpose. Ahead of us and a mile or so back from the highway, lying close to a crescent-shape beach, we saw a large cluster of buildings, evidently the ruins of fishing village, with interesting low-roofed structures which appeared to be storage chambers.

Here then were *our* clues — Cahua Marca where llamas were reconditioned, miles of agricultural terraces, a magnificently made road, a fishing village with large storage chambers, and the deviating road turning due east toward the Andes. All this was no accident, not "just there." As Dr. Raoul Porras Barranachea, Peru's eminent historian of the Spanish conquest, had stated it: "Why did Francisco Pizarro when he was trying to establish the vague outlines of his kingdom in Peru and was warring with his partner in rapine, Almagro the Blinkard, push his claim beyond the official line set at Chincha and want to include a place to the south known vaguely as Vilcaroca?"

Chala: the Fourth Quarter

Where was this mysterious region? For that matter, where did the Inca get his fresh fish from the sea in two days' time? Where in all Peru was the most direct route to Cuzco from the sea? "Silvia," I remember saying with mock heroics. "Hear this! I think this is the missing section of the 'world' — the Cuntu-suyu road, the one that leads from Cuzco to the sea."

At the end of the ravine we came to the ruins of the ancient fishing village. Here were the stone dwellings with their gabled roofs of the same type as those which crowned the heights of Cahua-Marca and the underground bottle-shaped storage bins, ten or more feet deep. Apart from the main village was a structure two hundred feet long, proportionately wide, with high walls and a formal entrance, the remains of what must have been a guardhouse; and within, sixteen enormous storage chambers intact with stone roofs. It was the only complete structure we had found in all Peru. In the shadow of these ruins I wrote a report to the Riddells urging them to consider Chala their next project once they had finished with the *tampu* of Acari. Even then I did not realize its full importance.

The next day Captain Leighton's bright red plane made an essay of the emergency landing field at Chala. Swooping down close enough to whisk away the remaining hairs from my head, he turned about and came in for a landing. From the airfield we could see to the south the three mile beach and the modern town of Chala, looking like an early American frontier village. To the north was the thin line of the descending Inca road and, on the bluff, the remains of what had been the *tampu* of the Imperial coastal highway.

I was elected to make the flight since I was to photograph out of the cockpit and the plane could only carry one passenger. Leighton was briefed, I climbed into the parachute harness, and we were up and gone. We located the ravine, and after I had photographed the ruins and the road, I saw again the trace of the turn-off. Leighton, like a blood-hound having been given a scent, was off. As we mounted, I explained what we had found and how we had found it.

Our course set northeast, we followed the dry canyon, and there was the road! Within five minutes we were flying over altitudes of five thousand feet and the road and the landscape were gray and desolate. Within fifteen minutes from the coast the hills were green and small farms began to appear and the ancient road had disappeared. But over the vacant *puna*, still flying due northeast toward Cuzco, we picked it up again. Then we were over Lake Parinacochas, round and not much more than ten miles in diameter. Around it were small farms and at its eastern edge rose Mt. Sarasara, its serrated cone encrusted with snow. Oddly the shores looked black with people until we swooped down and the people turned into hundreds of flamingos. It is from these beautiful birds that the lake takes its name — *Parina* [flamingo] *cocha* [lake]. At the northwest corner we saw the ruins of Inca structures, agricultural terraces curved to the natural contours of the hills, some of them still being used. Then we saw the road leading out from the ruins in the direction of Cuzco one hundred and seventy miles away.

"Why not follow the road to Cuzco?" I shouted.

In answer Leighton pointed to the gasoline gauge. Dangerously low, the high altitudes were rapidly emptying the reserve tank and the last I saw of the Cuntu-suyu road was when we banked to clear a flock of high flying flamingos. But I was satisfied that we had found the missing quarter that made up the Inca Empire and the great road which had traversed one of the four quarters — the Cuntu-suyu. Another piece of the puzzle had fallen into place.

A half hour later the motor coughed, spluttered and died with a sharp report just as our wings cleared the last western peak of the ndes. Ahead was the blue sea and the line of the exploding surf. It as no longer necessary to talk over the intercommunication phone. t was as quiet as eternity save for the hiss of the air as the plane ent into its glide. Leighton, calm as Buddha and as casual as if he ere reading the compass bearings of the map, gave me instructions:

"Tighten your parachute harness. I will try and glide in for a nding. If anything happens I'll go out to sea. Don't inflate your fe jacket until you hit the water. And don't forget to pull the ripord."

And that was all.

Briefly we disputed the air passage with two condors who, like urselves, were Pacific-bound, and when they found a wind current, Leighton followed them slightly upward. There was the emergency strip on the high bluff we had left three hours before and here was Silvia standing beside the trucks. There was one long moment more when I thought we would surely hit into a canyon, but Leighton skillfully avoided it and set us down on the Chala airfield. Our search, I felt, was becoming unpleasantly hazardous.

That night, with a water keg as my table and sharing my gasoline lamp with the insects, I wrote my dispatch for the *New York Times:*

INCAS' SIDE ROAD IS FOUND IN PERU

*Von Hagens Discover Lateral by Which Kings' Sea Food
Was Carried to Cuzco*

Chala, Peru, June 19, 1954 — We found today a fifteen-mile stretch of Inca road as wonderfully engineered as anything the Romans ever built. The same day, after a long search, my wife Silvia and I located the lateral road that led to Cuzco, the Inca capital — the road over which the Inca King received daily shipments of fish fresh from the sea.

Along the coast, we have followed and explored the high-

way from Lima for more than 500 miles, finding all the cities
through which the route once ran. We have left a team of archaeologists to examine four of these ancient settlements. Now
we pushed farther south to seek positive confirmation of the
evidence of the Incas — how they lived and their amazing engineering skills.

The Inca realm which was at its height in 1500 A.D. was held
together by its system of roads. Between the final decline of
Rome and the rise of Napoleon, who revised the Roman roads,
these Inca highways were the finest communication system de-
vised by man anywhere.

There were two main highways . . . the mountain road,
which began in what is now Columbia, then ran through Ecuador, Peru and Bolivia and split to reach into modern-day Argentina and Chile, a total distance of 2,700 miles; and, second,
the coastal highway which began at Tumbes, Peru, at 3 degrees
south latitude near the Ecuador line and traversed the entire
desert coast for 2400 miles to the Maule River in Chile, 35 degrees south.

Supplementing the two main roads was an intricate system
of secondary routes — the laterals that connected the two
main trunks at various parts of the empire. These are some of
the most spectacular thoroughfares; they climb the valleys
from the arid coastal desert to the snow-filled heights of the
Andes.

In our study they are important because they were the route
of the Incas' conquest and show us the extremes in the techniques of Inca engineering. We had plotted and followed most
of these important laterals. We had found all the important
laterals but one — the road that was said to have led directly
from the coast to the Inca capital of Cuzco. The Inca Kings
were said to have had fresh fish delivered daily to them from
the sea. If that was true, it must have come over the shortest
route from the coast.

When we found a turn-off from the main road and followed
it due east, we were certain that this was the road coming from
the sea — the Cuntu-suyu quarter moved directly to Cuzco.

Chala: the Fourth Quarter

Our exploration by land, a laborious one, was finally complemented by an aerial survey and we followed the road until it disappeared beyond Lake Parinacochas, 11,000 feet in altitude, and saw the road making its way toward Cuzco.

Many weeks later, when Silvia and I returned from following the Inca road south all the way to the border of Chile, we found the Riddells already deep in excavation at the ruins of the ancient fishing village at Quebrada de la Vaca on the sea coast of Chala. Over their tent as we approached the AGS flag still flapped, its now faded blue field giving some index of the time they had spent under Acari's menacing sun. About the tent and under the canvas, neatly labeled boxes filled with skeletal material they had gathered during this stay — pieces of cotton, textiles, rolls of mummy wrappings, bits of bone instruments, copper and bronze tools, fragments of quipas, and box upon box of scrubbed and labeled potsherds. No calendar was needed to tell us of the flight of time. We had only to look at Fritz Riddell's beard, now a luxuriant blond growth the same color as his hair, and generously coated with the dust of the centuries. Fritz, who presented a slight almost boyish appearance, was primarily a "dirt archaeologist." He had worked among the Indians of his native California, excavated in Alaska, and had dug up ancient villages of the prehistoric Tlingits. After several years of service as a marine in the Pacific, he returned to his work in the Southwest. His training in a field known for the paucity of its material, where the ground has to be searched expertly for every clue, fitted him for this work in Peru, where there were hundreds of different clue-bearing artifacts. We were to find that his conclusions concerning the Peruvian Indians' way of life gave us an excellent and well-rounded ethnographic picture of the people themselves.

Here on the coast the Riddells had been alone except for the reg
ular visits of Lawrence, who dropped in on them with fresh fis
and briefly photographed what had been done in the interval o
when Leighton had made a parachute drop of supplies and mai
Now and again local fishermen from the village of Chala had com
to the cove to search for molluscs or make a harvest of the seawee
that clung to the rocks. For company they had often had a red fox
drawn by the smell of their garbage and at last so tame that h
would sit and watch Fritz Riddell excavating the mummies. Con
dors paid them hopeful daily visits and frequently sea birds, dyin
of some strange malady, fluttered down to die in the camp. Once
moribund pelican, weak and clumsy, staggered into camp to fa
helplessly on its side. Dorothy propped it up with rocks and trie
in vain to feed it, but within an hour it died and the condor's danc
of death began. The detailed maps they had made of Acari, the nea
pile of reports on the findings with their careful analysis of the ru
ins and the scaled charts of the structures, showed how much the
had accomplished. These weeks too had given them the "feel" o
the climate — its mist-cold, the winds, the torrid heat, the ever
lasting dryness — which had forged the Indian way of life. So, in
sense, through them the dead became the living.

And what had they learned of Acari, that "buried city" on th
ancient road? To what culture or cultures had it belonged? Tha
the Inca had built their village city on top of an older village of th
Nascas, they had determined by their study of the architecture an
by comparing the potsherds they had found in the various layers o
Acari's history. The stylistic changes seen in the design, firing, mod
eling of the ceramics had much to say. The Riddells' first projec
had been a thorough analysis of this pottery in terms of its associa
tion with the architecture in order to establish a typology of the
artifacts. In so doing, they had learned that several cultures ha
had a part in the making of Acari.

Chala: the Fourth Quarter

The Nascas, that shadowy people whose identity was revealed by pottery of polychromic colors adorned with stylistic representations of birds, animals, trophy heads and elaborate stylized anthropormorphic monsters, had been in control of the Acari region from about 800 A.D. until the arrival of the Incas. In about 1450 A.D. Inca road-planners, marking the oasis villages where the Ica-Nasca tribesmen still lived, had laid down their road so as to connect the different valleys. Leveling the earlier Nasca buildings, they erected a formal administration center complete with pyramids, sun temples and a plaza with a north-south orientation. Into this they ran their road. The rooms of their buildings were large. Ancient wood stumps pointed to the fact that the rooms had been roofed and thatched with straw while building materials had come from close at hand — river cobbles set in clay mortar and covered with plaster painted white and yellow and the adobe which they used extensively. The *tampu* itself had numerous storage chambers, low-walled cubicles of loose stone construction known as *pirca* which are usually connected with house compounds. The repetitive use of these storage chambers indicated, so the Riddells had concluded, a construction used only at such places as had been halting stops on the Inca road.

The people who had lived in Acari and other coastal valleys wore tunics fashioned much like those of the Andean dweller, only theirs were more cotton than wool. Their agriculture was, as it is still today, the cultivation of corn, beans, squash and peppers. This basic food supply the native Peruvian supplemented with fourteen species of wild succulent roots, forty-two types of fish, twenty-one different forms of edible animals and at least forty varieties of game bird.

Still earlier the coastal civilization had been influenced by the Tihuanacu culture. That during this period there had been considerable trade with the jungles, the Riddells had discovered in their examination of the tell-tale artifacts — the jaguar, puma, parrot and monkey were common motifs on their pottery, and the iron-hard *chonta* wood, used for spindle whorls and combs, was only obtainable in the jungles. However, even after the Inca conquest early in the fifteenth century, the people of Acari had kept their own way of life and their pottery and textiles retained their traditional patterns. Also they spoke their own language although they were forced to learn Quechua, the tongue of the conquerors. Yet they became a part of the whole, and under Inca administrators and engineers they built the road along the coast and on it, the *tampu*-city of Acari.

Here the architecture, according to the study made by Fritz Riddell, showed clearly that the work on both road and city had been done under expert supervision and with a single unified plan and a pattern which pointed up the difference between the helter-skelter formless Nasca city and the purposeful compact Inca city which took its place. The latter, functional and utilitarian, was a fine example of the striking accuracy of Inca planning and attention to the details of arrangement. All that we had previously surmised about the over-all pattern of the Inca road, the careful planning that went into the road system, and the organization of the *tampus* was confirmed in these archaeological details the Riddells had found at Acari.

The Incas did not, of course, create these coastal cultures. They arrived too late for that and actually the aesthetics of their art was often inferior to those of the people they conquered. The Incas were organizers and their road became the connecting link which joined these competitive valleys skirting the thousand miles of Peru's desert. Local wars were stopped, the interchange of cultures began commerce and the well-being that trade causes brought a broader and a better organized life to the coastal tribes.

Proof of all this the Riddells found in the graves they examined and in the ruins of the kitchen middens. Engraved gourds, bits of dishes, pottery, spindle whorls, yarn, cordage, slings, nets and bags, beads and ornaments, fragments of figurines, stone and bone knives, pins, needles, awls for working leather and wood, weaving implements and carding combs, club heads and combs of chonta wood — from such as these the Riddells had drawn their conclusions regarding a lost way of life in ancient Acari, a caravan stop on the long Inca coastal road.

In order to determine whether Chala, as we suspected, was located on the road to Cuzco, the Riddells had made a survey of the radial road and had found where it broke off from the main coastal highway and where it ran up to the Parcoy Canyon. So, although there were indications that this had been only a small village, they had estimated that there had been at least two hundred and seventy underground stone storage chambers having a capacity from two to ten cubic meters. Only a fraction of this number would have been needed to maintain the village. One of these storage chambers, a walled structure two hundred feet long, Fritz had mapped in detail. In these the food obviously destined for Cuzco or for official use had been stored.

For food the people along the coast had fish and dry molluscs, along with corn, hot peppers and seaweed. The dry corn, boiled in lime juice, was made into a sort of hominy called *mote* to which peppers were added to give it flavor, and molluscs were boiled with the seaweed. These dehydrates and the fish were ample for a people of such limited tastes. The needs of the people were simple and the Inca had perfect genius for keeping them that way. Much of the year the climate was agreeably cool and pleasant and there were apparently few disease-carrying insects. From their examination of the mummy skulls, the Riddells found that tooth infections were the common affliction, with even the children suffering from diseased teeth as was shown by the traces of numerous cavities and abscesses in the jaw structures. Yet on the whole, their teeth were well preserved.

From their studies of the skeletal remains they fleshed the bones in this wise: they concluded that these Indians were of medium size, robust and broad-headed, with prominent "Roman" noses typical of the mountain Indians of present day Peru and with protruding chins which caused facial prognathis or a sort of lantern-jaw appearance. The hair, straight and black, was worn in various hairstyles — pigtails for the men, while the women wore braids intertwined with colored wool fringe wound very strikingly in back of the head with decorative ribbons. The men wore a breech clout and a *chusma*, "a kind of sleeveless waistcoat made by taking a fold of square cloth, sewing up the edge, leaving gaps for arms, and cutting a slit for the head in the fold." Both men and women wore the *chumpi* stomach band, an elaborately woven cummerbund, and leather sandals. The women wore a loose-shaped tunic called *anaco* reaching the toes and a sort of shawl which served a dual purpose as protection against the cold and baby carrier. Motifs in the textiles were different for men and for women, so much so that the sex of the skeletons could be determined merely by looking at the peculiar textiles that enveloped them. All of the dead found here were similar, suggesting that a homogeneous people had lived in the fishing village. Infant mortality seemingly was high; many a child had died of an ailment which had attacked the bone — the Riddells thought it might have been congenital syphilis. So well had they catalogued the motifs of the weavings in the mummies that they could tell from the burial textiles whether the little skeleton belonged to a boy or girl child. As everywhere in the world, the mortality among male children was higher than among the females.

In one of the more elaborate burial chambers the Riddells had found what they took to be the remains of the chieftains, judging from the quality of the textiles and the fact that the *quipus*, those string knots with which they kept records, had been buried with them. The architecture of the village also pointed to the fact that the formal house patterns facing the bay were the living quarters of an important caste. In the decimal classification of the empire by which all were ruled, such a village as this would have been run by a chieftain named to rule over five hundred people. But this had been the terminus of the Cuntu-suyu section, "one quarter of empire," and a direct route to Cuzco, so therefore an even greater chieftain would have been in command.

It was now abundantly clear from a study of the whole region that the three sites we had studied — Acari, Cahua Marca and Chala, all located within a twenty-mile stretch of boulder-strewn pampas — were related culturally and functionally. Here then the Inca road, important as the turn-off to Cuzco, had been particularly well constructed. The road-marker which we had noticed as we came in proved to be, when examined by the Riddells, a well-cut stone nicely fitted into a prepared base. It stood in the road just before the Cuzco-radial began, marking for the couriers the point at which they were to turn toward Cuzco.

However, Chala's *tampu* was another mile further along the road, on a high bluff overlooking the sea and the long beach. There a still larger site had played a different part in the life of this region. This the Riddells surmised from the skeletons of the people found there. Whereas here at the fishing village the people were homogeneous, at the site of the *tampu* at Chala they found all manner of skulls — flattened heads, long heads, "string heads" or those which had been artificially flattened, skulls which were elongated and deformed mingled with undeformed broad heads — which would seem to indicate that this *tampu* had been a mingling place of *all* tribes which used the Inca road.

These conclusions the Riddells stated with considerable caution, offering them as the dry bones of speculation. As Dorothy said, "this is the sort of information that is available in such a region and it is astonishingly complete, partly because of the unusual preservation of the evidence and partly because of the ethnographic historians and the Spanish chroniclers."

Time was nagging at our footsteps but the Riddells still had much to do and so would remain in Chala for some time. As for the rest of us, we were now ready for our northern journey. At our Ica headquarters Lawrence had finished the documentary film on the Riddells' archaeological work and was ready to go on with us along the Inca road from Lima northward to its end at Tumbes.

Dorothy and Fritz walked down with us over the connecting Inca road to the main Inca axial highway where our vehicle stood. We said our good-bys and then watched them turn back to their camp. They were a dedicated couple, re-creators of the dead. In their work with the complicated techniques of recording, reconstructing and classifying was the romance of treasure hunting; but in the slow process of mending the broken pots, the study and classification of the bones and the concentrated study of their findings, much of the patina of romance was of necessity rubbed off. Yet they had so given life to a long-dead people that as we stood on the road we seemed to see about us the hosts of those who had once traveled this highway and over this rock-dwarfed spot the ghosts of ancient man moved once more.

X V

The Kingdom of the Moon

As soon as we were north of Lima we felt the influence of the Chimus. There was not, to be sure, any physical change in the desert except that the valleys were more populated. The aridity was just as overwhelming and the sterile desert was even more encompassing if that was possible. There was still the same desolate pampas between the enveloping sand and the foothills of the Andes and still on its surface the ubiquitous Inca road. We followed it in our fashion.

In our two trucks specially equipped for this terrain we went around the sand dunes that loom up high and "impassable" along the Bay of Ancón and followed the track of the road through the valley of Chancay, then onto the pampas itself. The technique we had developed over the past year and more of exploration had become almost mechanical. We knew the characteristics of the Inca road so well that now we needed only to plot our direction, seek out the region, find the road, mark down its features, make measurements to check its width and then — once again — forward.

Near to the sea we passed Huara where the first Spaniards to come this way had stopped on the 28th of January, 1532, "at a very large village near the sea . . . where we were well served by the Indians who supplied us with what was required . . ." And then again turning eastward from the sea we took to the stretch of desolation between valleys and once again three miles back from the sea came on the Inca highway coursing across the pampa Medio Mundo. As soon as the influence of water appeared, all trace of the highway disappeared. It was completely eclipsed at the modern coastal city of Barranca, vehicular traffic going directly over it, and all we could do there was make an historical notation of the road's existence. Further on, on a high bank close to the large river the Incas called the Huaman-mayu, the Falcon River, was the site of an Inca settlement known as *Tambo Viejo* (Old Way Station). During the heavy rains in the sierra the river, practically uncontrollable, caused the Inca engineers considerable trouble. But at this one weak link in the coastal highway, they had managed to maintain a pontoon bridge made of reed boats across the river when it was comparatively dry. In full flood wayfarers "were conveyed across the river in balsa-boats, the horses swimming."

The further northward we journeyed, the more we felt the influence of the Kingdom of the Moon. Every crag, it seemed, on the grayish-brown verdureless hills was marked by a fortress with immense walls of adobe blocks, signifying that this was the territory of the ancient Chimor Kingdom.

The coastal highway had brought us to Paramonga in the Chimus' country. On one of the sandstone hills overlooking a river and the Pan American Highway which runs directly at its base was the remains of one of the great chain fortresses which the Chimu in their Kingdom of the Moon had erected to discourage any trespass by the Incas from the Kingdom of the Sun.

Even in its ruins, Paramonga is impressive. We passed under a massive gateway, once the formal entrance, and climbed the fallen stairway that led us into the fort through its only entrance. It was constructed much as a fortress in the Middle Ages would have been.

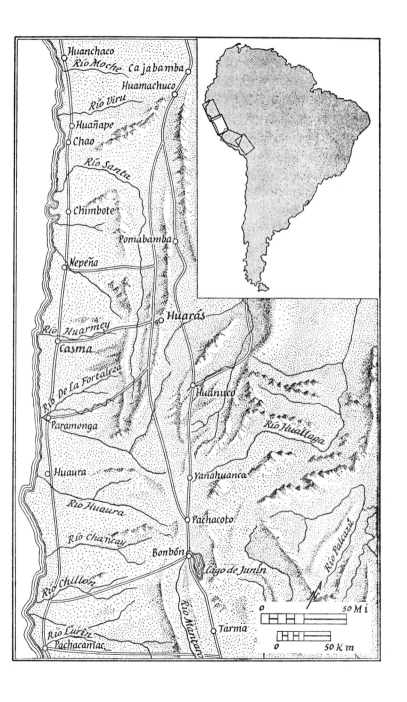

Huanchaco
Río Moche Cajabamba
Huamachuco
Río Virú
Huañape
Chao
Río Santa
Chimbote
Pomabamba
Nepeña
Huarás
Río Huarmey
Casma
Río De La Fortaleza
Huánuco
Río Huallaga
Paramonga
Huaura
Yanahuanca
Río Huaura
Pachacoto
Río Chancay
Bonbón
Lago de Junín
Río Chillón
Río Pacaza
Río Lurín
Pachacamac
Río Mantaro
Tarma

0   50 Mi

0   50 Km

In six tiers, with redoubts pushed out on the slope and salients to give the defenders the advantage of crossfire, Paramonga at any time would have been considered a powerful fortress. It marked the Maginot Line of the Kingdom of Chimor and a system of fortifications against attack by the Incas who since 1400 had sought to wrest from their resplendent rival the suzerainty of all the Perus. When it finally fell to the Inca legions, they merely incorporated the mighty fortress into their highway system, put their halt-station under its massive shadow and made it a key control point for the coastal way and a check point as well for the lateral road which connected with the highroad leading northeast up the valley to the white-peaked mountains of the Callejón de Huyalas. The walls of the Paramonga fortress, plastered with cement, still show the red pigment of frescos which were extant until the nineteenth century. Don Pedro, seeing them in 1548, wrote that the buildings were very handsome with "many wild beasts and birds painted on the walls which are now all in ruins . . . in these days the fortress only serves a witness to that which has been . . ."

Northward was country that has been described as "hollow and fainting" and destitute of beauty, and we hurried on through Huarmey, once a way-stop on the road and held, albeit briefly, by a Spaniard called Martin the Tongue. The land has not changed since he complained that he had been slipped a valueless thing, "a land full of dispeoplement." For a hundred miles we searched the sands and dry valley and found the road, but nothing else Inca. It seemed strange, after being so aware of the Argus-eyed Inca during the thousands of miles we had traveled, that now there were only these shadows of the once-powerful Moon Kingdom with its immense moldering mud-cast fortresses.

Such a fortress city was Casma in the next valley. Perhaps the Incas had no need to utilize the massive buildings they had taken along with the Chimus, their last opposition. For the Inca, master of three hundred and fifty thousand square miles of land and seven million people, it was essential that communications be kept open so that tribute could flow to the collecting stations, and that the road be always in good repair so that his legions could move without hindrance on the Sun's business.

Beyond this, in the Valley of Nepeña, we came upon the Inca road again and we camped that night close on to the little town of Huambacho, which formerly had been a night stop on the road. Like all coastal Inca villages, now as in 1548, "Huambacho . . . of which I shall say no more than that it resembles all the rest," stood on sterile ground while about it, watered by the constant river, was the richly cultivated valley.

Beyond that narrow verdant valley where a sea of sugar cane grew, once more the Inca highway continued northward. The road alone was Inca. The ruined cities were those of the rival Chimus while on every hill stood a ruined fortress and other barbarously beautiful remains of what the "Sun" had destroyed when it eclipsed the "Moon."

What better index of these Inca earth-conquerors and their passion for communication than to see the way this part of the road passed right through the protective walls? A towering wall had been raised to block a valley but the Incas had built their road right through it, tumbling down the ancient markers so as to reach the next valley without deviation.

Throughout all the long stretches of miles that we had passed between Nepeña and the desert of Chimbote, Lawrence had faithfully filmed the phases of the growth of Royal Road to Cuzco. Here where we found the best preserved section, we spent the whole of August 14 going back and forth over it for his cameras. The air was like a flame and there was not a tree nor bird-voice to lighten the burning air. All that suggested man had ever been this way was the seemingly always present road. These people, I thought, must have had a great capacity for sustained resolve and a stern, unrelaxing self-discipline. The Inca had said "Let there be a road" — and there was a road.

On we went northward through the desert of Chimbote where we were engulfed in a sand-storm. Later we climbed up the dunes to the Santa Valley where, past massive mud fortresses of the Chimu, past the cultivated strips of cotton, over railroads which had been laid on the passes marked out by the Inca, we followed the ancient road.

At midday on August 16, 1954, so my journal states, we went through the "Great Wall of Peru" and came to the last defense wall of the Kingdom of Chimor. The great wall, once towering to a height of eight feet and built of rough stone, began at the sea a few miles north of the bay of the Santa Valley and ran inland over the mountains for forty miles. At least, so thought Robert Shippee who discovered it in 1931 and followed it in air flight until it was lost in a tangle of masonry among the complex lower hills of the Andes. The wall which connected with a small fortress had evidently been a strong bastion of defense.

Next, in the Valley of Viru, we came to one of the oldest recorded and most systematically investigated valley-cultures in Peru. In 1944 a group of American archaeologists had pulled back the layer of history to find at the lowest level a people who lived in underground adobe-block houses and were without pottery — their date, 2500 B.C. Layer after layer of this record was examined to discover the past.

In 1000 B.C. a mountain culture known as the *Chavin* "introduced mirrors, finger-rings, carved stone . . . and corn." By the first century irrigation was being developed and the small Viru Valley two miles long, nine miles at its widest, extended its arable land. With increased population, it so attracted conquerors that in A.D. 800 a system of fortifications was erected on the dry hills. Then the valley was absorbed by the Mochicas, a people who knew how to govern, who came in from the north. For this culture the stratification showed fine pottery, gold casting, better textiles and, above the ground, impressive truncated temples, fortresses and walled roads. After A.D. 1000 came a new conquest, this time by a tribe coming out by Lake Titicaca. The shadowy figured Tiahuanacus brought with them their cult of the Weeping God, the Creator God who eternally weeps zoömorphic tears of condors, snakes and puma heads.

The Tiahuanacu conquered and rebuilt the fortresses and living compounds within the valley. Ceramics changed to fit the ideology of the Weeping God, with the dominant color black and most of the pottery mold-made. However, although the mountain people conquered, they did not know how to administrate the defeated, and after A.D. 1300 the desert land was reconquered by the Chimus. They, so archaeological evidence shows, spread their influence as far south as Lima and the valley of the Rimac and as far north as Ecuador and ruled until they were in turn defeated by the all-conquering Incas — who arrived in 1460 with all their heavy splendor and hideous litter of war and slavery. Utilitarian as ever, the Inca organizers did not even attempt to build onto forty-five hundred years of history. Instead they avoided the prebuilt sites and established their headquarters outside the Viru Valley on the pampas of Guanape where in 1549 there still were remains of the buildings and storehouses.

In the final analysis the Incas were civilizers, and so their practical engineers ran their Royal Road for twenty miles along the high land-bluff on the edge of the sea until it entered Chan-Chan, the capital city of the Kingdom of the Moon.

*   *   *

259

Worshipers of the Moon, the Chimus raised a city-state where it did not seem a city could be built — in the sterile desert hard upon the sward of the Moche Valley.

Slowly, with the years, the metropolis of Chan-Chan [1] took form. A city of pyramids, temples, house-compounds, streets, gardens and reservoirs, Chan-Chan in its day must have been the most populated city of the Americas. The immediate valley as well as the other valleys under Chimu dominance were extensively cultivated, and many irrigation canals brought water down from the mountains to channel it into reservoirs within the walls of Chan-Chan.

Everything here was large in scale. Their weaving, of exceptionally high quality, was a commonly practiced industry and there is evidence of widespread commerce hundreds of miles from their immediate realm. Ceramics, predominantly blackware pottery, were mass-produced in molds; golden ornaments were cast and hammered out by expert craftsmen. Within one of the ten great wall enclosures was an entire village of gold-workers where the dross of the melting ovens is still to be seen. The many golden Chimu ornaments — drinking cups, pendants, earplugs, necklaces and crowns — now in museums give an idea of the Arabian Nights unreality of this capital of the Chimu.

When the clash occurred in 1461 between the Sun (Inca) and the Moon (Chimu), it came, as war often does, unexpectedly. An Inca general on a raiding expedition in a sierra struck north at the tribal-state of Cajamarca — one hundred miles directly east of Chan-Chan — and in a short sharp conflict the raiding legions were victorious. Until that time, the Inca in Cuzco had not wished war with the Chimu, fearing their strength. But with the fall of

[1] I remain indebted to my friend Dr. John H. Rowe for considerable material for this chapter, adapted from his pamphlet, *The Kingdom of Chimor.* (*Acta Americana* Vol. VI, Nos. 1–2. 1948.)

Cajamarca, his massive armies began the siege of the Kingdom of Chimor.

An attempt made by the Chimu troops to relieve their mountain allies in Cajamarca had been beaten back with fearful losses. In turn the Incas' attempt to storm the Chimu defense positions had also ended in failure. Then a plan was made, the cleverness of which so charmed Indian folk singers who told of past events that for many years thereafter they sang of how "the Inca took into consideration the fact that the Chimus' valleys were irrigated by water and rivers from the highlands and that without it the Chimus could not get along; so that they sent many laborers accompanied by four thousand soldiers and in a few days they diverted the river of the Chimus into the sandy wastes which swallowed it entirely. They sent a messenger to the Grand Chimu saying that the Inca, the son of the Sun, had dominion over the waters and that he took them away and would keep them from the Chimu so long as they did not submit."

So the Inca conquered and thereafter the Kingdom of Chimor was ruled by the Sun instead of the Moon. And again, although the Chimus were forced to submit to Inca law, they were allowed their own customs and dress and local chieftains. Loot from Chan-Chan, the "richest ever," estimated at eight million dollars, was carried off, as was their lord Minchancaman, who was kept in honored exile in Cuzco. And from the conquered Chimu, possessors of a superior culture, the Inca learned. Town-planning, metal-working, mass production of textiles and tapestry — all became part of the Inca way of life, for the Incas with their capacity for conquering also knew how to assimilate different ideas and techniques. A Chimu colony was eventually established in Cuzco to teach these crafts. At the time of the Spanish conquest (which followed that of the Inca within fifty years) the traditions of the Chimu were still so much in evidence that a Spanish chronicler wrote: ". . . when the

King's Incas made themselves lords of these coast valleys they held the Chimu in great esteem and ordered large buildings and pleasure houses to be erected within the city walls. And the Royal Inca Road built with its walls was also made to pass through the valley.'"

We lingered on at Chan-Chan. Silvia, who had patiently endured the hardships of the road through the miles of sand, wished to stay longer at the ruins to sketch the few remaining wall arabesques, those last fragments of the rich decoration which once covered all the walls of Chan-Chan. Lawrence, as well, wanted to photograph it thoroughly, for it was obvious from the rapid pace of destruction that within a few brief years nothing would be left of it except mounds of amorphous mud.

Man and nature have combined to bring Chan-Chan to ruin. The coast that usually knows no rain is here subjected, by some twist of the meteorological dial, to a deluge of rain every thirty years. Since 1924 these rains have increased in violence and frequency so that most of the walls now resemble a piece of chocolate left in the noon-day sun. And of able assistance to this iconoclasm of Nature have been men in search of buried gold. Ever since a Spaniard in 1577 found two million dollars in gold in one of Chan-Chan's pyramids, treasure hunters have assiduously undermined its walls.

While the others worked in the ruins, I busied myself trying to find the route taken by the highway through the Moche valley into the ghost city of Chan-Chan and beyond, hoping I could discover how the Inca administrators had handled their highway when they brought it into a crowded city area. Would they have pushed it through Chan-Chan's high walls, tumbling them as they did in the desert when they came to the outer defense walls of the Kingdom of Chimor? Would it have been good policy to irritate the defeated by bringing a road through the heart of their city?

The Kingdom of the Moon

It has been suggested by historians that the Incas had done just that, and as proof they pointed to the numerous roads still seen to the north on a line with Chan-Chan. I was not of this school of thinking. There is something to be said for instinct, and instinct told me that we should look *without*, rather than within, these high walls, believing that the Inca engineers had tended to disregard the roads made by those they had conquered as not sufficiently utilitarian. Anything that slowed up such progress as could be made over their straight all-weather roads they regarded as a waste. The Incas measured distances by time — and while time is not precisely life and speed is not necessarily civilization, speed does cancel space, and the Incas had always to think about the time-space equation in this tortured landscape of desert and mountains.

So I turned to look without the walls. After some days of searching in the morass of grass-topped dunes between the old walls and the sea, I had found no trace of the road. There seemed no evidence of it — the sifting dunes and the long tufts of grass had usurped it.

We next tried an air view. Although the view from the air many times confounded the confusion, when an air survey was followed by an immediate ground examination the former had proven an invaluable aid. Fortunately in Chan-Chan there was an American aviator who operated a fleet of small dusting planes for one of the largest sugar-cane estates in the Chicama valley. And one day Frank Wellman dropped his yellow Cessna down on the airfield which lies immediately outside of Chan-Chan's walls. A curly-headed, one-eyed Californian, with a passion for hunting Chimu graves, he considered his Sundays well spent when, armed with his mine detector, a well-packed lunch and his family, he could scour the Peruvian earth for Chimu gold — one reason he was deeply interested in the route of the ancient roads. Knowing this, I had ventured to ask his assistance. He arrived on schedule.

"This shows the influence of Albrecht's clock at the hacienda," he said. "Over the face it reads *Hora tacit et labora*. I watched and labored and here I am."

That flight was well remembered. It was to be our last with Wellman. A few months later he went down in this very plane along with Silvia's cousins in the mountains just above the Inca road. It seemed to be our strange fate that, although we were exposed to physical dangers every day, we had escaped thus far while friends and family were struck down. Only recently we had been stunned to hear of the death of our friend Dr. Wendell Bennett who had guided the Expedition from the beginning and soon we were to have word of this latest tragic happening.

The Cessna had no sooner gained the air above the dry river canyon at Río Seco at the northern edge of Chan-Chan ruins than we saw four roads, and for five minutes we shifted excitedly from one side of the plane to the other, looking first at one, then the other. The larger road which we had already gone over was at least seventy-five feet in width and must therefore have been a Chimu processional road. We knew it was not Inca for they would have regarded such wide roads as a conspicuous waste of effort and land. The other three roads were more in keeping with the Incas' idea of road economy — each was narrow and bordered with walls. All disappeared from view in the windswept desert.

There was no great mystery about the appearance of so many roads. North of the Moche Valley is the valley of Chicama, the principal valley belonging to the Mochica's (A.D. 0–800) cultural predecessors on the coastal valley. But it was only after our plane had made its fourth sweep of the desert and we were again near the airport, which is located between the Río Seco and the first walls of Chan-Chan, that we saw what we hoped to see — the familiar parallel lines, the mark of the Royal Road. It was obvious why we had been unable to find it below. The airfield had been built directly on top of it! The line of the road was faint, yet we could see it going along the shore between Chan-Chan and the sea. So our instincts had not played us false. The Incas *had* kept, as we felt they would, their direct line of communication *outside* of Chan-Chan's walls. Now we could continue north on the Inca road.

Huanchaco, a village within sight of the ruins of Chan-Chan, lies close to the sea. In times past, large wood rafts sailed into this bay carrying tropical woods, gold, bird-feathers and chocolate from the north jungles. Anchored here and still used are small fishing fleets of *totora* reed balsa boats — made just as they appeared on pottery deposited in Chimu tombs. The natives call them *caballitos*, "little horses," of the sea.

Above the village of fragile houses made from the flattened withes of Guayaquil bamboo was the church of San José de Huanolaco, built directly over an Inca halting-place; and three hundred feet away from it on the desert was the Inca road. Like the other roads we had seen from the air, it too was soon lost in the sand.

This seemed to us as good a place as any to test the theory of the "directional straightness" of the Inca highway system. It is not true, as has sometimes been assumed, that the Incas always built their road in an undeviating line or that they always overcame physical obstacles rather than avoided them. Often in the coastal valleys where the road ran between a double array of hills, we had seen the road make a 45-degree angle rather than needlessly mount a hill. But because on the overall the road *was* constructed so that between two given points it would move in a straight line and acting on the assumption that variants always have to be built up against determinants, we began to lay down a theoretical line on the basis of what we knew.

On our Peruvian military maps, Lawrence plotted a direct line between the road on which we were standing and the next known Inca stop in the Chicama valley ahead. He drew a light pencil line over the intervening desert of Campana between these two points. The compass reading was 330 degrees north.

We started off in the early morning on a day hot enough to broil one's brains. In the vanguard, Silvia drove the jeep while I kept vigilance over the compass. I do not believe a vehicle had ever crossed this desert — none could unless it was, like ours, powered by double transmission. Even so the jeep had soon sunk to its hub-caps and we crawled forward at the pace of a mule's walk. It was as if we negotiated the sea. There was nothing to hold the eye, for the wind whipping up a whirlwind of sand had blotted out the 3000-foot mountain to the east, leaving us floating on an unlimited sea of sand.

The heat came as out of a blast furnace and sand, blown by the persistent gale of wind, cut like fragments of glass. Our calculations showed that we had approximately thirty miles of desert to pass through but even at our present speed of three miles an hour we felt that with luck we could reach the other valley by nightfall. But in a short time the jeep boiled over, and I crawled out in the high wind, pushing forward as a diver would walk on the floor of the sea. I could not open the hood of the motor, for it would have been sand-bound within moments. We could only wait for the Power Wagon. It was a long time in coming. Then we made it out, its fiery red clearly showing through the sand haze. It too was having trouble finding traction in the enveloping sand and, like the jeep, it was overheated.

So, while food was being prepared, I climbed on top of the jeep for a better vantage point and with my binoculars searched the sand. There was nothing to be seen in either direction. I wondered again if this desert had ever been traveled. Our map only confirmed the utter desolation of this region — there was nothing here to attract anyone. What if we stuck in the sand? What if the cars could not negotiate it? On foot one would have extreme difficulty getting out, and, even if help could be summoned, where was the vehicle that could cross this desert? I had grown so accustomed to our crossing the worst terrains that the thought of not being able to extricate ourselves from any situation had never occurred to me. But now . . .

Lawrence was still drinking coffee. I had long since stopped estimating how much coffee he drank but certainly it was more than the thirty cups that Balzac was supposed to have consumed daily. Silvia nursed a small cool drink with the last of the ice from the giant Thermos and the sand continued to blow in fine as blizzard snow. We discussed our prospects. For the moment, I felt it wiser to keep to myself the thought I had just had. Lawrence was only a little less certain of the ability of the trucks to withstand the heat than he was of the probability that we should find the road. At last Silvia came up with the suggestion that since we could not see anything anyway, why not wait and travel by moonlight? That indeed seemed sound advice. Surrounded by sand and desert, I felt the very opposite of that poor sheik who said: "The four wives I have are all ignorant and cause me much trouble. I want one with whom I can talk. If I can find the right one, I might be even willing to allow her to wear a hat."

Meanwhile we found that as we discussed our predicament the jeep had settled even deeper into the sand. The wheels threw up geysers of the stuff and the more I ran the motor, the deeper they sank. Lawrence finally managed to pull us out with the front winch of the Power Wagon, but then he was stuck. This was something else again for there was more than a ton of equipment in the trucks. In the fury of wind and sand, we emptied the truck and let the air out of the huge tires. Still it was not enough, so we fell to shoveling. For hours we dug at the rear wheels, hoping that in due course we might settle the tires on the hard pampas surface which lay somewhere down below the sand. As I alternately shoveled and wiped away the coursing perspiration mixed with grit, I fulminated against the Inca road — we would never be able to find it anyway in this benighted spot. Then, after digging out four feet of sand, we found that we had deposited the Power Wagon directly on the hardened surface of the road.

The night did not bring the moon. A veil of heavy mist settled about, so thick that our lights could not even penetrate it and the best that could be said of our night voyage was that it was cool and we were not forced to stop every half-hour to rest the motors. Although we kept to the 330-degree direction, we were soon well past the absolute maximum of time it should have taken us even at our slow pace to pass over the desert. More — we were exhausted. It was close to midnight and with the unchanging sand and mist acting as soporifics, even coffee could not keep us awake. Finally, with the firm conviction that we were utterly lost, we gave up, dragged out our sleeping sacks and, like seasick voyagers who are past caring whether they sink or float, we went to sleep.

In the morning the mist and wind were gone and the air was as if it had been rain-washed. With daylight came humiliation. We stood in the precise center of the Inca road! On either side were the remains of the high mud walls and in front of us was a tall, mud-black pyramid. This we climbed after we broke camp and before we set off again, and from the top we saw other pyramids such as the one on which we stood lying ahead in the sugar-cane fields. Unknowingly we had followed the road into the dead realm of ancient Mochica.

Today the Chicama Valley is the largest and most productive of all the coastal valleys and the site of the world's largest sugar hacienda. As we looked down we could see the faint impression of the ancient road running along through the canefield. In the course of hundreds of years of being traveled over, the ground had so hardened that even now crops did not grow well where the road once ran. Over the feathery gray plumes of sugar cane loomed the pyramid of El Ingenio, The Mill, where in 1540 the Spaniard Diego de Mora had planted the first sugar cane in Peru.

(The Mochica culture, the most advanced of the coastal region if not of all South America, was centuries ahead of all the others. Yet, overwhelmed about A.D. 800, the Mochicas were a memory long before the Incas even came into existence. However, while the Mochicas controlled the central coast area they built cities, and extensive irrigations works, as is evidenced at Ascope in the upper Chicama Valley, and road systems which in time were closely copied by the Inca. Although no Mochica house structures are extant, we know from their pottery that they were built with well worked-out floor plans, that they were constructed of adobe brick, and that the roofs were gabled with massive roof combs. That the Mochicas used mass labor is evident from the tremendous size of their pyramids. One mathematician has calculated that over thirteen million bricks were used in the construction of their great Pyramid of the Moon. Aside from these pyramids and the massive mud fortifications capping natural rock ridges, little is left of Mochica architecture. Yet few other civilizations have left so impressive a record of themselves.)

We lost the road again in this cultivated valley of Chicama and, making a detour to get to the desert on the other side, we came to the hacienda of Chiclin where the buildings had been calcimined a distinctive pink. The road to its administrative center parallels the course of a narrow gauge railway carrying sugar cane to the mill along a broad avenue planted with strangler fig trees.

Señor Rafael Larco Herrera, the hacendado of Chiclin, an exquisitely mannered eighty-year old patriarch and a former Vice President of Peru, met us and graciously conducted us to the museum which he had founded. An able — albeit amateur — archaeologist, his son Don Rafael Larco, present director of the museum, has for thirty years taken time from his business to pursue the ghosts of the Mochica people and other related cultures in this richly endowed sepulcher of Peru. To our delight we found that the museum housed a priceless collection of Mochica ceramics and thousands of other artifacts — textiles, gold pieces, wood carvings, exquisitely worked necklaces, bronze instruments, mummies, feather work — all "footprints" left by the Mochicas on the road of Time.

The revealing part of the Mochica history is in their pottery. The portraits in clay show a high level of realism combined with a charm and delicacy of modeling, painting and firing which has hardly ever been equaled anywhere in the world. Their sculptured heads are actually documents pertaining to a lost culture and the precise details of the faces make it at once apparent that they rank with the extraordinary art of the Egyptians.

There is in this pottery so wide a range of facial structures that we were able to form a good idea of their appearance. One head, that of an obese man with a cascade of chins, had the bemused expression of a sybarite while other sterner types with painted faces were evidently warriors. Some of the portrait vases — made from molds in the form of stirrup cups and designed to hold liquids — which had been taken from graves show Mochica tribesmen afflicted with disease. In fact a study of the portrait faces might give one a catalogue of the endemic diseases of the coast. We found the figure of a felon whose face had been purposely mutilated, and still other faces showed the effects of the disease which had eaten away the upper lip and nose leaving the face, when healed, with the appearance of a grinning skeleton. There was scarcely a facial feature from the piercing of the ears to the headdress which the Mochica artists did not realistically portray. Their headdress, a sort of turban, was their most conspicuous adornment, and in these the finest and most colorful materials were used. Distinctive turbans marked the priest, the medical curer, the soldiers and the couriers who ran the road.)

(There were infinite details to be seen in other ceramics. We saw models of houses and pyramids; an elaborate variety of realistic ceramics on plants was so well done that the species could easily be identified; landscapes simple and realistically graphic showed plants growing in cultivated fields; backgrounds were as delicately suggested as in Chinese paintings; cactus plants stud the pampas close to a walled road in a technique similar to those seen in Persian miniatures.)

The native animals, an intimate part of their lives, have been painted and modeled with a warm feeling that again is scarcely surpassed by the Egyptians. A red fox sat on a stirrup-spout jar with a lifelike sly look on his face; on another was a hunted fox with reddened tongue hanging from his mouth; on yet a third a deer lovingly nursed its fawn. There was a long parade of the bird kingdom, done with such exquisite modeling and careful attention to each feature and detail that we easily identified the pictured bird. Among the seabirds, a blue-beaked boobie-bird held its young affectionately under outstretched wing, and ducks swam with their peculiar dignity. The modelers of this pottery had caught the liveliness of the monkey, the humor of the sea lion, the feeling of animals. It was remarkably impressive.

These remarkable pictorial vases even recorded visitations to the tribal doctor, a practitioner always identified by the peculiar sash he wore. In one a skilled curer was removing a tumor from a man's shoulder; in another he trepanned the skull, removing pieces of broken bone that pressed upon the brain — the success of this operation is confirmed by the many trepanned skulls removed from graves. On another vase an old woman with eyes closed placed her hands on a patient's stomach to divine his plaint; in yet another, a curer hovered over the body of an inert patient trying to extract the "fairy dart," the symbol of his pain. There were vases showing cases of cretinism and syphilis, dwarfs, hunchbacks, Siamese twins and amputees.

But while it was socially profitable to be a doctor, it was also dangerous — for when the patient died under treatment, the doctor was held accountable, as was shown by one vase on which a doctor — naked, except for the usual badge of office — was tied to a dead man. The killed and the killer formed a spiritual bond; they belonged to each other, and so they were bound; they lay in the desert with a carrion bird poised above — and waiting.

Here then in this pottery collection was the history of a people. In one sense, an illustrated history is often more explicit than a written one, since the written word is, in the flight of time, always subject to interpretation. It has always been a mystery why these advanced civilizations did not invent some form of writing which would have enabled them to leave a record. The principal stimulation for the invention of writing, first used in Mesopotamia about the fourth millennium B.C., was economic and the earliest known written accounts are pictographic records of payments made to a temple. Such tribute was also paid by tribesmen in Peru's early history. This we know they did through their knot-string records, but beyond this there is no known "written" account. If writing was "an artificial creation impelled by the idea-diffusion or stimulus diffusion," the Mochica did not have it.

Yet they may have had a system of glyphic communication. Their couriers, a special class as seen by the form of their turbans, are often pictured on the ceramics as running along the desert roads carrying some sort of bag in their hands. Señor Rafael Larco once found such a bag of beautifully tanned light llama-skin in the tomb of a *chasqui*. He believes that the Mochica developed communication through the use of decorated painted beans in such stylized form as to be, in fact, ideographs, and that these glyph beans were carried in such a leather bag.)He has drawn these conclusions from thousands of ceramics which have the motif of the painted beans on them, often coupled with the running *chasqui* figure.

Death and the little gods were also present in this painted history. We came away with a complete idea of the Mochica military equipment and of their warriors. Their weapons were buinesslike: spears, sharply pointed javelins, war clubs weighted in bronze or stone. Each warrior was accoutered in a buckler and a shield on which was painted the heraldic totem of his clan. On vase after vase we saw scenes of carnage and battle, where sweeping vital figures clubbed and mutilated, and scenes of triumphs showing naked prisoners, disarmed and bound with rope around the neck, being led to a chieftain who was both judge and victor. Death too stalked the exhibit shelves with the vanquished trussed up and hanged or left to die in the pictured desert.

And woman — in Mochica art, woman is handled by the artist gently and tenderly. She appears as the mother-wife, an active, sympathetic role not always given her in other examples of primitive American art. The artist catches her as she washes her long hair and is in the act of wringing it out; she is found making a large bowl of intoxicant or cooking in the kitchen or weaving or perhaps removing a sand flea from the foot of her lordly spouse. Or she is found sitting contemplatively while arranging her hair. These are singular portraits of the primitive woman of the New World. Usually she emerges as a force in this society yet she waits to press her demands until her man has been made drowsy by the fumes of desire.

(The Mochica was a sophisticated society and that they caught all the humor and *accide* of great art is shown in their engagingly candid pictures of their sexual life. There is nothing in the whole range of erotic art — Greek, Egyptian or Indian — more libidinous than the intimate details that they modeled on their vases, where sex is fearfully and wonderfully displayed. Phallic worship — it would be better to say phallic admiration — abounds. In one vase, a man sits in such a state of desire and with so enormous a standard that it could have been characterized by an eighteenth-century courtesan as "not a weapon of man, nor the plaything of a youth, but a maypole." On another vase an outsized priapus is treated with Rabelaisian humor; on the very summit of this *instrument ingenieux* sits a small bird who looks down on it in a most curious expression of unbelief.

The positions of love on these vases are more numerous than those known to Montegazza, that nineteenth-century gazetteer of sexual aberrations. There is every approach, every position, thought up by man. So many and so varied that one recalls Remy de Gourmont writing that "the animal is ignorant of diversity of the accumulation of aptitudes; man alone is libidinous."

When the Inca conquerors arrived on this part of the coast they were shocked by this display of sodomy which involved both women and men. This fashionable way had been inherited by the Chimus from the Mochicas, and the Inca officials, who lived a comparatively Spartan life, regarded it as an abomination. They tried their best to stamp it out, first by destroying just those involved and then whole families and clans. But the practice was obviously too deeply ingrained to be stamped out, for after the arrival of the Spaniard fifty years later the religious phase of sodomy was still rampant.

Cieza de León said, "It is certain there were some Particular Places, where they kept Boys in Temples for that Purpose, and look'd upon that Abomination as a Piece of Religion, only to be practis'd upon solemn Occasions by the Priests and Caciques . . . for every Temple, or Place of Worship of Note keeps one or two more Men who are clad like Woman from their Infancy, imitating

274

them in their Tone, and all other Particulars. These on great festivals, the prime men us'd to have their Beastly Copulation."

The Incas seemed to have had no answer to sodomy except wholesale liquidation and when this failed they created artificial work-programs to keep the people so fully occupied they would have no time to slip out of the ritualistic rhythm of work. Accordingly they impressed thousands of these pleasure-loving coastal sybarites into their road construction.

And so over the tombs of the Mochicas which held, as in an eternal repository, those ceramics which told the well-defined story of a long forgotten and highly articulate civilization, the Inca ran his road, that highway which Humboldt characterized as "the most useful and stupendous work ever executed by man."

X V I

A Great City Called Tumpiz

No MONUMENT marked it; no one had penned an epic about it. Yet where we stood on what had been a truncated pyramid, the conquest of Peru had begun. We had come to the end of the great coastal road, near to Tumbes where the river of the same name flows into the sea. And here in 1532 Francisco Pizarro had landed with his small company of soldiers and the stirring drama that was to end in the death of the Inca Empire had its beginning.

Although at that time the Spaniards did not realize it, the road that they found outside of Tumbes, or Tumpiz as they called it, was the very road that would lead them to their goal. Never had a people so carefully made arrangements for their own downfall as did the Incas. Just as the Persians paved the way for their conquest by the forces of Alexander the Great, so did the magnificent roads of the Incas betray them to the Spaniards. As we stood on the ramparts of the pyramid where the first part of the drama took place, and looked at the not too distant sea, I thought about the man who had tumbled the Inca Empire.

Francisco Pizarro belonged to that company of Spanish *tercios* who, intermixing piety with rapine, had helped to double the world's landscapes. In 1532 with his little army he stood outside of this Tumbes at the margin of a wide road "made by hand, broad

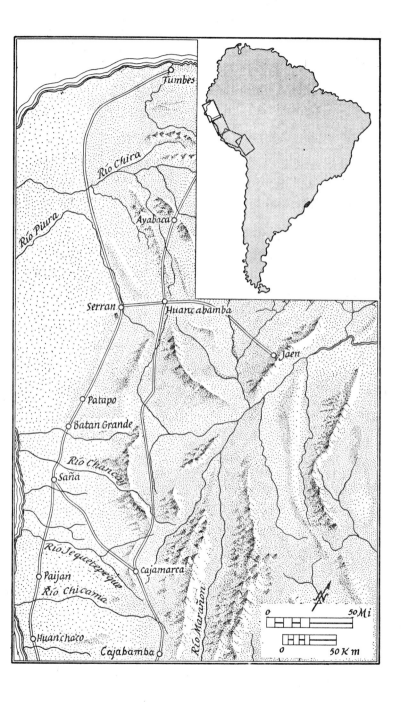

Tumbes

Río Chira

Río Piura

Ayabaca

Serran   Huancabamba

Jaen

Patapo

Batan Grande

Río Chancay

Saña

Río Jequetepeque

Paiján

Río Chicama

Cajamarca

Huanchaco

Cajabamba

Río Marañon

N

0   50 Mi

0   50 K m

and well built and in many places paved," and as Balboa had once claimed all the land which the Pacific touched, so Pizarro now laid claim to all the land that this road serviced. It was a large and generous gesture since the road spread, as the Spaniards were to learn, over all of Andean South America. Chilli-masa, the corpulent Indian chieftain of Tumbes, who with a retinue of his people including buffoons and dancers had turned out to welcome the steel-clad strangers, was amazed by the proceedings — the furling of the Imperial flag of Spain, the drums, the bugle and the reading of the proclamation by the Royal Scrivener. Of the last he could make nothing, and even the garbled version supplied by the Indian translator attached to the Spaniards was of no help. Since the road went to every part of the "four quarters of the Sun" and embraced the desert, the Andes and the jungle, and therefore the lands belonged to the Inca, how then could these people claim it? Or how, if this claim was denied them, could they take it by force, since his people were seven millions and the Spanish army consisted of a mere one hundred and eighty men, thirty-seven horses, two cannon, twenty crossbows and one white woman? The whole thing had an air of utter improbability. But that Francisco Pizarro was not a man to be crossed the Indians were soon to learn. They were dealing with the most deadly fauna ever to walk the Peruvian earth.

Three years earlier, on July 26, 1529, Francisco Pizarro had made a contract with his Queen to make a conquest of these lands in her name. As a reward, he was to have 750,000 maravedis annually, the title of Governor and the prerogatives of a Viceroy. He had spent many years searching for this Golden Kingdom and now bore at his temples the snow of fifty-six winters and in his heart an infinite bitterness. Born illegitimate and nursed, it was said, by a sow, able neither to read nor write, he had come to the "new founde worlde" to change this outrageous fortune. Life in those times was a lottery. Chance has a way of elevating one man while she buries others in mud and infamy. The great prizes were few and the odds in this game of conquest were frequently stacked against the player. Fortune had eluded Pizarro during his first decades in America. Then after the discovery of the Pacific by Balboa, copious accounts began to filter up to Panama of a great kingdom of gold that lay to the south.

In search of this kingdom, Pizarro and his one-eyed partner, Almagro, spent a weary five years moving south along the seacoast until, after vicissitudes which would have ruined a less demoniac man than Pizarro, they arrived at last in 1527 in the port of Tumbes where they took refuge when their single ship sprung a leak. To their amazement they found they were facing a city with roofs which appeared to be gold — while about it, the usually dry desert was a mass of color. Invited to land by the gestures of the city's inhabitants who thronged the beaches, Pizarro sent one Alonzo de Molina ashore. He returned presently with descriptions of a place which rivaled the splendor of the Arabian Nights. The women "were as beautiful as suns," every one wore gold in her ears, about her neck, and wrists and ankles. The houses were well made, luxurious, the finest that he had ever seen. Believing that their comrade spoke out of the stardust of the imagination, Pizarro sent another, this time Pedro de Candia, the "Greek," who went ashore in full armour freshly burnished and stayed the night. His tale was even more wonderful than the other.

The great city called Tumpiz is inhabited entirely by Indians and close to the shore is a great house belonging to the lord of the country with walls built of adobes like bricks, very beautifully painted with many colors and varnished. I never saw anything more beautiful. The roof is straw also painted so that it looks more like gold. About a large temple was a garden with fruits and vegetables of the country imitated all in gold and silver. The women wore a dress large and broad like a morning gown, and the chieftains went dressed in mantles and shirts and wore a thing like a turban adorned with gold and silver beads which they called *chaquira*. The country itself was desert, but the Indians had made it bloom by irrigation. They said they were the vassals of a great lord named Old Cuzco who lived in the mountains and that he had much gold and the people spent many days and nights at drinking bouts and it is certainly marvelous the quantity of liquor *chicha* that these Indians drink.

The Spaniards were mad with joy. They had found at last the outpost of the Golden Kingdom. They bartered for golden ornaments, took aboard several llamas which they called "sheep," traded for vicuña-wool weavings which they thought were silks, and managed to persuade several Indians to return with them to Spain. In turn it was agreed that Alonzo de Molina, the first Spaniard who had gone ashore, would remain at Tumbes alone with his Negro slave Gines to await their return.

That return took five years. In 1532 Pizarro was back with his "contract" for the conquest and his titles and his emoluments. He found the Spaniard dead and Tumbes destroyed. The "golden gardens" of which de Candia had sung and the houses plated with gold leaf were all gone. The Golden Kingdom about which Pizarro had spun beautiful stories, where gold gushed out of the earth midst emeralds and pearls, was gone. There were mutterings of revolt. Pizarro, "who was as proud as he was poor and whose eagerness for gain was in proportion to his poverty," rose to the occasion. He sought to buoy up the hopes of his men by having his scrivener write a note which he claimed was given to him by an Indian: "Know ye," said the note, "whoever you may be that may chance to set foot in this country, that it contains more gold and silver than there is iron in Biscay."

Failing by this ruse to satisfy his followers, Pizarro left a crew behind to await reinforcements coming from Panama and, after three days in the ruins of Tumbes, moved off and so came onto the wide road.

"On the first day," said the scrivener, "the governor departed from Tumbes which was the 16th of May, 1532, and he arrived at a small village. From there they began to march south on this wide road in search of this 'Old Cuzco.' "

The Spaniards were amazed by the road.

Along this Coast and Vales, the Caciques and prime Men, by his order, made a Road 15 Feet wide with strong Walls on both Sides above the Height of a Man. All the Way was very clean and shaded with Trees, whose Boughs in many Places hung over heavy with Fruit, and Abundance of Parrots and other Birds were everywhere among the Woods. In each of these Vales the Incas had stately Apartments for themselves and mighty Magazines for their Soldiers being so much Fear'd that none durst omit to provide for them . . . The Walls were carry'd along on both sides of the Road . . .

At the end of August 1954 in the second year of our Expedition and precisely four hundred and twenty-two years after the Spaniards set off in search of the Golden Kingdom, we ourselves were searching for the remains of this 15-foot wide road with "strong Walls on both Sides."

We had begun, as Pizarro had begun, at the end of the beginning. It was soon apparent that modern Tumbes on the banks of the Tumbes River was not the old city. But on the advice of one or two in the valley who seemed to know something of the road's history, we traveled four miles southwest to San Pedro de los Incas. There in that little village, with its wickerwork and mud-covered dwellings, we found the ruins of the first Tumbes. Around them now a skein of irrigation ditches nourishes the fields of rice, and through them and over them runs the new four-lane vehicular Pan American Highway. A small house sits atop the Sun Temple first seen by Pedro de Candia. Cows and goats wander up its steep sides where still to be seen are the adobes "painted with many colors and varnished." With an archaeological map of the place supplied to us by Dr. Georg Petersen, an oil geologist, we moved through the little village and traced the outlines of those first Inca buildings seen by Pizarro and his men in 1527. There were the courts, the enclosures and the walls, and we could still see faint traces of the old road which Pedro de Candia marched over when, fully armored, he came in from the ship to visit "golden Tumpiz." It is now little more than a flooded ricefield.

But the ancient road was gone. We found nothing but a memory of it as we moved back toward the mountains in search of the route of the conquistadores. The land itself has changed. Floods have ravaged the region and there have been devastating earthquakes, while for four hundred years the natives have been busy turning over every available piece of arable soil.

Thirteen miles due south of the village, we passed the remains of an Inca *tampu* called Ricaplaya. This had been the first "small village" which the army of Pizarro reached on its first day out of Tumbes. The landscape was now much like the velds of Africa. The mimosa stood tall with flat-spreading foliage and stalks of shrubs stood bare of leaf in the coarse soil with the cactus. Large algaroba trees which had reminded the early Spaniard of the Karob trees of Arabia appeared now in profusion.

It was a trackless place. No car had been there before us and we rumbled over the ground as a battle tank might have done. Southeast and to our left were the Mountains of Amatope — rising, so our maps indicated, to a height of 3000 feet and completely covered with vegetation. Had the Inca road climbed that mountain or had it hugged the plain at the mountain's base? And where was the "village among hills" where the Spaniards stayed on their third day out of Tumbes?

That night we camped in the dry forest. With the rising moon came the animals. A red fox loping by stopped to look at us for a moment, a deer with its spotted doe leisurely walked in front of our lights, and above the sibilance of the night cicadas there was another deep throbbing sound. It was the cry of the howling monkeys. Somewhere high in those mountain woods the deep-chested males were beating out their song.

Along the lower foothills of the mountain spur where the trees were the largest, we came on the old road again. Under the detritus, gift of the sun and the rain, there was a dim but definite line that marked a continuing wall. Lawrence drove the Power Wagon slowly over the rock-strewn ground as Silvia and I walked ahead with our guide. It was when we saw parallel walls which were distanced twenty-four feet that we knew we were on that wide road "with strong Walls on both Sides."

I had long wondered what part of Peru the conquistadores had referred to when they said the road they walked had been shaded by trees. This region was the only place in the entire twenty-five hundred miles where such a situation could exist. Here were the trees and large blue morning glories that bloomed in profusion, the same flowers they had seen, and vines that had a large melon-like fruit which, when dead, emitted a dry ash like the Apples of Sodom found in Arabia Deserta. This then was the place of the shaded trees and the fruit. And so, alternately finding and losing the road over which the myrmidons of Francisco Pizarro had marched in May of 1532 on their way to find the Lord Inca, we came at long last to the banks of the Rio Chira in the first valley south of Tumbes. And on a high embankment in the same type of terrain where the rolling dry earth was studded with cactus and mimosa, we found Poechos. Here Pizarro, following the Inca road, had come to "the banks of rivers which were well peopled and yielded abundance of provision of the country and flocks of sheep [llamas]," and here he made camp in a large village called Poechos.

After this we never lost for long the track of the ancient road. It ran along through ancient villages, up the sides of hills, through a desolate country, moving from valley to valley.

In order to reach the place the Spaniards had called Zaran [Serran], we had to take the winding vehicular dirt road that wound up and around the sides of the lower Andes and back through the semidesert land. Zaran is now a hacienda lying in a valley where several small rivers meet but in 1533 it was a place of considerable importance. Ruled over by a "great lord," its fortress guarded the Inca lateral road which there connected with the Royal Road through the mountains not more than fifty miles to the east and upward. It was at Serran, where we found more ruined structures, that Pizarro had waited for the return of Hernando de Soto who with his twenty soldiers had gone into the mountains to seek out the whereabouts of the fleeing Inca King.

We fortunately had an account of this search as it had been reported by de Soto's soldiers. Don Diego Trujillo told how, after Pizarro had seen at Serran a road which appeared to go up to the mountains, he sent "Hernando de Soto with forty men. I went with him, and we continued up the road for twenty leagues until we came to the road which led to Caxas, the operation taking two days and one night without resting except for meals."

Eight thousand feet above the Rio Tabaconas, in June 1532, de Soto and his forty soldiers came upon "a village surrounded by mountains." Here at Cajas (which still exists) they saw the first evidence of the grandeur of the Golden Kingdom, "fine edifices and a fortress built entirely of cut stones, the larger ones being five or six palms wide and so closely joined that there appears to be no mortar between them." Since the natives were under the strictest orders from the Inca not to attack, the two thousand Indian warriors withdrew into the mountains, leaving de Soto master of the place. In time a chieftain appeared and through an interpreter offered to guide de Soto out to a "road made by hands and broad enough for six men on horseback to ride abreast."

Thus Hernando de Soto became the first white man to see the Royal Road of the Incas, the "same road that traverses all the intervening land between Cuzco and Quito, a distance of more than three hundred leagues." The distance is actually one thousand two hundred and thirty miles. The same Indian described Cuzco, the Golden Kingdom's capital, "as a league around, and the house of the Lord Inca as four crossbow shots in length," and he told of the civil war between the two brothers who had been rivals for the Inca-ship of all the Perus. The victor, Atahualpa, was even now not far distant from this same Cajas, taking the hot water baths at Cajamarca.

It was not long after this that the soldiers found "a great and strong building in the town of Caxas [Cajas] surrounded by adobe walls in which there were many women spinning and weaving cloth . . . and there were no men with them except the porters who guarded them." At the entrance the bodies of three Indians were found hanging by their feet, punished because they had entered the houses of the chosen women. Even in this ferocious drama of conquest there was a parenthesis now and then for other pastimes and de Soto's men, who had not seen women for months, could not be restrained. Five hundred of the Virgins of the Sun were forced out into the plaza, and while some of the crossbowmen mounted guard, the Spaniards had their way with them. Finally the soldiers left off and de Soto marched on down to Serran.

That the conquistadores were brave men, I will be the last to deny. To march in such small numbers into an unknown land must have required courage of an uncommon sort. But I can only suggest that any who have traveled as we traveled, changing from vehicle to horse, from horse to foot, sleeping out here, taking a hurried meal there — over the same terrain — would agree that the Spaniards in those early days were less inconvenienced than we. They at least found a road in a fine state of repair; the *tampu* rest-stations were well provisioned; and if the proper pace was maintained, in the evening there were night quarters for the traveler. It is true that for us there was no hostile people ready to fall upon us. On the contrary, a more peaceful people than the present-day Peruvian scarcely exists. Still even in those June days of 1532 the Spaniards went unmolested along a road wide enough "for six horses to go abreast." Such a road we never saw in its entirety, only fragments, and yet it seems amazing to us who followed the traces of these roads back and forth across mountain and desert that any part of this once great highway system should be intact.

It was in this same region between Cajas and Huancabamba that in 1802 Alexander von Humboldt, "traveling for the acquisition of knowledge," made a scientific study of the highway. After following it for hundreds of miles through Ecuador, he wrote: "The roads of the Incas were the most useful and stupendous works ever executed by man." He went on to speak of the ". . . solemn impression which is felt on beholding the deserts of the Cordilleras, increased by the remarkable and unexpected fact that in these very regions there *still* exists wonderful remains of the great road of the Incas, that stupendous work . . ."

On the sides of this road and nearly at equal distances there are still small houses built of well-cut free stone . . . answering the purposes of caravan-series or *tambos* . . . While we journeyed onward on the heights of Pullal, our eyes were continually riveted on the hard remains of the Inca road upwards of 20 feet in breadth; this part of the road had a deep understructure and was paved with well-hewn blocks of black-trap porphyry. None of the Roman roads which I have seen in Italy, in the south of France and in Spain appeared to be more imposing than this work of the ancient Peruvians; and the Inca road is the more extraordinary, since according to my barometrical calculations it is situated at an elevation of 13,258 feet . . .

We saw still grander remains of the Peruvian Inca road not far from Huancabamba and also in the vicinity of Ingatambo near Pomahuaca. On our travels northward in the Cordilleras between Cajas and Huancabamba, we had no less than twenty-seven times to ford the Rio Huancabamba, compelled to do this on account of the numerous sinuosities of the stream, which on the brow of the steep precipice near us we had continually without our sight the vestiges of the rectilinear Inca road . . .

In time, following this important lateral that joined the two main axis roads — the coastal and the Andean — we too came to the same "vestige" of the road near Huancabamba mentioned by Humboldt, and so found and later explored the Inca road that led east into the jungle realm of the headhunters. But that is another story. . . .

On that night we slept in the same Serran where Pizarro had once stayed for eight days awaiting the return of de Soto. Then, hearing his captain's story of the "things" of empire, he had gathered up his whole army and continued south on the wide road "with strong Walls on both Sides." And now here were we taking the same coastal route.

We moved our trucks through little towns with old Inca names — Copiz, Motupe "where there are great fields of cotton with which they make their clothes," through the next valley-village of Jayanca, "where a pleasant river flows with artificially made channels which serve to irrigate all the land that the Indians choose to sow." All along the way we found ruins of pyramids, outlines of structures and occasionally a section of the Inca road. As always, it measured twenty-four feet and even in its decay, it was ever a wide road "with strong Walls on both Sides." At the end of several weeks, the canvas top of the Power Wagon was torn, the paint on the cars marred and faded from the constant sun, and we ourselves burnt to a crisp. Yet like a beagle following the scent, we kept to our pursuit of history and the roads.

By now we had formed a clear picture of the over-all Inca road. In the south, and in the north, it had measured the same — twenty-four feet. Whether the land through which it ran was desert or semi-desert, along the entire route were remains of *tambos* and pyramids. Always our inexorable itinerary found the roads and measured them; found the *tambos* and measured the distances to determine the intervals between stations; surveyed the ruins and made a plan of them; searched for potsherds. All this, recorded and catalogued, was building toward an ever more complete picture of the Inca Empire. We were taking the extraneous legendary material of history and giving it archaeological foundation. The dead cities we discovered were not resting places wherein we sat and indulged in "sententious reflections on the transitory nature and decay of empires" as Volney did in his *Ruines*. Ours was the task of rediscovering the direction the roads had taken, and the reason why the roads entered this rather than that geographical avenue, the utilization of terrain, the history of those who had come and gone over them. We were seeking to revitalize a dead civilization with its cities, its division of labor, its methods of communication, its manner of handling surplus, its system of records, and along with these to gain some knowledge of the people and their multifarious activities in the social complex.

An important part of this phase of our study had to do with our attempt at ferreting out the *chasqui*-courier system. Ever since

288

we had found those courier stations in the mountains and had made our test, we had been searching along the roads for the communication posts. The stations were turning up more frequently. We came across a number of them well-spaced along a section of the desert road which had perhaps remained untouched since the Spanish abandoned it after the conquest. Speed was the important factor of communications "for the Inca King thought he should be as a heart in the midst of his realms," and the newsbearing *chasquis*, who were as blood flowing along the arteries, carried information with the greatest speed. It was as a solution of the time-space problem that the *chasqui* system had been established.

On our way south we stopped for a breather at Cinto [Zana, Zaña, or Saña] once a populous oasis watered "by a great and rapid river." In 1532 the conquistadores in their search for the Inca had traveled along this stretch of the Royal Road which they found "paved and bound on each side by a wall and so wide that two carts could be driven upon it . . ." into Cinto. Now we were driving our vehicles abreast over the same road, looking as the Spaniards had then for the road to Cajamarca.

I do not know what Zana was like when it was Indian nor how "the road, made for Old Cuzco when he visited his dominions" looked then. Now sand surrounds it and there is a small village with a little square and houses of painted adobe, windowless to keep out the mosquito plague at night. In the seventeenth century, this village had been the place of an "experiment in God," and several beautiful churches, whose ruins were still visible as we drove by in the semidarkness had been built in what then was an extensive agricultural region. These offered no place to set up camp, for with the twilight the insects were out in thick swarms and our only escape was to find a place where we would have the strong wind from the sea. So we forced our trucks to climb the sides of a demolished pyramid. There in dust ankle-deep we set up camp. But tired though we were we could not sleep, and presently in the hope of finding someone who could give us some information about the old road, Silvia and I went down to the dark streets of the village.

Fortune favored us this evening for we found Mayta. Small and precise, this little man with the Inca name wore pince-nez glasses containing but a single glass perched at an angle on his nose. He welcomed us into his bare room and fetched out another candle. We had no need to tell him our business. He had seen our truck with its emblazoned INCA HIGHWAY EXPEDITION and the running *chasqui* figure. He had been reading news of our Expedition in the Lima papers and he had hoped that we would come this way.

Mayta was an antiquarian, or better, a *huaquero* — there is at least one in every village — one touched by interest in things past who collects information, digs up graves, records the facts. He was exceedingly helpful. He knew, he said, the part of the road for which we searched, the part that broke off from the main coastal road and moved east to the mountains, the one that Pizarro took when he searched out the Inca King. His grandfather had accompanied the great Antonio Raimondi, the Italian-born Peruvian geographer, when he too sought it out in the last century.

Then he brought out the collections of ceramics he had found in graves. We saw the black polished ware of the Chimu; the beautiful polychromic pottery of the Mochicas on which deer, fox, and people were naturalistically portrayed; and Inca pottery. When we asked how he had managed to find these, he brought out a notebook covered with diagrams and figures. He opened it, furtively glancing over his shoulder first one way then the other, leaned toward us and said, "I work in the occult sciences." He had, it seems, a co-worker among the unseen forces, an Inca spirit called "Claudio." On proper contact, Claudio would inform him where to dig and at what level he would find the antiquities. It was Claudio who had told him of the Inca lateral road which led to the sierra. Then he rose and, taking the candle in hand and moving in front of us so that his small shadow was large on the wall making it seem as if we were following the genie rather than Claudio, he led us to a dusty back room furnished with only a bed and a crucifix. There he showed more treasures — ceramics, wood carvings, bronzes and mummies. He then excused himself, saying that he had to contact Claudio for word about the morrow's trek.

With Mayta and "Claudio" as our guides, we found the Inca road in splendid condition to the south of Zana. As soon as the influence of the water canals ended, the desert began and there we saw their road, direct and wide as it had been described by the first white men who traveled it. The soil, waste gravel baked hard in the eternal everlasting drought, glowed underfoot and the air was like a flame in the sun as we walked toward the remains of a way station. The ground was a fallen desolation of stone of dry-laid masonry which had once formed the *tampus* for this part of the road. Our measuring tapes out, we set to work in the brazen sun. One station measured one hundred and fifty feet by one hundred and twenty feet and was broken up in several rooms. These were right on the road which had been indented so that the structures could be keyed to the road. The stones used had been brought from the upthrust rock-hill a few hundred yards behind, a hill Mayta called "the Hill of the Gallows."

Here the road bifurcated to the east and, along a lateral road which climbed toward the mountains, Francisco Pizarro and his small army, thinned by disease and fear, marched toward the lair of the Lord Inca. A member of that expedition against an empire wrote: "From Zana we took the road to the sierra."

It seemed that we moved for hours, so slowly did we creep through the skein of small trees toward our goal, the blue haze of mountains rising in the east. We passed several small haciendas thriving somehow in the aridity where we stopped just long enough to assure ourselves that this was the lateral road through the mountains to Cajamarca. It was essential that we get to the coast as and when we had planned and we could not now make the long and arduous climb over the 12,000-foot mountains that lay between Cajamarca and ourselves.

With extreme difficulty we worked the trucks around the Nancho River which here snaked between the lower foothills of the towering Andes. At San José de Nancho we left our trucks and set out on foot to see the traces of the Inca road. We found it close to the pass that led up the mountains, a pathway still used by mules. There rising ahead of us was the now familiar step-road of broad treads, broken and out of line, but the same step-road which Pizarro had used to seek out the Inca.

With an emissary sent as an escort by the Inca Atahualpa, and his one hundred and thirty foot-soldiers and forty horses and the numerous Indian porters who had been pressed into his service gathered about him, Francisco Pizarro, who knew how to make fine speeches at solemn moments, mounted a rock close to the road and addressed his men. The import of his words was recorded by his scrivener:

> He exhorted all his men to make up their minds to act as he hoped they would, to have no fear of the great numbers of soldiers in the army of the Inca. Though the Christians might be few in number, they had been blessed with divine aid for the confounding of their enemies. He would be with them seeing that they went hence with the good intention of bringing these infidels to a knowledge of the truth.

So we left the conquistadores climbing up the sides of the Andes over the Inca road, climbing into history, into glory, as they carried death and destruction to the Inca's sanctuary.

292

X V I I

The End of the Road

Was it fortuitous or had it been subconsciously planned that the Expedition should end at Cajamarca where the end of the Inca Empire took place? I do not know. I remember only that in putting together the last links of the Royal Road in the Andes we had woven back and forth between mountain and coast and that our second anniversary — and our journey's end — found us in the environs of Cajarmarca.

In our two years of travel we had linked by direct exploration almost the entire road system of ancient Peru. We had followed the Royal Road up and into Ecuador marking its way accurately; we had entered Huancabamba, famous in history as the first Inca city seen in the mountains by Hernando de Soto, who there had had his first glimpse of the opulence and wealth of a mysterious empire; and out of Huancabamba we had followed the until now unbroken road built by the Incas in 1470 over which they had moved seventy-five miles east to the banks of the Marañon River and eventual defeat by the head-hunting Aguaruna Indians.

All through the last months of the Expedition we had been at work joining together those roads in the highlands which we had been forced to bypass on previous trips. Now to mark the end, we had come north to Ichocán along the vehicular dirt road. On the plain near Cajamarca we put up what was to be our last formal camp. We were but three now — Silvia, Richmond Lawrence and

myself. The Riddells had finished their work and gone, and our
native helpers and assistants were down on the coast preparing the
final packing of our collections. Here I began to write the last
dispatch:

EXPLORERS FINISH INCA ROAD SEARCH
U.S. EXPEDITION WENT 22,000 MILES IN UNCOVERING VAST
HIGHWAY NET IN PERU

ICHOCÁN: DECEMBER 7, 1954: WE HAVE MADE OUR LAST
RUN ALONG THE INCA ROAD AND OUR LAST DISCOVERY . . .

WE HAVE SOUGHT THE REMAINS OF THE FABULOUS ROYAL
ROAD OF THE INCAS BY TRUCK, BY MULE, BY AIRPLANE, ON
FOOT. WE HAVE FOLLOWED THE INCA ROADS THROUGH DESERT
AND TOWERING ANDES INTO THE JUNGLES IN ONE OF THE
FIRST EXTENDED STUDIES OF COMMUNICATION SYSTEMS OF
PREHISTORIC MAN. OUR LAST . . .

I broke off from this summary to think how I might say exactly
what it was that we had accomplished in these two years. I turned
abstractedly to watch Silvia busy in the last light of day. She had
been only twenty-three years old when we began, young and un-
tried in this arduous work. Now bronze and lean, she had a knowing way about her and an awareness. She had won her spurs as an
explorer; working, drawing, collecting, helping to gather the material which I would draw upon in framing my over-all report. I
turned to Lawrence, at work as always on his cameras. For two
years, often under the most miserable conditions, he had photographed the history of a people through their roads and had taken
in all 60,000 feet of color film without the loss of a single roll. Our
archaeologists, our draughtsmen, our guides, the aviators — all had
worked with us in our search for the answers to the questions we
asked: Where had the Inca roads gone? Who built them? What part
had they played in creating an Empire? "Rich man, poor man, beg-
garman, thief" — all along the way the people of the road had

shown a very real interest in our search for the horizons of the past. I shall be ever grateful for their helpfulness and inherent kindness.

Had we found only a road? Much more! We had found a road *system,* a vast network of communications which had bound all the discordant elements of geography and of peoples into an empire. This we had followed wherever it led us and so had given substance to those first incredulous reports of the Spaniards. We had measured these roads at thousands of different points; had studied structures, techniques, the engineering which made passage through bogs and fens and over high mountains possible; had seen how tunnels were constructed through the living rock and the way in which the courier-system of communications was set up and maintained. We had found, after following an estimated five thousand miles of these ancient roads, that we were dealing with a *master plan,* that the Incas — out of the pale of history as we know it — had conceived and put into operation under a uniform plan a road system which extended from Colombia to Chili and into Argentina, a total of no less than ten thousand miles of all-weather roads which climbed to heights over which Man had never until then maintained communications.

Whatever we had accomplished, I thought, could not be measured in mere numbers of photographs nor in the vacant figures of mileage nor in the menacing piles of notes, maps and surveys. It was our hope that because of our study and traverse of the roads we had brought the story of the Inca civilizations into the focus of world history, and that these ubiquitous, these overwhelming, highways — which climbed mountains, pervaded jungles, crossed deserts — could now take their place among the major achievements in the history of the world along with other great roads of Europe and Asia. I thought, too, of the shock our findings had given to complacency.

Highway of the Sun

Scholars have long been aware of the great influence of Early Man's roads and his communications, yet few of us who take for granted the present-day roads which now encircle the world have any clear idea of the extent of prehistoric communications. Early Man was a far-ranging animal, willing to undertake great journeys to obtain something which would alter his humdrum existence. He built a road from the Black Sea to the Baltic to get out amber, "that special act of God." He laid the Silk Road halfway around the world to get material in order that he might enjoy the luxury of soft cloth. He pushed roads to the turbulent sea to obtain Tyrian dyes so that he might wear garments of royal purple.

It is not possible to minimize the importance of the world's roads, for every prehistoric road is a wish that has gone to work, every road built an accumulation of persistence. These roads were the refusal of Man to accept his environment as fixed. Roads took Man out of himself to seek for something beyond his own borders of experience. We are surprised to learn that men were laying down brick roads in India as early as 1600 B.C. in response to a demand for all-weather roads for the wheeled vehicles, that the Greeks in 500 B.C. were preparing a manual on road repairs, that the Romans laid down fifty-two thousand miles of road with traffic regulations, milestones, maps and an *itineraria*, or travelers' handbook, for the road.

If we forget how deep our roots go into the past, we have only to peel back the layers of roads. London's Watling Street was an ancient route two thousand years old before the Romans arrived. They found it straight enough to put their own road on top of it, and that in turn became the King's Highway and is today a great traffic artery. Similarly more than one fifth of Peru's modern roads are laid upon or utilize the strategic alignments of the ancient Inca road. The coastal Pan American Highway runs for miles alongside the ancient one, and in some places is actually laid over it. In Huncayo in the Andes, the Royal Road was first Inca, then the King's Highway, and now the modern road.

A road is like a man. When he is dead he remains thus only for as long as he is not remembered, and so it is with a road — when it is not maintained or used, it disintegrates and dies. History is built in layers and what we do not use or see we are likely to forget. Roads are our routes to the past. A road is the first thing that an archaeologist seeks to discover and through stratigraphical excavation he attempts to find the layers of history. We separate the present from the past by many artificial barriers, finding it extremely difficult to perceive that the past is not past but a permanent part of life, just as ontogenesis is part of our physical evolution.

Civilization is a road. And if civilization can be defined as the building of cities, the division and exploitation of labor, the conversion of resources, the creation of large social units, the complex religious organizations, the keeping of records, the building of monumental architecture, the linking of cities with roads and their corollaries, communications and bridges, then our Expedition has followed a path that has led us back through the centuries to the Inca civilization. Had time, endurance and money permitted, we could have extended our search for thousands of miles more into Argentina and Chile and north into Ecuador. Yet, in spite of these limitations, we have taken *this* road from the many general statements of the old chroniclers and have given it physical reality by finding it and following it through an inhospitable land, and so established something of the way of a people. In following the itinerary of these roads we gained what we believed to be the first comprehensive view of the extent of the Inca Empire, and more, by our excavations, provided an ethnographic picture of the people who built the road and used the road.

We fleshed the dry bones, breathed on them and gave them life.

The road and the people who built it were no longer technical archaeological terms who moved by some orphic feeling. Together they showed us conclusively by their ever-present road which traveled from the suffocating sands of the desert to the moonscapes of the Andes that Man, wherever he is or whatever he is, accepts none of the frontiers laid out for him by Nature.

It is this, then, that we have accomplished, apart from actually rediscovering large sections of the road and innumerable cities and *tampus* along the way, and it is only when this immense amount of material has been evaluated and written into the record that we shall really know how much has been found. At least we know with Emerson that "he who builds a great road earns a place in history."

So at the end we were at Cajamarca, which today has no resemblance to the place once described by one of its Spanish conquerors. Following along on what had been the Inca road, we had come late one afternoon to the hot sulphur baths a few miles south of Cajamarca where the Inca had been with his troops on the evening of November 15, 1532, taking the baths and performing various religious purifications. Then we moved on to Cajamarca. It is a small city laid out like a checkerboard with carefully spaced streets and a large plaza dominated by a colonial fountain and bordered by eighteenth-century churches. On the outskirts are masses of eucalyptus trees and blue-green fields of lucerne and alfalfa. Cajamarca has never been a strategically important city. Lying as it does in a complicated fold of the Andes at 10,000-feet altitude, it is not today of any vital importance nor was it in that year 1532. Except that it was here that the Spaniards finally caught up with the Incas.

A crossbow-shot from the plaza, as our Spaniard would have

described it, is a small hill about five hundred feet high, once capped by an Inca fortress overlooking the square. We left the Power Wagon and climbed the hill, surmounted now by a cross, and sat down on stone seats carved out of the rock. About us lay the panorama of Cajamarca.

The Spaniards had come into the city of two thousand inhabitants from the north, arriving on Friday, November 15, 1532, at the hour of vespers. In this city was a plaza "larger than any in Spain" surrounded by a high wall and entered by two doorways which opened upon the streets of the town. The buildings were long, strongly built, three times the height of a man and roofed with straw. "They were," the scrivener said, "the finest we had seen." In the distance steam could be seen rising from the sulphur baths where the Inca was taking his pleasure, while nearby white tents "covered the ground as thick as snow flakes." Thirty thousand battle-tired soldiers were encamped about him. "It filled us with amazement," wrote the Spaniard, "to behold the Indians holding so proud a position." On the hills were fortresses "of a strength as not before seen among the Indians" and the small army of the Spaniards passed along beneath several such fortifications which, had the Inca been so inclined, could easily have stayed its progress.

Why then had not the Indians attacked? Why had the conquistadores been permitted to reach this Cajamarca without harm? Why had Pedro de Candia been allowed to mount his small cannon on a nearby hill, thus enabling him to dominate the square?

These were questions which Atahualpa himself later answered. He had thought them at first to be followers of the returning Kontiki Viracocha, the Inca's Creator God who, so the legend went, had once brought them civilization but later, dissatisfied with his handiwork, had sailed away from Peru thereby setting a pattern for an amazing twentieth-century sea voyage on a balsa raft which bore the now familiar name *Kontiki*. The devastating civil war in Peru between the time of the first and second comings of the Spaniards, in which brother was pitted against brother for the leadership of the empire, had ended in triumph for Atahualpa and his generals. The way to Cuzco was open and the victor was on his way to the sacred city to be officially proclaimed Inca King when two *chasquis* from Tumbes — five hundred miles distant — arrived at the baths with a message: "People have arrived by a big ship from out of the *hatuncoca* [sea], a people with different clothing, beards and animals like llamas only larger."

At first Atahualpa was hardly puzzled. He remembered how, in his youth, the "Viracochas" had come to their coast and then had sailed away. Now they were here again. After consultation with his priests, he ordered a general rejoicing. Had not the Kontiki Viracocha returned to add divine sanction to his recent victories? He sent a message back that he was to be kept informed of the movements of these visitors, forgetting in his eagerness the real Viracocha's departing warning: "A people will come who will say that they are Viracocha the Creator and they are not to be believed."

As the Spaniards marched inland, Atahualpa was told of every incident of their advance. He knew when they killed some of the natives and put others into chains. He knew too when Hernando de Soto's men, climbing to the Royal Road, entered the village of Cajas and ravished the Sun Virgins — it was then that the white man lost his divinity. Still the Inca held back and still his people were under strict orders not to attack the Spaniard nor provoke him. The concept he had formed of the nature of the danger which threatened him was to prove disastrous. The reports which reached him indicated that the strangers and their horses were one and that, dismounted, the "manpart" was ineffective and therefore incapable of fighting; that their "fire-sticks" were animated thunderbolts;

and that the Spaniards' steel swords were no more effective than a woman's weaving battens. Yet the Indians' llamas, like horses, were four-footed; the Indians' bronze weapons were like the white man's swords; and their own military tactics of flank, envelope and charge were similar to those of the Spanish.

However, their *fatal* mistake was that they underestimated the ability of the Spaniard to get reinforcements from the sea. To the land-bound Indian, the sea was an impassable barrier and once an enemy was encircled, that was his end. The plan, then, was not to give battle to the Spaniards, not to attack; rather to give them encouragement by the lack of resistance, to draw them into the mountains away from their ships, and then strike and end it all at once. How was an Inca King surrounded by his thousands of battle-tried troops, ruler of seven million people and a land extending throughout all the latitudes south, to know fear of a paltry one hundred and two soldiers on foot and sixty-two on horseback?

To the Spaniards the moment called for audacious action. De Soto rode boldly into the Indians' camp to invite the Inca King into theirs, taking no more notice of the thousands of armed warriors than he would of a handful of flies. Invited to sit on a seat of gold, he was waited upon by two Indian girls "as beautiful as suns." De Soto's talk was of the King of Spain, the Vice-regent of God, and of how he had sent Francisco Pizarro and his companions to bring the divine truth and holy law to these realms. The Inca agreed to go to their camp as invited, with his warriors unarmed, so as not to give offense to Pizarro.

Toward the evening of November 16, the retinue of the Inca advanced into the plaza. First came a squadron of Indians dressed in livery of different colors "like a chess board"; they advanced sweeping the road clear of any obstacles. Next came more Indians, beating drums, blowing their conch horns, dancing and singing. Then

301

came the Inca himself on a litter adorned with plumes of parrot feathers and plates of gold and silver, carried on the shoulders of eight blue-liveried nobles of the Rucaña tribe. To the bleat of the horn and pounding of the drum they entered one of the gateways of the plaza. The rest is history.

The Spaniards were hidden in the surrounding buildings, the plaza was vacant of white men and to the annoyed inquiry of the Lord Inca as to the whereabouts of the intruders, a solitary figure crossed the plaza. It was Friar Vicente. He stopped before the litter of the Inca: "I am a priest of God and I teach Christians the things of God . . . and I come to teach you." Offered the Bible and unable to make any sense out of it, the Inca threw it to the ground in proper rage. That was enough. The war cry *"Santiago!"* splintered the air and from the houses the armed Spaniards poured down on the trapped Indians.

It was all over in thirty-three minutes, one of the most fateful half-hours the world has ever known. Within the space of time it took for the Spanish bugles to blow and the falconets to explode, for the shock of Spanish cavalry charging into the ranks of naked bodies, for slaughter of the bodyguard and the capture of the Inca, an empire which had been thousands of years in the making fell in the dust and gore of that plaza at Cajamarca. The people never fully recovered from the first shock.

Within days, realizing that his captors suffered from a malady for which gold was the only remedy, Atahualpa offered to ransom himself with the gold and silver of the Empire. He would, he said, standing on tiptoe, "give enough gold to fill this room twenty-two feet long and seventeen wide to the white line which is halfway up the wall." As for silver, he said he would "fill the whole chamber with it twice over."

"Atahualpa," so a chronicler wrote, "a man of thirty years of age, good-looking, somewhat stout, with a fine face, handsome and

302

fierce, the eyes bloodshot," sent his *chasqui* runners out over the Royal Roads with orders to all Indian officials that they deliver up the gold and silver.

In the eight months during which the Inca was held as hostage, the ransom poured into Cajamarca, filling the room "twenty-two feet long and seventeen wide" which he agreed to fill once with gold and twice with silver. Several hundred Indians arrived carrying litters filled "in greater part, of gold plate . . . taken from the walls, for holes showed where they had been secured." Native goldsmiths were put to work melting it down into ingots. An account was made — the gold alone came to 326,539 pesos, equivalent now to $20,000,000. . . .

While the royal assayer of the ransom "with the fear of God before his eyes evoked the assistance of heaven to do the work of dividing the gold, conscientiously and justly," the captains about Francisco Pizarro pressed for Atahualpa's death. Rumors of the mobilization of Indian warriors were rife and Pizarro knew that he and his men would never get out all their golden loot once the Inca was set free. So in a feigned rage Pizarro, who had taken the precaution of having the Inca chained, went to him and remonstrated: "What treason is it that you have prepared for me, Lord Inca — I, who have treated you with honor like a brother and have trusted your word?"

"Do not make nonsense with me," the Inca answered.

There were many Spaniards, among them de Soto, who protested against this travesty and who thought that only the King of Spain should have the right to try a monarch. It is ridiculous now to speak of justice, for codes of action are founded upon necessity. The whole thing was improbable, ridiculous, fantastic — a king captured in his own realm, obedient to his own laws, held in chains and for ransom, only in the end to be tried for crimes against humanity.

There was a trial in which Atahualpa had twelve accusations

leveled against him; among these that he was a bastard, he had many wives, he was an idolator, he waged unjust wars and he spent tribute which rightfully belonged to the Spaniards. He was found guilty and condemned to be burned alive. In great distress, Atahualpa asked if there were not some way he could escape. He was offered a way out.

"If you will become a Christian, I will promise that not a drop of your blood shall be shed," said Pizarro. The Inca agreed and the Spaniard kept his promise. On that 29th day of August, 1533, when the Inca was finally led out to the square, not a drop of his blood was shed. He was strangled by the garrote.

Disintegration began immediately with the Inca's death. This empire, which was the apogee of many other ancient native civilizations, began to fall apart at once. The roads were first to go. Each tribe had had the responsibility for the upkeep of that section of road which ran through his particular land. The victors, not at first aware of this, gave these border-line villages to deserving soldiers in fief and with them the Indians who lived in them as vassals. These were then marched off as burden-bearers to their new lords. One by one the villages and *tampus* whose function was the maintenance of the roads were depopulated, and beneath the hammering blows of climate and conquest the roads themselves fell into disrepair. The Spaniards, soon realizing their mistake, wrote their "Ordinance for Roads and Tampus" which required the Spanish owners of the villages through which the roads passed to do various things, one of which was that each should keep his section of road in good condition. But by this time the Spaniard was used to making his own terms on the principal of "I obey but I do not comply." After the dissolution of the roads, the rest of the culture that had been the Incas' followed.

Yet in 1548 the road was still a wondrous sight and young Pedro Cieza de León, a soldier of but twenty-three years, rode along it and, moved by all that he saw, decided to write down an account of the wonders of the Indies. "One of the things which I admired most, in contemplating and noting down the affairs of this kingdom, was to think of how or in what manner the Indians could have made such grand and admirable roads as we now see and what number of men would suffice for their construction and with what tolls and instruments they can have leveled the mountains and broken through the rocks to make them so broad and good as they are. It seems to me that if the King, our Emperor, should desire to give orders for another Royal Road to be made such as this which goes from Quito to Cuzco, and the other from Cuzco to Chile — even with all his power I believe that he could not get it done. O! what greater things could have been said of Alexander the Great or any of the other powerful kings who have ruled the world than that they could have made such a road as this . . . the grandest and longest road in the world."

Silvia von Hagen, 26, co-leader of the Expedition, at the American Geographical Society, before dimensional map of the Cuzco Valley which she made.

Expedition on the coast near Huacho. Hans Disselhoff, archaeologist, Victor von Hagen, Silvia von Hagen.

Henrik Blohm, 21, Harvard undergraduate. Expedition volunteer, discoverer of ruins of outlying Vilcabamba.

The Riddells with Captain Henry Leighton, USA, pilot to Expedition.

Victor von Hagen in Puno, with Expedition mascot, vicuña Afidea, and an Indian helper for the Expedition.

Lawrence and von Hagen ascend canyon of Apurimac, on way to "Bridge of San Luis Rey."

Members of the Expedition

The *chasqui* symbol of the Expedition and its living counterpart, an Indian

Lake Titicaca beyond the city of Puno.

The entrance gate to Puno, City of the Lake.

Around the lake adobe houses, windless, thatched with straw.

Puno and the Titicaca Lake

First seen by white man in 1553, the basin about the lake has held South America's oldest cultures since the earliest times. At 12,500 feet altitude, freezing at night, sun-bright during the day, Titicaca is one of the highest lakes in the world — and the most populated area in the Andes.

...sas in their alignment before playing down of matting.

...e floating bridge from Squier's *Peru*
...877).

Llamas cross the newly made balsa
in simulation of the old crossing.

The Balsa

*The reed pontoon balsa bridge, the floating road invented by the Indians
for river crossing in a treeless land. Thirty or more reed balsas were strung
together, filled with straw, matted for the pontoon road which spanned the
Desaguedero at Lake Titicaca. The bridge, pictured by Squier in 1866,
endured for 1000 years.*

The square and round *chullpas* near Qutimbo, Lake Titicaca.

Towers of the De

Various *chullpas* on the west of Titicaca, close to the Inca highway.

Entrance to the interior of the *chullpas,* with carvings of *viscachas* (related to chinchillas).

Chullpas (*Towers of the Dead*), *found around all of Lake Titicaca. They are pre-Inca, made of well-fitting stone as fine as anything Incaic. The* chullpas *were built to house the dead. "They once outnumbered the houses of the living," said an early Spaniard. They are a great mystery; rifled for four centuries, there are not enough remains to determine age, epoch, or culture.*

An old Inca causeway resurfaced at the northern end of Titicaca.

San Jeronimo de Asilla (built 16? 1696), village of Asillo, entrance in Carabaya.

Detail of façade of San Jeronimo de Asillo.

Carabaya Country

Around the northern end of Titicaca flows the Inca causeway moving through the little-known Carabaya region into the eastern montaña. In the smallest villages, such as Asillo, stand churches built by Hispanized Indians, marking the wealth that once came from the "verie riche river of Carabaya."

A bridge across the Carabaya River. The suspension cables are still used, but taken out in the rainy season.

apacheta ("burden depositor"), a ne propitiatory cairn at 13,800 feet the road to Carabaya.

The Inca road entering Tambillo on the Carabaya River.

Carabaya Country

e ancient Inca roads of the Carabaya still used. Here it is cold, remote, de-pulated. Still to be seen are highway ne cairns (apachetas), the stone undations of suspension bridges, an-nt drainage and a road entering the a village of Tambillo.

Drainage on the Inca road which was built *circa* A.D. 1400.

Cuzco from the air, showing the Plaza.

The Four Quarters of the World

All roads lead to Cuzco, capital of the Inca Empire. In an 11,000-foot valley, the Incas, about A.D. 1200, began to build; they continued until the Spanish conquest in 1533. The four great roads entered the Plaza, called Huayka-pata from the four cardinal directions. The southern, lake, or Colla-suyu road, enters at Piquillacta.

The main entrance to Cuzco from the south of Piquillacta and the ruined pre-Inca site close to it.

The Sun Festival

Inti-raymi marked the summer solstice when the Sun God returned to be among his people. A modern version of that Festival, done with authentic costuming.

The llamoids (below), *related to camels; domesticated by the Inca for wool and as beasts of burden; also, like the camel, for great zoological mysteries. The vicuña, which Silvia von Hagen holds, was never domesticated, but protected by the Incas for the fine wool seen* (below) *hanging from the male vicuña chests. The inquiring face is an alpaca, the real wool provider, living high in the snow. Llamas are fine beasts of burden, but poor wool yielders.*

Vicuñas down from the hills of the Carabaya for shearing.

Face of a young alpaca, close to Macusani, Carabaya.

Llamas resting on Inca roadway to Cuzco.

A herd of mixed alpacas and llamas close to Allin-Capac mountain.

Somewhere, Lost Vilcabamba

Machu Picchu, in the jungle, or Anti-suyu section of the Inca road system, is on top of a mountain in the Urubamba Gorge, at 10,000 feet. It is notable for being the only Inca city found intact and gives a good idea of Inca city planning. It is the climax of an Inca road network and terraced cities. One road leads to Cuzco. From 1000 feet higher on top of Huayna Picchu, where Victor and Silvia von Hagen stand, Machu Picchu and the road leading southwest from it can be seen.

In the valley north of Machu Picchu is Salcantay. The river valley cuts through tropical jungle, is ringed with ancient roads, and goes under the great 20,000-foot-high Salcantay massif. It is reached by mule over log bridges and through freezing temperatures.

The Bridge of the Great Speaker

The Apurimac-Chaca, the Bridge of the Great Speaker, a suspension bridge over the gorge of the Apurimac. It entered literature as the "Bridge of San Luis Rey." Squier, who made an engraving of it in 1866, measured it accurately as 200 feet long and 118 feet above the river. It was built circa 1350; lasted until 1890. Its rope cables were replaced every two years. The tunnels, and the steps to the road, still exist.

Victor von Hagen with Spanish documents dated 1541, at Ayacucho.

Sanctuary of the Hawk

Consulting colonial documents was one way to find the elusive Inca Road. These showed that the Road bypassed Ayacucho to move on to Vilcas-huaman, where the Sun Temple is still intact. Built during the apogee of the Inca Empire, this Sun Temple is now the only such edifice in the whole extent of what was the Empire.

The Sun Temple at the ruins and village of Vilcas-huaman.

Silvia von Hagen walking
down the step-road between
Jauja and Bonbón.

Highway of the Sun

The great military Highway of the Sun between Jauja and Bonbón was found in good state. Technology in road building varied with the terrain. On the hard puna *a surface was not needed, and the road was walled and drained with steps placed on all hills to prevent erosion. On a steep hill, steps* (pata pata) *were used. Silvia von Hagen essayed descent on the Royal Road. Over this* puna, the chasqui *ran 1250 miles in 5 days, resting at terraced villages such as Tarma-tambo.*

A member of the Expedition walks over the Jauja road where small treads were placed to prevent erosion.

An Indian garbed as a *chasqui* makes the "run" between stations on the road at Inka-katana.

Terraced village Tarmatambo, a halting place on the Royal Road, which is seen climbing the sacred hills above the modern village.

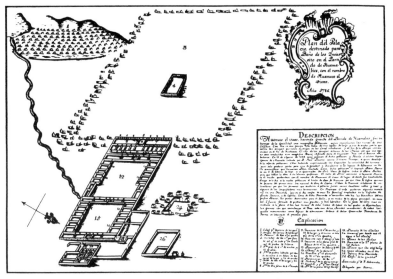

Map of Huánuco drawn by Spanish Expedition, 1786.

One of a series of ornamented doorways in the main palace.

Road to Chachapoyas

Huánuco, the greatest city between Cuzco and Quito, was built late in the Inca Empire period as a strategic city for the conquest of Chachapoyas, the Chimu on the coast, and for Quito. Three roads entered and left it. It had a population of 30,000. The map of 1786 shows this Huánuco. The larger building had doorways of crouching lions shown in the photograph. Huánuco is 12,000 feet high, desolate; one reaches it by an ancient causeway after going up a series of steps to reach the high plain.

The causeway of the Royal Road which reaches Huánuco.

The staircase road on the way to Huánuco, close to Banos.

The fortress of Torre-Pukro high on the crown of a hill.

The staircase highway beyond Pataz.

The paved Inca road entering the jungles close to Leimebamba.

Road to Chachapoyas

All along the route of the conquest road to Chachapoyas, the empty way is crowned with fortresses raised to prevent Inca troops from entering, and stone stairway roads marching across the silent jalka and then entering the jungles. It is 450 miles in length, and is the longest fully paved road in the entire Inca road system.

In the matted jungles close to where the Inca road enters the forest, the Expedition found countless stone ruins. One, the site at Choquillo, was found almost intact. Stone-laid dry walls were part of a fortress, while, within the jungle, rounded stone buildings with square windows were covered with orchids, and about the outside a fret design coursed its rounded sides.

Tambo Colorado from the air lies on the Pisco River.

Detail of decorative frieze and rooms with step windows within Tambo Colorado.

Details of windows.

Unliving Desert

Tambo Colorado lies in the next valley south of Cañete and Incahuasi and is connected by the coastal road. It is built on the Pisco River and is a planned official highway stop, a garrison and a sacred Inca bath. A lateral road also ran up this valley and connected with Vilcas-huaman in the high sierra.

The desert about Ica.

Unliving Desert

On the coast rains never come. In the northern desert nothing grows; in the south, date palms were introduced by the Spaniards. In the Cañete Valley are the remains of an Inca lateral road which connected coast and Andes — near the ruins of Huasi or Incahuasi, the Incas' "New Cuzco." It is built of adobe. This was the largest Inca city ruin on the entire coast, and lies back 40 miles from the sea.

The lateral road moving between coastal road and royal Andean road in the Cañete Valley.

View of the storage chambers of Incahuasi used for storing corn and sea food.

The Tres Cruces or Tree of Life at Paracas. Its direction is true north-south.

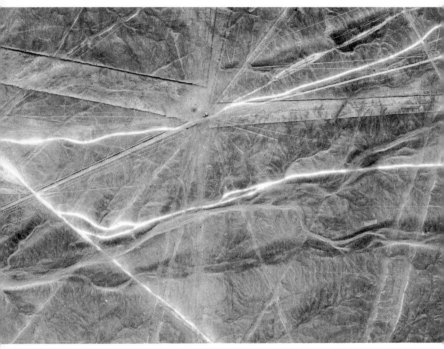

The Nasca lines, found between the Ingenio and Nasca Valleys. (Taken by the Peruvian Air Force at an altitude of 10,000 feet.)

Marked Desert

The southern desert, which is eternally rainless, has many surface mysteries. The dead are fully preserved from the desiccating sands. On a hill facing the bay of Paracas is the "Tree of Life" buried in the sand. It is 602 feet high and at least 2000 years old. And father south, in the Nasca Valley, are mysterious radiating lines in the form of platforms, animals and abstractions. They fill hundreds of square miles of desert.

Skeletal dead pulled from graves at the Caverns of Paracas. The 2000-year-old textiles in which the bodies are wrapped are of such imaginative beauty that museums treasure them as some of the finest weavings in the world.

Ilvia von Hagen looks down to the sea, the beach and to the ruined *tampu* station on t coastal road.

Chala

Chala lies at the edge of the sea in the south desert. It is the terminus of the Cuntu-suyu (coast) road coming out of Cuzco. It is from this place that the Inca had fish fresh from the sea. It has excellent roads, stone stairways, tampu road markers, and immense official storage areas.

The road leading to Chala, on which run Indians in *chasqui* dress.

An ascending stone stairway, one of the many on the coastal road. As with all Inca work, they are laid in dry masonry. Silvia von Hagen ascends.

Chala

The Inca fishing village at Quebrada de la Vaca, where the Expedition found the skeletal remains of those who fished for the seaweed and sea food destined for Cuzco, two days distant by runner over this road made with rock fill.

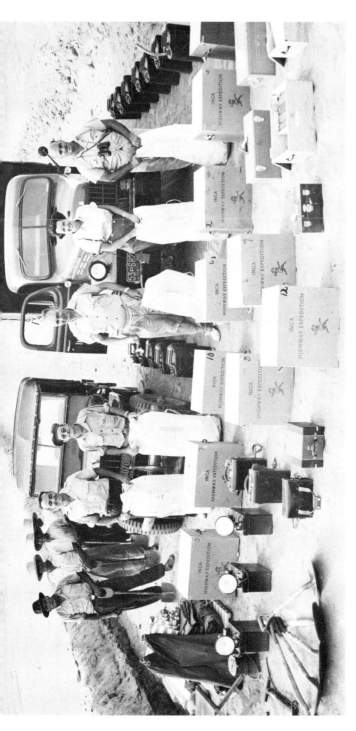

On the Inca Highway Expedition

Charles Daugherty (topographer-photographer); Richmond Lawrence (cinematographer); Hans Disselhoff (archaeologist); Silvia von Hagen (artist); Victor von Hagen (ethnographer).

Kingdom of the Moon

The northern coast belonged to the Moon, the deity of the Kingdom of Chimor, but in time (1460) it was eclipsed by the Sun and the Inca ran his ubiquitous road directly through the conquered lands. Beyond the pre-Inca Mochica pyramids at Chiquitoy in the Chicama Valley runs the Highway. Chan-chan, capital of the Chimu, was built between 1200-1400. It ruled a kingdom of 600 coastal miles. The Chimu medium was mud cast in molds, colored. Rain and Man have brought it to its amorphous state.

Kingdom of the Moon

The Mochicas, who were centered in the Chicama Valley, were the finest pottery makers of the world. Their time: 1 B.C. to A.D. 800, when they were overwhelmed by the Chimu. Their pottery techniques reached into Inca times. (a) The head of the man is a portrait; (b) sea birds, a study in bird observation (note the young birds, and their wings); (c) llamas shown with eye fringe to keep away glare from the sun; (d) the house jar is a coastal house: round, thatched, made of mud. It was made during Inca occupation after 1450.

Inca Artifacts

The Incas were a disciplined, almost Spartan, people living within the framework of a society in which almost everyone was his own artisan. Their artifacts are practical: a large aryballus which falls on its side when it is empty of drink; a gold llama to propitiate the gods; a long-necked drinking vessel used for ceremonial occasions.

Acknowledgments

The Expedition was successful in its quest. It found what it sought, and more. But all of this could never have been done without the aid of the many individuals and organizations whose material aid gave us the tools to make these discoveries possible. Foremost of those who aided us was Herr Sigmund Gildemeister of Bremen and São Paulo, Brazil, whose death just a few months before the Expedition's end did not allow him to see what his interest had wrought. And so we wish to give him homage, and to thank also the following individuals and organizations who made this expedition possible:

His Excellency, the President of Peru
The Minister of Education of Peru
The Minister of Finance of Peru
Dr. Wendell C. Bennett
Dr. John H. Rowe
Sr. Rafael Larco Hoyle
Dr. Albert Giesecke
Mr. Roderick Rawlins
Mr. Junius Bird
Lt. Col. John Miles, U.S. Army
Capt. Henry Leighton, Jr., U.S. Army
Col. Truman Smith, U.S. Army (Retired)
Mr. Gordon MacDonald
Mr. Tage Nielsen
Mrs. Harriet Gibney
Dr. G. H. T. Kimble

Highway of the Sun

DR. CHARLES B. HITCHCOCK, DIRECTOR, AND RAYE PLATT, OF
THE AMERICAN GEOGRAPHICAL SOCIETY
MR. JOHN SCHELL
MR. FREDERICK HAHN
ABBOTT LABORATORIES
ANSCO
THE COLLINS COMPANY
THOMAS A. EDISON COMPANY
FAUCETT AIR LINES
GOODYEAR TIRE & RUBBER COMPANY INC.
GRAFLEX INCORPORATED
HOMELITE CORPORATION
INTERNATIONAL PETROLEUM CO. LTD. (ESSO)
JOHNSON & JOHNSON
LIFE MAGAZINE
LAURITZEN LINES, COPENHAGEN
NESTLE'S INCORPORATED
THE NEW YORK TIMES
THE NORTH AMERICAN NEWSPAPER ALLIANCE
PAILLARD PRODUCTS INC. (BOLEX)
PARKE DAVIS & COMPANY
REMINGTON ARMS COMPANY, INCORPORATED
WEST COAST LINE INCORPORATED
CARL ZEISS INCORPORATED

> *The maps and end papers were drawn by*
> *Messrs. Lee Hunt and Victor B. Harris, Jr.*

Bibliography

ALCEDO, ANTONIO DE (1786–1789) — Diccionario Geografico Historico de las Indias Occidentales o America. Madrid.

ANONYMOUS (1881–1897) — Breve relacion de los pueblos de espanoles del Peru con sus principales distancias (approx. 1573). *In* RGI.

ANONYMOUS (1906) — Relacion de los pueblos que median en el transito de la Ciudad de Lima a la de Chuquisaca, y descripcion de las 25 provincias que se ofrecen en el camino &. (No date.) *In* Prueba Peruana, by Maurtua: Juicio de limites . . . , Vol. III.

ANONYMOUS (192–) — Descripcion de la ciudad de la Plata, Cuzco y Huamanga y otros pueblos del Peru (Approx. 1650). *In* Col. Libr. Doc. Ref. Hist. Peru, 2d ser., Vol V. (Urteaga.)

ANONYMOUS (1934) (Silva y Guzman, Diego de) — Relacion del sitio del Cusco y principio de las guerras civiles del Peru hasta la muerte de Diego de Almagro (1535–1539). *In* Col. Libr. Doc. Ref. Hist. Peru, 2d ser., Vol. X. (Urteaga.)

BANDERA, DAMIAN DE LA (1881–1897) (Corregidor) — Relacion general de la disposicion y calidad de la provincia de Guamanga, llamada de San Joan de la Frontera y de las viviendas y costumbres de los naturales della (1557). *In* RGI.

BAUDIN, LOUIS (1928) — L'Empire socialiste des Inka. Institut d'Ethnologie, Travaux et Memoires, No. V. Paris.

———— (1922) — Inca Land. Explorations in the Highlands of Peru. Boston.

———— (1930) — Machu Picchu, a Citadel of the Incas. New Haven.

BOGGIO, PABLO A. (No date given) — Estudio del F. C. Huancayo — Cuzco. *In* Atlas de planos publicado por el Ministerio de Fomento. Peru.

BOWMAN, ISAIAH (1916) — The Andes of Southern Peru. New York.

BUENO, COSME (1872) — Descripcion de los Partidos o Provincias (1764–1770). Second edition by Coronel Manuel de Odriozola. Documentos literarios del Peru, Vol. III, Lima.

CABELLO DE BALBOA, MIGUEL (1920) — Historia del Peru bajo la dominacion de los Incas (1576–1586). Col. Libr. Doc. Ref. Hist. Peru, 2d ser., Vol. II, Lima. (Urteaga.)

CAMACHO, J. M. (1923) — Note in the translation of Markham's "On the Geographical Positions of the Tribes Which Formed the Empire of the Incas." *In* Col. Libr. Doc. Ref. Hist. Peru, Vol. IV, 2d ser., Lima. (Urteaga.)

CARBAJAL, PEDRO DE (1881–1897) (Corregidor) — Descripcion fecha de la provincia de Vilcas Guaman (1586). *In* RGI.

CARRASCO, EDUARDO (1849) — Calendario y Guia de Forasteros de la Republica Peruana para el ano de 1849. Lima.

CIEZA DE LEON, PEDRO DE (1880) — Segunda parte de la cronica del Peru, que trata del senorio de los Incas Yupanquis y de sus grandes hechos y gobernacion. *Ed.* Marcos Jimenez de la Espada. Biblioteca Hispano-Ultramarina, Vol. 5, Madrid.

———— (1881) — Guerra de Chupas. *In* Col. Doc. Ined. Hist. Espana, Vol. 77 (76 in Regal). Madrid.

———— (1877) — Guerra de las Salinas. *In* Col. Doc. Ined. Hist. Espana, Vol. 68, Madrid.

———— (1924) — La Cronica General del Peru (1553). Vol. I. Ed. H. H. Urteaga. *In* Coleccion Urteaga, Historiadores classicos del Peru, VII. Lima.

———— (1947) — La Cronica General del Peru. *In* Biblioteca de autores espanoles, Vol. 26. Ed. Don Enrique de Vedia, Madrid, pp. 349–458. (First publ. in 1849 ed.)

COBO, BERNABE (1891–1895) — Historia del Nuevo Mundo (1642–1653) . . . Ed. Marcos Jimenez de la Espada. Sociedad de bibliofilos andaluces. 4 vols. Seville.

CONCOLOCORVO (1908) — El lazarillo de ciegos caminantes desde Buenos Ayres hasta Lima (1773). Bibliot. de la Junta de Hist. y Numismatica Amer. Vol. IV, Buenos Aires.

CONTRERAS Y VALVERDE, VASCO DE (1881–1897) — Relacion de la cuidad del Cuzco, de su fundacion, descripcion, &c (1650). *In* RGI, Vol. II.

COSIO, JOSE GABRIEL (1913) — Expedicion cientifica de la Universidad de Yale. Inf. del Delegado del Gob. *In* BSGL, Vol. XXXIX, Dec. 1913.

Bibliography

CUSI YUPANQUI, TITO (1916) — Relacion de la Conquista del Peru y hechos del Inca Manco II. Col. Libr.

DOERING, HEINRICH (1941) — Auf den Koenigsstrassen der Inka. Berlin.

ESTETE, MIGUEL DE (1918) — N[oticia] del Peru. In El descubrimiento y la conquista del Peru. Relacion inedita de Miguel de Estete. La publica con una introduccion y notas Carlos M. Larrea, Bol. Soc. Ecuatoriana Estud. Hist., Vol. 1, No. 3, pp. 300–350. (1534.)

———— (1924) — Noticia del Peru. Col. Libr. Doc. Ref. Hist. Peru, 2d ser., Vol. VIII, pp. 3–56. (Urteaga.)

FEGOS, PAUL (1944) — Archaeological explorations in the Cordillera Vilcabamba, southeastern Peru. Viking Fund Publ. Anthrop., No. 3.

FERNANDEZ, DIEGO (1876) — Primera y Segunda Parte de la Historia del Peru (1571). Publicac. de Manuel de Odriozola, In Col. Doc. Hist., Vol. VIII, Lima.

FORNEE, NICULOSO DE (192–   ) — Descripcion de la Tierra del Corregimiento de Abancay (1586). Col. Libr. Ref. Hist. Peru, 2d ser., Vol. V. (Urteaga.) RGI.

GARCILASO DE LA VEGA (1919) — Los Comentarios Reales de los Incas. Publicacion de Urteaga. Lima.

———— (1943) — Los Comentarios Reales de los Incas. EMECE, Buenos Aires. 2 vols.

GASCA, PEDRO DE LA (1866) — Cartas al Consejo de Indias. In Doc. Ined. para la Hist. de Espana, Vol. XLIX, Madrid.

GIBBON, LARDNER (1854) — Exploration of the Valley of the Amazon, Part II. Under the Navy Department of the United States, Wash.

HERRERA Y TORDESILLAS, ANTONIO DE (1601–1615) — Historia general de los hechos de los castellanos en las islas i tierra firme del mar oceano. 4 vols. Madrid.

———— (1726–1727) — Historia general de los hechos de los castellanos en las islas i tierra firme del mar oceano. 9 vols. in 5. Madrid. (Another edition of the 1601–1615 edition.)

LEHMAN, WALTER; DOERING, HEINRICH (1924) — The art of Old Peru. New York.

LEVILLIER, ROBERTO (1926) — Nueva Cronica de la Conquista del Tucuman. Lima.

LIZARRAGA, FR. REGINALDO DE (1907) — Descripcion y poblacion de las Indias (1599). Publ. de Carlos A. Romero In Revista Historica, Vol. II, Trim. III a. IV. Lima.

LIZARRAGA, FR. REGINALDO DE (1909) — Descripcion breve de toda la tierra del Peru, Tucuman, Rio de la Plata y Chile. Nueva Biblioteca de Autores Espanoles, Vol. XV. Madrid. *Also* in Historiadores de Indias, publ. by M. Serrano y Sanza, Vol. II, pp. 485–678.

LOPEZ DE VELASCO, JUAN (1894) — Geografia y Descripcion Universal de las Indias recopiladas en los anos 1571–1574. Publ. Justo Zamora, Madrid.

MARKHAM, CLEMENTS ROBERT (1920) — Los Incas del Peru. Transl. by Manuel Beltroy, Lima.

——— (1923) — Las posesiones geograficas de las tribus que formaban el Imperic de los Incas. Transl. by Manuel Vicente Ballivian. *In* Col. Libr. Doc. Ref. Hist. Peru, 2d ser., Vol. 4, Lima. (Urteaga.)

MAURTUA, V. M. (1906) — Juicio de limites entre el Peru y Bolivia. Prueba Peruana presentada al Gob. de la Rep. Argentina. Barcelona.

MEANS, PHILIP AINSWORTH (1919) — La Civilizacion precolombina de los Andes. *In* BSEH, Vol. III, Nov.–Dec., 1919.

——— (1931) — Ancient Civilizations of the Andes. New York.

MERINO, DAVID (1903) — Croquis del Camino del Inca en la Prov. de Tayacaja (Feb. 1903). *In* Archivo de la Secc. Tecnica de FF. CC. y Caminos. Lima.

MIDDENDORF, E. W. (1893–1895) — Peru . . . 3 vols. Berlin.

MIRANDA, CRISTOBAL DE (1906) — Relacion de los oficios que se proveen en el Peru (Lima 1583). *In* Prueba Peruana & by Maurtua, Vol. I.

MOLINA, CRISTOBAL DE (of Cuzco) (1916) — Relacion de las fabulas y ritos de los Incas. Ed. Drs. H. H. Urteaga and C. A. Romero, and preceded by a Biography by Dr. Romero. Col. Libr. Doc. Ref. Hist. Peru, Vol. I.

MOLLINEDO Y ANGULO, MANUEL (1906) — Resumen de lo que se ha obrado en el Obispado del Cuzco (January 1678). *In* Prueba Peruana & by Maurtua.

OCAMPO, BALTASAR DE (1907) — Account of the Province of Vilcapampa and a Narrative of the Execution of the Inca Tupac Amaru. (Written in 1610.) Transl. from a MS in the British Museum by Sir Clements Markham, Ed. Hakluyt Society, Ser. 2, Vol. XXII, pp. 203–247. (This captain had been in Peru for 44 years, under the Viceroy Toledo also, and had returned to Spain to write his memoirs.) (Orig. in Maurtua.)

OLAECHA, TEDORICO (1901) — Apuntes sobre el Castillo y Fundicion de Curamba. Anales de la Escuela de Ings. del Peru. Lima.

Bibliography

PETROCOKINO, A. (1903) — Along the Andes. London.

PHILLIPS, F. (No date given) — Monografia de Tarma. *In* BSGL, Vols. XXVII, XXVIII and XXIX.

PIZARRO, PEDRO (1944) — Relacion del descubrimiento y conquista de los reinos del Peru y del gobierno y orden que los naturales tenian, y tesoros que en ella se hallaron, y de las demas cosas que en el han subcedido hasta el dia de la fecha. Arequipa 1571. Buenos Aires, Ed. Ernesto Morales.

POLO DE ONDEGARDO, JUAN (1916–1917) — Informaciones acerca de la Religion y Gobierno de los Incas (1571). *In* Col. Libr. Doc. Ref. Hist. Peru, Vols. III and IV. (Urteaga.)

POMA DE AYALA, FELIPE GUAMAN (1936) — Nueva coronica y buen gobierno (codex peruvien illustre). Inst. Ethnol. Trav. Mem., Vol. XXIII. (Universite de Paris.)

———— (1944) — Primer Nueva coronica y buen gobierno. (Written between 1584 and 1615.) Ed. Arthur Posnansky, Editoria del Instituo "Tihuanacu" de Antropologia, Etnografia y Prehistoria. La Paz.

RAIMONDI, ANTONIO (1875) — Mapa para la Historia de la Geografia del Peru. Lima.

———— (1876) — El Peru. Historia de la Geografia del Peru. Lima. Mapa del Peru. Scale 1–500,000.

———— (1929) — Itinerario de sus viajes. Publicac. del Banco Italiano de de Lima.

REGAL, ALBERTO (1936) — Los caminos del Inca en el antiguo Peru. Lima.

Relaciones Geograficas de Indias, Peru. (1881–1897) — 4 vols. Published by Marcos Jimenez de la Espada. Madrid.

ROMERO, EMILIO (1928) — Monografia del Depat. de Puno. Lima.

ROWE, JOHN H. (1942) — Sitios historicos en la region de Pucara, Puno. Revista del Instituto Arqueologico, Cuzco, pp. 66–75.

———— (1944) — An introduction to the archaeology of Cuzco. Pap. Peabody Mus. Amer. Arch. Ethnol. Harvard Univ., Vol. XXVII, No. 2.

RUIZ FOWLER, JOSE R. (1924) — Monografia Historico-Geografica del Departamento de Ayacucho. Lima.

SANCHO, PEDRO (1917) — Relacion para S.M. de lo sucedido en la conquista y pacificacion de estas provincias de la Nueva Castilla y de la calidad de la tierra, despues que el capitan Hernando Pizarro se partio y llevo a su Magestad la relacion de la victoria de Caxamalca y de la prision del cacique Atabalipa. Ed. H. H. Urteaga and C. A. Romero, Col. Libr. Doc. Ref. Hist. Peru, 1st ser., Vol. V, pp. 122–202.

SARMIENTO DE GAMBOA, PEDRO (1906) — Segunda Parte de la Historia General llamada Indica (1572). Berlin. (Geschichte des Inkareiches. Abhandl. Koenigl. Gesellsch. Wissensch. Goettingen. Philologisch-historische Klasse. Vol. VI, No. 4.) Berlin, Ed. Richard Pietschmann.

SQUIER, E. GEORGE (1877) — Peru, Incidents of travel and explorations in the Land of the Incas. London.

STIGLICH, GERMAN (1922) — Diccionario Geografico del Peru. Lima.

TELLERIA, MANUEL (1925) — Reconocimiento para trazado del ferro-carril de Ayacucho al Cuzco. Anales de Ob. Publ. Lima.

TSCHOPIK, MARION H. (1946) — Some Notes on the Archaeology of the Department of Puno, Peru. Papers of the Peabody Museum of American Archaeology and Ethnology, Harvard University, Vol. XXVII, No. 3.

UHLE, MAX (Ms) — Letters to Mrs. Phoebe Apperson Hearst, dated Huaitara, October 9th, 1901, and San Francisco, January 1902. *In* Field Catalogue, Museum of Anthropology, University of California, Vols. IV, V.

URTEAGA, HORACIO H. (1928) — El Peru. Monografias historicas. Lima.

VACA DE CASTRO, CRISTOBAL (1909) — Ordenanzas de tambos, distancias de unos a otros, modo de cargar los indios y obligaciones de las justicias respectivas hechas on la ciudad del Cuzco en 31 de mayo de 1543. Ed. C. A. Romero. Revista Historica, Vol. III, No. 4, pp. 427–92. Lima. (1543.)

———, addressed to (1917) — Declaracion de los quipucamayos (1541–1544). *In* Col. Libr. Doc. Ref. Hist. Peru, 2d ser., Vol. III. (Urteaga.)

VARGAS UGARTE, RUBEN (1942) — De la conquista a la republica. Lima.

VASQUEZ DE ESPINOSA, ANTONIO (1942) — Compendium and description of the West Indies. Smiths. Miscell. Coll., Vol. 102, Washington. (Spanish edition in 1948.)

VEGA, ANDRES DE (1881–1897) (Corregidor) — La descripcion que se hizo en la provincia de Xauxa por la instruccion de S.M. que a la dicha provincia se invio de molde (1582). *In* RGI.

VILLAR CORDOBA, PEDRO EDUARDO (1929) — Las ruinas de Willcas Waman. Diario "El Comercio," Dec. 29, 1929.

WIENER, CHARLES (1880) — Perou et Bolivie. Recit de voyage. Paris.

WIESSE, CARLOS (1913) — Las civilizaciones primitivas del Peru. Lima.

INDEX

Index

ACARI, 230–233, 234, 235, 240, 246–249, 251

Acosta, Father José, 48

Aguaruna Indians, 293

Allin-Capac, 62, 67

Almargo the Blinkard, 102, 240, 279

Alvaredo, Alonzo de, 201–202

American Geodetic Survey, the, 221

American Geographical Society, the, 11, 12, 32, 57, 117, 170, 233, 245

Andachuaylas, 136, 137, 176

Anti-suyu quarter, 84, 98

Apurimac River, 103, 105, 117, 120, 121–135, 138

Arequipa, 8

Asia, 208–209

Asillo, 59–60

Atahualpa, 82, 122, 285, 292, 299–304

Atiquipa, Hills of, 235, 236

Ayacucho, 139–141, 160

Ayala, Poma de, 35, 152, 185, 225

Ayapata, 57, 70

Ayaviri, 28, 59

BANNISTER, DR. ROGER, 179

Barrios, Juan de, 220

Bellevista, 123, 126

Bingham, Hiram, 106, 110–111, 112, 124, 134

Blohm, Henrik, 91, 111–114, 125–126, 140

Bonbón, 26, 182–185

Bridge of San Luis Rey, 120, 122, 129

CACHA-MARCA, 37

Cahua-marca, 235–237, 238–239, 240, 241, 251

Cajamarca, 82, 88, 128, 189, 260–261, 285, 289, 292, 293, 298–299, 302–303

Cajas (also Caxas), 284–285, 300

Candia, Pedro de, 279–280, 282, 299

Canete, 209

Carabajal, Francisco de, 96–97

Carabaya, (also Kara-waya), 56–80

Casma, fortress of, 256

Cassamarca, 231

Chachapoyas, 139, 170, 189–190, 200, 201–203

Chala, 178, 241–244, 245, 249–250

Chancas, (also Yachas), 95–96, 137–139, 176, 191–192, 200, 211–212

Chan-Chan, 259–260, 262–265

Chasquis, 18, 84–86, 87, 132, 177–181, 272–273, 288–289, 300, 303

Chicama Valley, 264, 265, 268–269

Chiclin Museum, 269–275

Chimbote, Desert of, 257, 258

Chimor, Kingdom of, 176, 254–256, 259, 261, 262

Chimus, 206, 253–274, 290

Chincha, 240

Chinchas, 212, 213

Chinchay Lake, 161, 182

Chinchay-suyu quarter, 83, 93, 168, 182

Choque-quirao, 113, 123, 124

Choquillo, 197–200.

Chupas, Battle of, 141, 145

Index

Cieza, Pedro de Léon, 3, 4, 23, 25, 26, 37, 44, 45, 59, 68, 93, 128–129, 131, 133, 138, 144, 150, 151, 167, 171, 179, 180, 213, 219, 234, 256, 274–275, 304–305
Colla-suyu quarter, 84
Contay, 149
Cuntu-suyu quarter, 84, 241–242, 243–244, 251
Cuntur-marca, 190, 192
Cuzco, 3, 6, 11, 26, 35, 50, 55, 60, 78, 79, 80, 81–97, 102, 125, 138, 171, 241, 285, 300, 305

DAUGHERTY, CHARLES, 15–16, 30, 34, 41, 53, 64, 77–78, 91, 112–114, 140
Desaguadero, 37–40, 44
Deza, Francisco, 52–53
Don Luis, 64–66

ESPINOSA, FATHER VASQUEZ DE, 232–233

FRIAR GABRIEL, 105–106

GILDEMEISTER, SIGMUND, 14, 15, 307
Gölz, Willi, 56–57, 62

HAGEN, VON, SILVIA, 8, 13–14, 18, 30, 31, 34, 47, 71–74, 114–120, 141–143, 158, 163–164, 165, 169, 182, 196, 197–198, 293, 294
Hanco-Hualla, 138, 176, 191–193
Haqui, 19, 23, 44, 50
Herrera, Señor Rafael, and Don Rafael Larco, 269–270, 272
Highway of the Sun, 165, 166
Huaca-punca, 93
Huadquina, 111–112
Huambacho, 257
Huampu, 105
Huancabamba, 286–287, 293
Huancas, (also Yanchas), 167, 168
Huancayo, 163, 166–167, 297
Huanchaco, 265
Huánuco, 170, 184, 186–189
Huara, 253
Huaymango, 104, 105
Huayna Capac, 132, 147–148
Huayna Picchu, 110
Huayuri, 225–226, 230
Humboldt, von, Alexander, 275– 286–287

ICA, 216, 217–220, 224–226
Ichocan, 293, 294
Inca-Huasi, 124, 211–212
Inca Roca, 129, 135
Ingapirca, 10
Inti-raymi Festival, 78, 92–93
Ituata, 57, 70
Izcu-chaca, 165

JAQUI, 234, 238
Jauja, 166, 167, 168, 170, 172
Juli, 34
Juliaca, 56, 58
Junin, 161, 182, 183

KARMENKA, HILL OF, 81, 88, 93
Kontiki Virachoa, 79, 299, 300
Kuelape, 200

LA VENTA, 225, 230
Lawrence, Richmond, 16, 30, 34, 42, 77–78, 91, 111–114, 126–128, 141, 164, 165, 212, 218, 252, 265, 267, 293, 294
Leighton, Capt. Henry, 221–229, 241
Levanto, 201–203
Lima, 31, 33, 102, 105, 206, 220, 253
Lucanas, 150

MACHU PICCHU, 106–111, 215
Macusani, 62
Manco Capac II, 101–105
Marañon River, 138, 170, 190, 293
Marcavalle, 166
Marquez, Don Felipe, 220
Mayoc, 162, 163, 166
Mendoza, Pedro de, 234
Mesapata, 177
Moche Valley, 262, 264
Mochicas, 258, 259, 268, 269–275, 290
Molina, Alonzo de, 279
Mollepata, 119, 126
Montaro River, 161–163, 166, 183

NASACARA, 40, 41
Nasca (Nazca), 125, 218, 223, 224, 226–229. See also end paper.
Nascas, 247–250
National Archives (Lima), 187, 220
New York Times, 14, 33, 50, 76, 112, 165, 228–229, 243–244, 294
North American Newspaper Alliance, 14

318

Index

OCAMPO, FRANCISCO DE, 190, 193–194, 199
Old Cuzco, 280, 281, 289
Ollachea, 70
Ollantay-tambo, 103
Oma-suyu quarter, 28, 59
Ordinance for Roads and Tampus, 169–170, 304

PACHACAMAC, 167, 206–207, 214
Pachacutic, 146
Pampaconas River, 103, 106
Pampas River, 151, 152
Pan American Highway, 216, 225, 235, 254, 282, 296–297
Pancorvo, Pepe de, 107, 111, 113–114
Paracas, 221–224, 227
Paramonga, 254–256
Pariabamba, 151
Pariacaca, 48
Parinacochas Lake, 242, 244
Paulla-Inca, 90
Pisac, 98
Pisco, 218; Desert of, 216; River, 214
Pizarro, Francisco, 82–83, 101, 104, 151, 168, 206, 240, 276–281, 282, 283–284, 287, 290–291, 292, 301–304
Pizarro, Gonzales, 96
Pizarro, Hernando, 185
Plain of Blood, 138, 176
Poechas, 283–284
Pomacocha, 153–160
Pomata, 35, 36
Pompo, 184
Pucara, 151
Pukuta, 72, 75–76
Puncuyoc, 112, 113
Puno, 8, 18–21, 24, 29, 45, 50, 53–54

QUITIMBO, 46
Quito, 3, 6, 176, 305

REICHE, FRAULEIN MARIA, 227, 229
Riddell, Dorothy and Fritz, 16, 18, 206–207, 211, 212, 218–219, 230, 232–233, 241, 245–252, 293
Road, Royal (Huayna Capac Ñan), 93, 132, 147–149, 152, 167–169, 172, 184, 189, 206, 211, 215, 231, 257–258, 264, 284–285, 289, 293–294, 297, 300, 303, 305. *See also* end paper.

Road, Royal, of Conquest, 169–172, 176, 189–203
Roads, Old World, 5, 6, 130–132, 237, 276, 287, 295–296

SACSA-HUAMAN, FORTRESS OF, 90, 92
Salcantay Mountain, 103, 114–117, 123
Saminez, David, 120, 121
San Pedros de los Incas, 281
Sancho, Pedro, 127, 150, 152
Soras, 150
Soray, 118, 122
Soto, Hernando de, 81–88, 284–285, 287, 293, 300, 301, 303
Squier, E. George, 38, 40, 41, 119, 122, 133–134

TAMBILLO, 68–70
Tambillo River, 201
Tambo Colorado, 214–215, 216
Tanaca, Desert of, 234, 236
Tanquihas, 146
Tawantin-suyu, 84
Tiahuanacan Empire, 227–228, 247, 259
Titicaca, 7, 8, 10, 11, 18, 28, 34, 37, 42, 43, 50, 53, 56–57, 58, 59, 79, 227, 259
Topa Inca, 147, 185, 188, 200, 211–212
Torre Pukro, 195–197
Tres Cruces, 221–223
Tucuman, 11
Tumpiz (*also* Tumbes), 204, 244, 252, 276–282, 300
Tupac Amaru, 105

UCTUBAMBA RIVER, 195, 200
Uran-marca, 150, 152–153
Urcos Lake, 79
Urumbamba River, 100, 103, 106–107

VALLEY OF VIRU, 258–259
Vega, Garcilaso de la, 129, 133, 200
Vilcabamba, 98–120
Vilcanota River, 79, 98
Vilcas, 143–148
Vilcas-huaman, 139–148, 153, 184
von Hagen, Silvia. *See* Hagen, von.

WANKAS, 167, 172
Wellman, Frank, 263–264
Wilder, Thornton, 120, 122, 129, 133–134

Index

XAQUI-XAHUANA, 94–95, 96

YAHUAN HUACAC, the Bloody Weeper, 152
Yucay, 100
Yupanqui, 138, 147

ZANA, 289–291
Zaran (*also* Serran), 284, 285, 287
Zepita, 96
Zuñigo, Don Inigo, 187–188
Zurite, 94